Palaeozoic Fishes

PALAEOZOIC FISHES

J. A. MOY-THOMAS

SECOND EDITION
EXTENSIVELY REVISED
BY

R. S. MILES

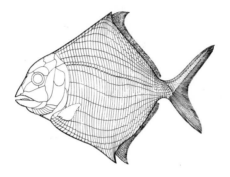

W. B. SAUNDERS COMPANY
PHILADELPHIA · TORONTO

American and Canadian distribution rights assigned to
W. B. SAUNDERS COMPANY
West Washington Square, Philadelphia, Pa 19105
1835 Yonge Street, Toronto 7, Canada
Library of Congress Catalog Card Number: 79-157532
SBN 0-7216-6573-X

First published in Great Britain 1939
Second edition extensively revised
by R. S. Miles 1971

© *1971 J. Moy-Thomas and R. S. Miles*

Photoset in Malta by St Paul's Press Ltd.
Printed in Great Britain

Contents

CONTENTS

Preface to the Second Edition

I have revised Moy-Thomas's widely used book on Palaeozoic fishes in an attempt to incorporate some of the considerable advances that have been made in this field over the last 30 years, which have in some respects made the first edition seriously out-of-date. The book is now inevitably longer, but its scope remains the same and the original approach has been maintained as far as possible. I have, however, undertaken a certain amount of re-arrangement of the contents, consonant with our changing views of fish evolution, and have tried to reflect some of the current preoccupations of students of fish evolution in expanded sections on mode of life and relationships. The illustrations have been completely replaced, and in selecting the figures I have been faced with an embarrassing richness of source material. In an attempt to keep the figures down to a reasonable number, I have decided that it is better to have a few species illustrated with clear drawings than give thumb-nail sketches of all the forms mentioned in the text, and as far as possible to restrict the illustrations to Palaeozoic species. All the illustrations have been redrawn to a common style, and in some cases they have been specially prepared or modified for this book. Authors' names are now included in the text and a list of references is given at the end of each chapter. The great flood of literature in recent years has raised many problems, not least in the compilation of the lists of references. To conserve space it has been necessary to restrict these very largely to papers published in the last 20 or 30 years, but I am confident that the writings of earlier workers can be reached through these papers. The small glossary of the first edition has been omitted, as I feel that its function is better fulfilled by the labelled drawings and by the Bibliography in the Introduction. Finally the classification has been divided among the individual chapters to make it more accessible for the reader.

I wish here to express my gratitude to Dr. Mahala Andrews and Dr. C. Patterson who have read the manuscript, corrected mistakes and provided much good advice. I am also indebted to Dr. R. P. S. Jefferies who has critically read the first two chapters, and to Dr. B. G. Gardiner for comments on Chapter 5. The opinions expressed and any mistakes that remain are, of course, my sole responsibility. I should also like to thank these colleagues and Drs. D. L. Dineley, L. B. Halstead, A. Ritchie, E. I. White, H. P. Whiting and Miss Susan Turner for the information they have provided on particular points. Drs. Andrews, Gardiner and Halstead have kindly permitted me to see work in manuscript, otherwise I have made no use in the text of works that reached me after June, 1970. Dr. B. G. Gardiner has kindly assisted me by reading the proofs.

R. S. M.

July, 1970

Preface to the First Edition

During the past twenty years no branch of Palaeontology has advanced more rapidly than that of the fishes. Modern methods of examining fossils with low-powered binoculars under various liquids, the introduction of powerful lamps, the use of acids and fine mechanical hammers, and the method of restoring fossils from serial sections have all contributed to this. Not only have the methods of studying fossils improved and made it possible to give far more accurate descriptions than has been done hitherto, but this rapidly advancing field has attracted a greater number of workers. In this respect our knowledge of the Palaeozoic fishes has particularly benefited. The tremendous influx of literature due to this stimulus to research has caused text-books to be out-of-date almost as soon as they are published, and although it is highly probable that this book will in many respects be shortly out-of-date, it is intended to be an attempt to bring the latest research on the early history of fishes to the student of both zoology and geology. The more accurate knowledge of early fishes increases, the more clear it is becoming that they are not only interesting as an evolutionary study, but are also important to the geologist for stratigraphical purposes. At the present time they are only commonly used in the stratigraphy of the Devonian, but it seems probable that further research will also make them of value in other formations.

It has not been found entirely practical in this work to confine the descriptions to the Palaeozoic fishes only, and in certain cases it has been necessary to draw on later forms to enable the accounts of the Palaeozoic members to be more exact. This book is naturally not intended to be a complete work on fishes, and many terms may be introduced without explanation which will be familiar to the zoologist but possibly not to the geologist. However, as these terms are explained in all current text-books on fishes, reference to these should overcome any difficulty in understanding such terms.

It would be outside the scope of this book to give chapter and verse for all the statements in it, and the list of literature cannot refer in detail to all the valuable works on which our knowledge of early fishes is based. Care has, however, been taken to refer where possible to recent works not listed elsewhere and to papers in which most of the references to any particular group can be found.

I would like to express my thanks to Professor E. S. Goodrich for his encouragement, for many helpful criticisms, and for reading the proofs of this book. I am also very grateful to Dr. E. I. White and Mr. B. W. Tucker, who assisted me greatly by reading the proofs and providing valuable suggestions, which have been incorporated in the text.

J. A. M.-T.

March, 1939

CHAPTER ONE

Introduction

The term 'fishes' as used in this book includes all those free-living, aquatic, cold-blooded, gill-breathing craniates in which fins and not pentadactyl limbs are developed. This is the popular usage of the term, and if fishes are defined in this way the group is composed not only of the true jawed fishes but also the jawless agnathans of which the lamprey is a living representative.

Fishes begin their evolution in the early Palaeozoic and by the end of the era forms have been evolved which are very little different from those that are living today. The Palaeozoic is, therefore, the most critical and interesting period of their history. Although recent research has advanced our knowledge of their evolution very greatly, much still remains to be learned of their early history, both of the actual origin of the group itself, and of the two principal divisions, the agnathans and gnathostomes, and their main subdivisions. All the fossil and living fishes that are known fall readily, unfortunately too readily, into one of these subdivisions, for in no case have convincing intermediate forms been described. Consequently, although the evolution of each independent group is tolerably well known, the phylogeny of the fishes as a whole can only be reconstructed in its broadest outlines.

1.1. CONSPECTUS

The agnathans include two distinct groups, the cephalaspidomorphs and the pteraspidomorphs. The former include both groups of living agnathans, the petromyzonids or lampreys and the myxinoids or hagfishes, as well as diverse, armoured Palaeozoic forms. The latter include two extinct groups, the heterostracans and thelodonts, and are the first vertebrates to appear in the fossil record (Fig. 1.1). In older works the Palaeozoic agnathans are frequently brigaded together as the ostracoderms, and the living species as the cyclostomes; but this practice results in two artificial assemblages which obscure the true relations, and is best avoided.

The gnathostomes also contain two groups, the elasmobranchiomorphs and the teleostomes. The elasmobranchiomorphs include the elasmobranchs

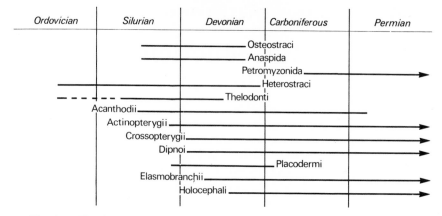

Fig. 1.1. The time-range of the main groups of fishes during the Palaeozoic.

with all the living sharks and rays; the holocephalans with the living rabbit-fishes; and the placoderms, an exclusively Palaeozoic group. The tele-ostomes contain two well-marked subdivisions; the acanthodians, also an exclusively Palaeozoic group; and the osteichthyans. The latter include the actinopterygians with most of the living bony fishes, the dipnoans or lung-fishes with three living genera, and the crossopterygians. The last fishes are particularly noteworthy as the group closest to the ancestors of the tetrapods in the Devonian; they include one living representative, the coelacanth *Latimeria*.

1.2. EVOLUTION OF JAWS

One of the most outstanding features in the evolution of fishes is the change which has taken place from the microphagous jawless condition of the proto-chordate ancestors to the macrophagous jawed condition of the gnathos-tomes. The orthodox history of this event has both used and strongly in-fluenced the study of Palaeozoic fishes, and is worth repeating here in outline. The head of a hypothetical primitive agnathan was assumed to have had a terminal mouth and to have been segmented in a manner similar to the rest of the body, each segment having myotomes and dorsal and ventral nerve roots. Between each segment in the head region a pair of gill-slits, related to the dorsal nerve root of the segment behind, connected the pharynx with the outside; and each gill-slit was supported posteriorly by segmental skeletal elements, the skeleton of the visceral arches. This condi-tion was said to be fulfilled to a great extent in the early agnathans, which were interpreted as bony fishes with a terminal mouth, no true jaws and gill-slits between the first (premandibular) and second (mandibular), and second

2

and third (hyoid) arches. In the gnathostomes or fishes with gill-arch jaws, which fed on bigger prey, the mouth has become greatly enlarged and extended backwards obliterating the most anterior gill-slits. As a result of this the visceral arch skeleton of the mandibular segment supposedly became modified into jaws, the palatoquadrate above and the meckelian cartilage below. Also the dorsal nerve root of the mandibular segment, the trigeminal, came to innervate the jaws. This condition, with a complete spiracular gill-slit and the hyoid arch still unmodified, was said to be found in the acanthodians and placoderms, collectively termed the Aphetohyoidea. Other jawed fishes, the chondrichthyans and osteichthyans, represent a more advanced condition in which the mouth was more backwardly pro-longed, and dorsally part of the visceral arch skeleton of the hyoid segment had become modified into the hyomandibula giving support to the jaws. In addition to this the lower part of the spiracular gill-slit was obliterated, leaving only the dorsal spiracle, which itself tended to disappear.

Recent work, however, has undermined much of the support that this theory has drawn from palaeontology and comparative anatomy, and has resulted in a re-examination of the interrelations of the early fish groups. With regard to the first stage in the evolutionary sequence, the objection may be raised that the first gill-slit in fossil agnathans is probably neither premandibular nor mandibular in position but spiracular, i.e. between the mandibular and hyoid segments (Chapter 2 §3.1). In the living lampreys the mandibular gill-pouches of young embryos soon disappear as develop-ment progresses, to become part of the buccal cavity as the stomodaeum invaginates to form the lining epithelium of the mouth. As exactly the same invagination takes place in the development of all vertebrates, it is doubtful if mandibular pouches could ever have existed at an adult stage (Jollie, 1968). Certainly no fossil or living agnathans correspond to the first hypothetical stage of jaw development, with complete mandibular and premandibular arches. In some crossopterygians a 'prespiracular' groove in the roof of the mouth has been interpreted as a vestige of the mandibular gill-slit, and attempts have been made to trace the premandibular arch in the skeleton (Jarvik, 1954; Bertmar, 1959). But this groove is probably the ventral part of the spiracular groove (Patterson), which is well known in actinopterygians, and it is difficult to find other evidence of the existence of a premandibular arch in gnathostomes.

Some workers now claim that there are even grounds for disputing the serial homology of the first three and more posterior segments (Jefferies, 1968). Whether or not this is the case, the hypothetical primitive gnathos-tome condition, still with a complete gill-slit between the mandibular and hyoid segments, seems to be no more firmly grounded than the first, primitive agnathan stage of the sequence, and is shown by neither acanthodians

3

(Chapter 4 §2.1) nor placoderms (Chapter 8 §3.1). In fact, a complete hyoid gill-slit has not been demonstrated unequivocally in any gnathostome, and appears to be found only in some fossil agnathans and larval lampreys, where it is the first gill-slit. It is possible that the gnathostomes never passed through an aphetohyoid stage in their evolution, for the formation of jaws from the mandibular arch and corresponding enlargement of the mouth probably did not leave the hyoid segment and the intervening gill-slit untouched. The most primitive gnathostomes in this respect seem to be the holocephalans, in which the hyoid arch skeleton is not modified to form a hyomandibula, although in other respects the jaw apparatus of these fishes is highly specialized (Chapter 10 §2). Even in the living agnathans, which are completely cartilaginous, the hyoid slit has been lost, either in connection with the modification of the mouth for 'biting' with a pair of horny toothplates (myxinoids), or with the development of a rasping tongue (petromyzonids).

The crucial point is that the agnathans and gnathostomes are divergently specialized. This is well shown by the gills, which face inwards from the inside of the gill-arches in agnathans and outwards from the outside of the arches in gnathostomes (Fig. 1.2). As it is unlikely that one condition has been derived from the other, it seems that the agnathans cannot be ancestral to the gnathostomes, and therefore the two principal stocks of vertebrates must have diverged from a common ancestor and are of equal antiquity (Jarvik, 1964, 1968). Although we are now left without a simple story of the evolution of jaws, we have in its place a less complicated picture of changes in the head in the diverging agnathous and gnathostomatous lines, which is more in accord with the palaeontological and embryological evidence, and we have a clearer concept of the relationship between the Agnatha and Gnathostomata (Fig. 1.3).

1.3. FOSSIL RECORD

The conclusion that the agnathans and gnathostomes are of equal antiquity is not supported by the time of appearance of the groups (Fig. 1.1), which has been used to demonstrate a progressive evolutionary series from jawless to fully jawed forms. The agnathans are the first to appear, in the Middle Ordovician; they flourish during the Silurian and Lower Devonian, become rarer in the Middle and Upper Devonian and a few stragglers survive to the present day. The first gnathostomes, the acanthodians, do not appear until the Upper Silurian, some 50m years after the first agnathans. The late appearance of the gnathostomes in the fossil record, however, may be due to biassed sampling, for all Ordovician and Silurian faunas are from the western half of the Northern Hemisphere, and the first gnathostomes may have had a limited

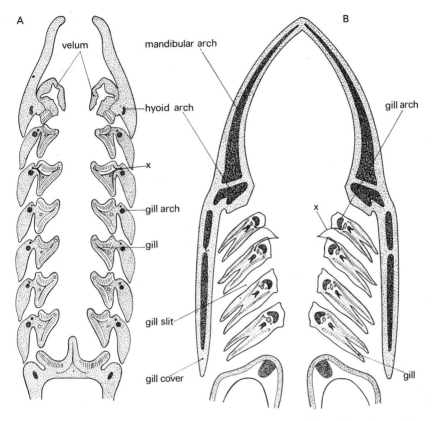

Fig. 1.2. Horizontal sections through the heads of an agnathan (A) and a gnathostome (B) to show the different positions of the gills. (After Jarvik.)

geographical range that has not been sampled. On the other hand they may
have lived in environments in which they were not readily fossilized, such as
true marine environments or upland areas that were regions or erosion
rather than deposition (Romer, 1955; Obruchev, 1967); or they may have
been without bone and therefore incapable of fossilization in normal circum-
stances. Whatever the explanation, numerous fully-formed, well-armoured
gnathostome groups appear suddenly in the Lower Devonian, and clearly
they have a long evolutionary history behind them. Another possibility to be
considered is that the first members of the Gnathostomata have been confused with true Agnatha, for there is no need to suppose that the first gnathostomes had fully-formed, gill-arch jaws. The heterostracans have been tentatively advanced to fill the position (Halstead, 1969), but the evidence is
slight (Chapter 3 §6).

5

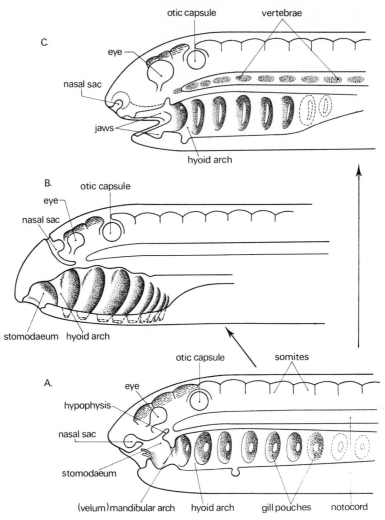

Fig. 1.3. Evolution of the head. Sagittal sections of a hypothetical basic vertebrate (A), a hypothetical agnathan (osteostracan) (B), and a hypothetical gnathostome (C). (After Jollie.)

1.4. ENVIRONMENT

Recent analyses of the habitats of early fossil agnathans have led to the conclusion that the vertebrates were originally a marine group (Denison, 1956; Robertson, 1957; White, 1958), as surely were their protochordate ancestors. It is particularly noteworthy that this conclusion is in harmony with the results of research into the physiology of excretion in living fishes, which implies that the glomerular kidney must have been a preadaptation that enabled vertebrates to penetrate fresh waters. The blood plasma of myxinoids is isosmotic with seawater, which is probably a primitive state inherited directly from early marine agnathans. All other groups of fishes, however, seem to have passed through a freshwater stage at least some time in their evolution, as a result of which their blood plasma contains less salt than seawater.

The marine agnathans of the Ordovician were succeeded by marine, brackish and freshwater species in the Silurian and Devonian. The osteostracans and anaspids were predominantly freshwater, whilst some of the heterostracans may have been euryhaline. Most living agnathans spend some part of their lives in the sea. Silurian acanthodians were marine, but later the group invaded freshwater where they were particularly successful in the Devonian. Of the osteichthyans, the actinopterygians include both freshwater and marine species almost from the beginning and they have become the dominant group of fishes in both environments. Lower Devonian crossopterygians and dipnoans include marine species, but subsequently they are overwhelmingly freshwater. Some of the placoderms remained entirely freshwater, where the group is first found in the Lower Devonian, but others migrated early into the sea. Placoderms flourished particularly in fresh waters in the Middle Devonian and in the sea in the Upper Devonian. The elasmobranchs and holocephalans, on the other hand, are typically marine fishes, and in only a few cases have they come to inhabit fresh water.

1.5. CLASSIFICATION

The following chapters of this book treat Palaeozoic fishes in systematic order, according to the following outline classification.

Superclass Agnatha (= Cyclostomata)
  Class Cephalaspidomorphi (= Monorhina)
    Subclass Hyperoartii
      Infraclass Osteostraci (= Cephalaspida)
      Infraclass Anaspida
      Infraclass Petromyzonida
    Subclass Hyperotreti
      Infraclass Myxinoidea
  Class Pteraspidomorphi (= Diplorhina *sensu stricto*)
    Subclass Heterostraci (= Pteraspida)
    Subclass Thelodonti (= Coelolepida)

Superclass Gnathostomata
  Class Teleostomi
    Subclass Acanthodii
    Subclass Osteichthyes
      Infraclass Actinopterygii
      Infraclass Crossopterygii
      Infraclass Dipnoi
  Class Elasmobranchiomorphi
    Subclass Placodermi (= Arthrodira *sensu lato*)
    Subclass Chondrichthyes
      Infraclass Elasmobranchii (= Selachii *sensu lato*)
      Infraclass Holocephali (= Bradyodonti *sensu lato*)

REFERENCES

Bertmar, G. (1959) 'On the ontogeny of the chondral skull in Characidae, with a discussion on the chondrocranial base and the visceral chondrocranium in fishes'. *Acta zool. Stockh.*, **40**, 203–364.

Denison, R. H. (1956) 'A review of the habitat of the earliest vertebrates'. *Fieldiana, Geol.*, **11**, 359–457.

Goodrich, E. S. (1930) 'On the relationship of the ostracoderms to the cyclostomes'. *Proc. Linn. Soc.*, **142**, 45–49.

Halstead, L. B. (1969) *The pattern of vertebrate evolution*, (Oliver & Boyd, Edinburgh).

Jarvik, E. (1954) 'On the visceral skeleton in *Eusthenopteron* with a discussion of the parasphenoid and palatoquadrate in fishes'. *K. svenska VetenskAkad. Handl.*, (4)**5**, 1–104.

Jarvik, E. (1964) 'Specializations in early vertebrates'. *Annls. Soc.r.zool. Belg.*, **94**, 11–95.

Jarvik, E. (1968) 'Aspects of vertebrate phylogeny'. *Nobel Symposium*, **4**, 497–527.

Jefferies, R. P. S. (1968) 'The subphylum Calcichordata (Jefferies 1967) primitive fossil chordates with echinoderm affinities'. *Bull. Br. Mus. nat. Hist., (Geol.)*, **16**, 243–339.

Jollie, M. (1968) 'Some implications of the acceptance of a delamination principle'. *Nobel Symposium*, **4**, 89–107.

Obruchev, D. V. (1967) 'On the evolution of the Heterostraci'. *Colloques int. Cent. natn. Rech. Scient.*, **163**, 37–43.

Robertson, J. D. (1957) 'The habitat of the early vertebrates'. *Biol. Rev.*, **32**, 156–87.

Romer, A. S. (1955) 'Fish origins—fresh or salt water?' *Deep Sea Res.*, **3** (Suppl.) Papers in marine biology and oceanography dedicated to Henry Bryant Bigelow, 261–80.

White, E. I. (1958) 'Original environment of the craniates', in *Studies on fossil vertebrates*, ed. Westoll, T. S. (The Athlone Press, London.) p. 212.

BIBLIOGRAPHY

de Beer, G. R. (1937) *The development of the vertebrate skull*, (Oxford University Press).

Berg, L. S. (1958) *System der Rezenten und Fossilen Fischartigen und Fische*. (Veb Deutscher Verlag der Wissenschaften; Berlin).

Grassé, P. P. (Ed.) *Traité de Zoologie: Anatomie, Systématique, Biologique*, T. 13, fasc. 1–3, (Masson, Paris, 1948).

Goodrich, E. S. (1909) 'Vertebrata craniata. Fasc. 1. Cyclostomes and Fishes', in *A treatise on zoology*, ed. Lankester, E. Ray, (Adam & Charles Black, London).

Goodrich, E. S. (1930) *Studies on the structure and development of vertebrates*, (Macmillan, London).

Jarvik, E. (1960) *Théories de l'évolution des vertébrés*, (Masson, Paris).

Jollie, M. (1962) *Chordate Morphology*, (Reinhold Book Co., New York).

Marshall, N. B. (1965) *The life of fishes*, (Weidenfeld & Nicholson, London).

Miles, A. E. W. (Ed.) *Structural and chemical organization of teeth* 2 vols, (Academic Press, New York and London, 1967).

Norman, J. R. (1963) *A history of fishes*, Revised by Greenwood, P. H., (Ernest Benn, London).

Orlov, J. A. (Ed.) *Osnovy Paleontologii*, Vol 11. (Izdatel 'stvo 'Nauka': Moscow, 1964). (Throughout this book references are given to the English translation, *Fundamentals of Paleontology: 11., Agnatha, Pisces*. Israel Program for Scientific Translations: Jerusalem, 1967.)

Piveteau, J. (Ed.) *Traité de Paléontologie*, T.4, vols. 1–3, (Masson, Paris, 1962–1969).

Romer, A. S. (1970) *The vertebrate body*, 4th. ed., (Saunders, Philadelphia).

Romer, A. S. (1966) *Vertebrate paleontology*, 3rd. ed., (University of Chicago Press).

Westoll, T. S. (1960) 'Recent advances in the palaeontology of fishes'. *Liverpool, Manchr Geol. J.*, **2**, 568–96.

Woodward, A. S. (1889–1901) *Catalogue of the fossil fishes in the British Museum (Natural History)*, (Brit. Mus. (Nat. Hist.), London). Pt. 1, 1889; pt. 2, 1891; pt. 3, 1895; pt. 4, 1901.

Young, J. Z. (1962), *The life of vertebrates*, 2nd. ed., (Oxford University Press).

CHAPTER TWO

Class Cephalaspidomorphi

2.1. CLASSIFICATION

SUBCLASS 1, Hyperoartii

  INFRACLASS 1, Osteostraci

  Order 1, Tremataspidida

    e.g. *Dartmuthia*, U. Sil; *Didymaspis*, L. Dev; *Oeselaspis*, U. Sil; *Saaremaspis*, U. Sil; *Sclerodus*, L. Dev; *Tremataspis*, *Tyriaspis*, U. Sil.

  Order 2, Cephalaspidida

    e.g. *Alaspis*, U. Dev; *Benneviaspis*, L. Dev; *Boreaspis*, L. Dev; *Cephalaspis*, U. Sil—M. Dev; *Escuminaspis*, U. Dev; *Procephalaspis*, U. Sil; *Securiaspis*, L. Dev; *Thyestes*, U. Sil—L. Dev.

  Order 3, Ateleaspidida

    e.g. *Ateleaspis*, U. Sil; *Hemicyclaspis*, *Hirella*, L. Dev; ?*Witaaspis*, U. Sil.

  Order 4, Kiaeraspidida

    e.g. *Acrotomaspis*, *Axinaspis*, *Ectinaspis*, *Kiaeraspis*, *Nectaspis*, L. Dev.

  Order 5, Galeaspidida

    e.g. *Galeaspis*, L. Dev.

  INFRACLASS 2, Anaspida

  Order 1, Jamoytiida

    e.g. *Jamoytius*, U. Sil.

  Order 2, Endeiolepidida

    e.g. *Endeiolepis*, *Euphanerops*, U. Dev.

  Order 3, Lasaniida

    e.g. *Lasanius*, U. Sil.

  Order 4, Birkeniida

    e.g. *Birkenia*, *Pharyngolepis*, *Pterygolepis*, *Rhyncholepis*, U. Sil.

  INFRACLASS 3, Petromyzonida

    e.g. *Lampetra*, Extant; *Mayomyzon*, U. Carb; *Petromyzon*, Extant.

SUBCLASS 2, Hyperotreti

  INFRACLASS 1, Myxinoidea

e.g. *Eptatretus*, Extant; *Myxine*, Extant.

Incertae sedis *Palaeospondylus*, M. Dev.

L., Lower; M., Middle; U., Upper; Sil, Silurian; Dev, Devonian; Carb, Carboniferous.

2.2. CEPHALASPIDOMORPH CHARACTERISTICS

As we have seen in the previous chapter, agnathans are characterized by the absence of true, gill-arch jaws, their development having been prohibited by the position of the gills on the inner face of the gill-arches. These fishes also lack or have only poorly-developed paired fins, although pectoral fins analogous to those of gnathostomes evolved within the group more than once, from lateral ridges. Other characters include the fusion of the neurocranium and gill-skeleton, and the presence of only two semicircular canals in the ear.

Much of the interest of agnathans, as they radiate in the Upper Silurian and Lower Devonian to fill numerous ecological niches later occupied by gnathostomes, lies in the methods they adopted in feeding and control of swimming in the absence of jaws and paired fins of gnathostome structure. We can reasonably assume that ultimately the gnathostomes were biologically superior in their feeding and swimming, and probably in other respects as well, as they rapidly replaced the agnathans in the Middle and Upper Devonian. Agnathans declined rapidly in these times, and thenceforth survived only as the eel-like lampreys and hagfishes, which are narrowly specialized predators and scavengers with either a rasping tongue or a biting mechanism employing a pair of horny tooth-plates on the floor of the mouth. There is no doubt that this adaptive type appeared early, as remarkably 'modern' lampreys are found in the Carboniferous.

The cephalaspidomorphs are agnathans with a single nasohypophysial opening and numerous gills, with up to 15 external openings. The embryology of living forms shows that the monorhinal condition is secondary and that the group evolved from ancestors with paired nasal sacs and openings. It has been suggested that the hagfishes (Myxinoidea) are derived from the diplorhinal pteraspidomorphs (Chapter 3 § 2), but this is improbable and the cephalaspidomorphs seem to be a natural group. Nevertheless the lampreys and hagfishes are distinct fishes with long separate histories (see Relationships of agnathans, Chapter 3 §6), and this is recognized in our classification.

Most early agnathans have a thick bony skeleton (the 'Ostracoderms'). This has led some workers to believe that the primary skeletal material of the vertebrates was bone and not cartilage as has usually been held to be the case; cartilage, it is suggested, is an embryonic adaptation allowing easier three-dimensional growth than bone. If this were true, the living agnathans must have lost their bony skeleton and secondarily degenerated into possessing a

11

cartilaginous skeleton. The geological record is, however, so notoriously imperfect and cartilage so rarely fossilized that further evidence is necessary before this point of view can be accepted (Romer, 1942; Denison, 1963). The adaptive significance of the bony armour is disputed. Where an immobilizing dermal armour is possessed by living bony fishes, it clearly has a defensive function, and by analogy it has been suggested that the armour of early agnathans afforded protection against predators, such as eurypterids, which are often found in the same deposits (Romer, 1933). This view is supported by the well-marked correlation that is found between the reduction of the armour and the change from a bottom-haunting, mud-grubbing mode of life to a free-swimming, predatory mode. However, physiological explanations have also been advanced (Westoll, 1945; Halstead, 1969; see also Denison, 1963). One theory supposes that deficiencies in the control of calcium metabolism were significant, another that bone originated as a store for phosphates. A related point concerns the weight of the armour. It is often supposed that it was invariably burdensome and heavy, but this was not necessarily so. In many species it was thin and highly cancellous. As in later vertebrates, the strength of the skeleton lay in the structure of the bone rather than in its mass. Even in the earliest agnathans the bone was deposited in plates of reasonably constant pattern in given regions of the body, presumably under the influence of interrelated factors such as mechanical stress, equilibrium, buoyancy and protection (Schaeffer, 1961).

2.3. INFRACLASS 1, OSTEOSTRACI

The osteostracans range from the Upper Silurian to the Upper Devonian and are anatomically by far the best known of all fossil agnathans. As the connective tissue of the head is ossified and all the spaces in it lined with perichondral bone, Stensiö (1927, 1932) found it possible to describe fully the shape of the brain and the course of all the nerves of the head in a way previously undreamed of in fossil fishes.

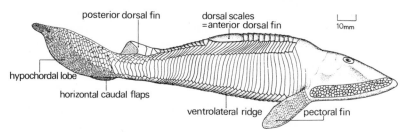

Fig. 2.1. *Hemicyclaspis murchisoni.* Restoration in lateral view. (After Stensiö and A. Heintz.)

Osteostracans are usually rather small fishes, although the Middle Devonian *Cephalaspis magnifica* must have been about 600 mm in length.

2.3.1. Structure

Typically osteostracans have an undivided bony head-shield extending some distance down the body, which is covered with bony scales with a well-differentiated area of overlap. The scales are arranged in dorsoventral and longitudinal rows and articulate with one another in a characteristic way. The head is dorsoventrally compressed, but the body becomes more and more laterally compressed, being triangular in cross-section directly behind the head-shield, but oval at the hind end of the body (Figs. 2.1, 2.3).

The exoskeleton (Fig. 2.2) is formed of three layers (Stensiö 1932; Denison, 1951b; Wängsjö, 1952; Gross, 1961). There is an outer layer of dentinal substance, a middle vascular layer and a basal lamellated layer. The first layer (mesodentine) sometimes and the latter two layers usually contain enclosed bone cells. The structure of the skeleton is thus like that of other armoured agnathans, except for the presence of the enclosed bone cells in all but a few specialized species (Ørvig, 1965). The outer dentinal layer is less easily discernible as distinct denticles than in heterostracans (Chapter 3 §3.1). Cellular bone has been described from the Middle Ordovician (Ørvig, 1965), which, if its osteostracan nature is confirmed, greatly extends the range of the group back in time.

The exoskeleton is permeated by vascular canals, and in the middle layer by a ('mucous') canal system which opens to the outside through pores or slits in the outer surface. The main horizontal canals of this pore-canal

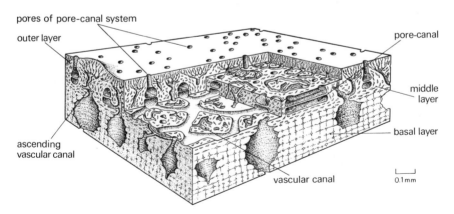

Fig. 2.2. *Tremataspis mammillata.* Diagram to show structure of fully developed exoskeleton. (After Denison.)

13

system, the circumareal canals, usually divide the outer region of the middle layer into polygonal areas. These polygons become exposed on the outer surface of the shield in species with a reduced outer layer. The function of the pore-canal system is not clear, but possibly it was part of the laterosensory canal system (Denison, 1947).

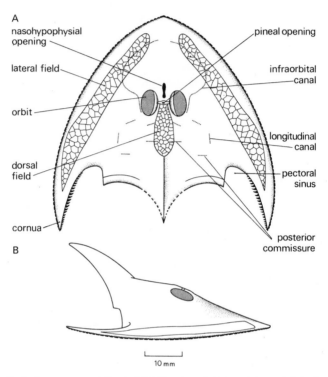

Fig. 2.3. *Cephalaspis pagei*. Head-shield in dorsal (A) and lateral (B) views. (After Stensiö.)

The orbits are situated dorsally, close together, and near the middle line, and are separated by the pineal foramen, immediately anterior to which lies the median nasohypophysial opening (Fig. 2.3). The skull, therefore, as in the living *Petromyzon*, has a greatly enlarged prenasal rostral portion. The mouth (Fig. 2.4) is anterior but ventral. The head-shield, which is comparatively small, forms a continuous plate enclosing the brain, and is produced downwards both anteriorly and laterally to form a large oralobranchial chamber (Fig. 2.5), which has its floor formed ventrally of a mass of small polygonal plates (Fig. 2.4). The mouth opens into this oralobranchial chamber anteriorly. Ventrally at its lateral edges the

14

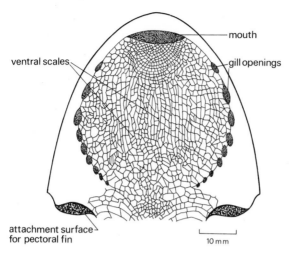

Fig. 2.4. *Hemicyclaspis murchisoni*. Ventral view of head-shield. (After Stensiö.)

gill-slits, usually about nine or ten pairs, open separately to the outside. The roof of the oralobranchial chamber is divided into paired branchial chambers by the interbranchial ridges and pierced by segmental nerves and blood vessels. The ridges are to be regarded as the undifferentiated dorsal parts of the branchial arches. The shape of these branchial chambers suggests that the gills had deep lamellae as in living agnathans, and were organized into anterior and posterior hemibranchs. In some species (e.g. *Cephalaspis signata*) the chambers bear cross-striations which may show the positions of the gill lamellae, although it is also possible that they were muscle attachment areas.

The head-shield is usually drawn out at its posterior corners into cornua, in the angles of which the shield is notched (Fig. 2.3) for the attachment of the pectoral fins. On the dorsal surface of the shield directly behind the eyes is a small median depressed area covered with tiny plates, and a pair or several small pairs of similar areas are found at the lateral margins of the head-shield. These areas are connected to the vestibular region of the ear by between three and six large canals, which may have transmitted nerves or contained fluid. These areas must have functioned as sensory fields. They may have been part of the laterosensory system served by branches of the facial (VII) nerve. Alternatively they may have been a development of the ear functionally replacing the laterosensory system, with the lymph-filled canals conveying pressure pulses to the ear.

The exact segmentation of the gill chambers and the identification of the branchial nerves is disputed (Allis, 1931; Lindström, 1949; Wängsjö, 1952;

15

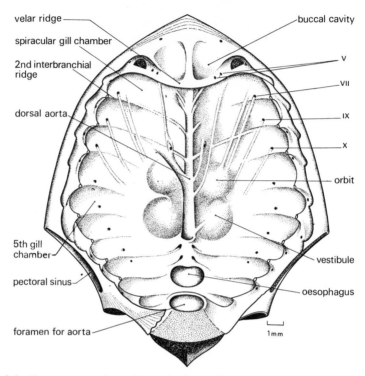

velar ridge
spiracular gill chamber
2nd interbranchial ridge
dorsal aorta
5th gill chamber
pectoral sinus
foramen for aorta

buccal cavity
V
VII
IX
X
orbit
vestibule
oesophagus

1 mm

Fig. 2.5. *Nectaspis areolata*. Ventral view of oralobranchial chamber. (After Stensiö.) The foramina for the branchial nerves are indicated by the usual Roman numerals; V, mandibular nerve; VII, facial nerve; IX, glossopharyngeal nerve; X, vagal nerve.

Damas, 1954; Stensiö, 1958, 1963, 1964;). In *Nectaspis* (Fig. 2.5) the buccal cavity is large and separated from the rest of the oralobranchial chamber by a prominent ridge which carried the velum. In living agnathans (e.g. *Myxine*, larval lampreys) the velum is a mandibular arch structure separating the buccal cavity from the pharynx, and there can be little doubt that the velar ridge of osteostracans represents the dorsal part of the mandibular arch. The first gill chamber immediately behind it thus housed the hyoid (spiracular) gill sac. In osteostracans the branchial nerves lack pretrematic branches, as they do in lampreys, and generally they pierce the roof of the oralobranchial chamber slightly in front of the arch to which they belong, to innervate the anterior hemibranch of their own arch and the posterior hemibranch of the arch in front (Stensiö, 1958). As in other fishes, the hyoid gill must have been innervated by the facial (VII) nerve, and this is the case if Lindström's interpretation of the branchial nerves is followed (Jefferies, 1968), as in Fig. 2.6. Wängsjö and Stensiö have proposed a different interpretation, with the

16

number of each branchial nerve raised by one; but it is difficult to harmonize their scheme with the obvious interpretation of the buccal cavity and branchial chambers; and the expediency of reinterpreting the chambers to match the nerves leads to the mechanically impossible situation of having gills in front of the mandibular arch, i.e. before the velum, in the buccal cavity.

Nectaspis is an evolved genus with an enlarged buccal cavity. Usually the velar ridge and buccal cavity are not so distinctly formed, but homologous structures can be traced throughout osteostracans. The position of the most anterior cross-striations, in species that possess them, confirms that the first gill chamber lies immediately behind the velar ridge. Some workers have taken lateral fossae in the buccal cavity to be gill chambers (e.g. in *Kiaeraspis*), but more probably they housed glands; at any event there are no gill openings in the shield corresponding to these fossae. The important conclusion to be drawn here is that the osteostracans possessed neither one nor two prespiracular gill sacs, but that the first sac belonged to the hyoid arch, as in lamprey larvae.

The auditory capsules are relatively rather large, but there are only two semicircular canals, the horizontal one being absent as in modern agnathans. The brain (Fig. 2.6) resembles that of *Petromyzon* very closely, parti-

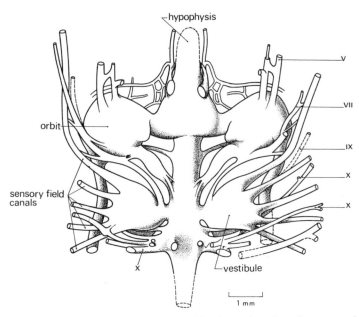

Fig. 2.6. *Nectaspis areolata*. Restoration of brain cavity, dorsal segmental nerves and canals to lateral fields. (After Stensiö.) Canals for nerves lettered by same Roman numerals as in Fig. 2.5.

17

cularly in the shape of the olfactory lobes, diencephalon and myelencephalon, but the bilobate cerebellum is more reminiscent of the hagfish *Myxine*. The hypophysial sac opens to the outside by a common pore with the olfactory organ (the nasohypophysial opening) and also as in *Petromyzon* the right habenular ganglion is larger than the left. In general the cranial nerves also resemble those of lampreys, especially in the alternation of the spinal and spino-occipital nerves of the right and left sides; the separation of the dorsal and ventral nerve roots in the adult; the presence of a general cutaneous fibre in all the cranial nerves; the absence of pretrematic branches in the branchial nerves; the position of the branchial nerves in relation to the visceral endoskeleton and the mode of exit from the skull of most of the cranial nerves; especially the closeness and shortness of the olfactory nerves. There are, however, certain marked differences between the brains and cranial nerves of osteostracans and lampreys. For example, the large canals that pass from the vestibular region of the ear to the sensory fields are represented, if at all, only by short pocket-like outgrowths of the labyrinth in lampreys (Jarvik, 1965); the glossopharyngeal (IX) nerve of osteostracans passes through the otic capsule, a fact which is probably a consequence of the anterior position of the foremost gill chambers relative to the brain, and the large size of the capsule.

The blood vessels of the head are on much the same general plan as those of the ammocoete larva (Stensiö, 1927; Wängsjo, 1952).

The lateral-line system (Fig. 2.3) is not embedded in the bony exoskeleton, but merely leaves a few frequently interrupted superficial grooves to indicate its course. The general pattern has been fairly successfully compared with that of lampreys (Stensiö, 1927, 1932; Wängsjo, 1952). There are, in forms like the Upper Silurian *Tremataspis* (Fig. 2.7) where the shield extends some distance down the trunk on the dorsal surface, both dorsal and lateral longitudinal lines, the latter meeting in two transverse commissures behind the dorsal sensory field. In *Cephalaspis* only the anterior of these may be present. There is also another more anterior commissure behind the pineal, and an infraorbital line. There are no supraorbital lines, but this is clearly due to the dorsal position and closeness of the orbits. Ventrally there is an oral and a main ventral canal. The acustico-lateral system would thus seem to have been poorly developed, although this was not the case if the pore-canals prove to have been part of the system. It has also been suggested that the sensory fields of the head-shield were a hypertrophied part of the acustico-lateral system, correlated with the poor development of the lateral lines (Watson, 1954).

In some genera such as the Upper Silurian *Ateleaspis* (Ritchie, 1967) there are two dorsal fins, but in the majority of forms there is only one (Fig. 2.1), the anterior being represented by a row of dorsal scutes. The caudal fin is

18

heterocercal (Stensiö, 1932; Heintz, 1967a), and the hypochordal or lower lobe is subdivided into two parts, the anterior of which consists of paired horizontal caudal flaps (Heintz, 1967b). There are paired pectoral fins covered, like all the other fins, with numerous small imbricating scales. The pectoral fins arise in the sinuses at the posterior corners of the head-shield, but are sometimes absent, as in tremataspids (Fig. 2.7). The pelvic fins appear only to be represented by ventrolateral scale-covered ridges on the trunk between the pectoral and caudal fins. Unfortunately, in none of the fins is the internal structure known, apart from some simple rods in the second dorsal and caudal fins of *Escuminaspis* (Jarvik, 1959). There are no special articulating surfaces for the pectorals, although these fins were well supplied with blood from a 'subclavian artery', drained by a large venous sinus, and innervated by spinal nerves, like the pectoral fins of jawed fishes.

2.3.2. Growth and life-history

As the shield of osteostracans is generally a sutureless capsule, the question arises as to whether these fishes could have grown once they reached the fully ossified adult condition. Conceivably they could have done so either by moulting the armour like an arthropod or by loosening joints in the shield; but there is no evidence of the first process, which would not in any case have permitted growth in species with an ossified endocranium, and the second is improbable in the majority of cases. It seems, therefore, that most osteostracans acquired their bony skeleton only at full growth, which explains the limited size range known for each species (Heintz, 1939; Westoll, 1945; Denison, 1952).

In *Tremataspis* (Denison, 1947, 1952) the bone formed first in the outer layer of the shield and around the canals of the pore-canal system, later being deposited around the other canals of the middle layer and added as successive lamellae below to form the basal layer. Not only was the outer layer formed first, but it differs from the other layers in lacking any sign of subdivision into polygonal areas; it may well have had a different ontogenetic history. One suggestion (Westoll, 1945) is that it was formed by the concrescence of superficial tubercles in the 'leathery' skin of the unarmoured larval stage. Genera like *Dartmuthia*, which have a much more strongly tuberculated outer layer than *Tremataspis*, may be cited in support of this view. The outer layer is also odd in that unlike the middle and basal layers it never shows signs of bone resorption and redeposition. This confirms that growth of the exoskeleton must have stopped once the outer layer was fully formed. However, it is a moot point whether resorption and redeposition permitted extensive growth in genera with the outer layer restricted to the top of superficial tubercles or completely missing (Denison, 1952); there

19

is no strong evidence that it did, except perhaps in the Upper Devonian *Alaspis* where the shield is reduced to separately growing polygons (Ørvig, 1968).

It has also been concluded that osteostracans had an unarmoured larval stage on the grounds that the head-shield must have developed from the oral hood of a lamprey-like ammocoete (Watson, 1954; but see Strahan, 1958). In some lampreys the change from the larval to the adult condition is associated with a migratory life-history, and it has been suggested that osteostracans migrated from the sea into lagoons or freshwaters at maturity, where calcium ions were more readily available for the growth of the skeleton (Westoll, 1945).

2.3.3. Diversity and tendencies in evolution

The tremataspids (Fig. 2.7 A, 2.8) are mainly Silurian species, characterized by the great length of the head-shield, which includes several trunk segments and may reach back to the anus, the absence of pectoral fins and the absence or slight development of pectoral sinuses and cornua. The morphological and stratigraphical evidence shows that these are primitive characters, and there is no doubt that the order Tremataspidida as used here is a heterogeneous group of primitive species, and oddly-specialized species with primitive characters, that are not all closely related.

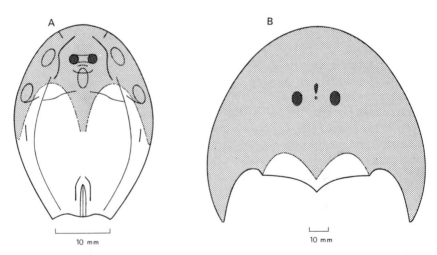

Fig. 2.7. A. *Tremataspis mammillata*. Dorsal view of head-shield; B. *Cephalaspis powriei*. Dorsal view of head-shield. These forms may be regarded as end terms in a series illustrating the evolution of the shield. Extent of endoskeleton shown by grey tone. (After Denison and Stensiö.)

A series of osteostracans can be arranged from those with neither sinuses nor cornua through those with short cornua and small sinuses to those with long cornua and well-marked sinuses, to illustrate the evolution of pectoral fins and correlated shortening of the shield (Fig. 2.7) (Westoll, 1945, 1958; Denison, 1951a). The relative extent of the endoskeleton does not change throughout this series: in the early stages it has posterolateral processes which lie within the anteroventral ridges which reach forward on to the shield from the trunk; in the later stages with fins the processes come to lie within the cornua and form the 'shoulder-girdle' region of the endoskeleton.

There is no doubt that this series illustrates a common and important trend in the evolution of osteostracans, associated with an increase in the power and control of swimming. There is evidence that pectoral fins evolved independently from ventrolateral ridges several times within the group, although the development of cornua was not always involved. Other evolutionary tendencies include the lengthening of the prepineal part of the shield, which is certainly correlated with the elaboration of the buccal cavity and feeding mechanism; and the increase in total area of the lateral fields and number of canals serving them, which may be correlated with a more active life as the shield is shortened and pectoral fins developed (Denison, 1951a).

Tremataspis and *Dartmuthia* are typical tremataspids. In some forms, like *Didymaspis*, the cornua are very short and the pectoral sinuses small, whilst in others like *Tyriaspis* (Heintz, 1967a) the cornua are long and broad (Fig. 2.8). *Sclerodus* (Stensiö, 1932) is a highly specialized genus often classi-

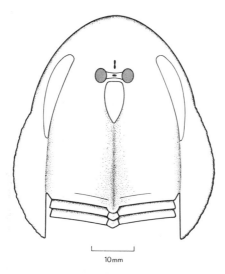

10mm

Fig. 2.8. *Tyriaspis whitei*. Dorsal view of head-shield. (After A. Heintz.)

21

fied apart from the tremataspids, with very long, anteriorly fenestrated cornua and a greatly shortened shield. The cephalaspids (Fig. 2.3, 2.7B) are typical osteostracans with a short shield, long cornua and well formed pectoral fins. Probably they evolved from a tremataspid like *Dartmuthia*. *Procephalaspis oeselensis* (Denison, 1951*a*) is a primitive Upper Silurian species with a short prepineal shield. The Lower Devonian *Boreaspis* is peculiar in having the shield drawn out anteriorly into a long rostral spine (Fig. 2.9). The ateleaspids (Fig. 2.1, 2.4) are a group which never developed

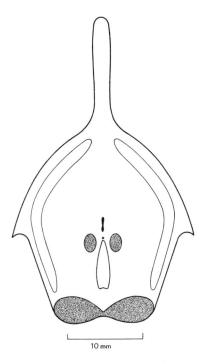

10 mm

Fig. 2.9. *Boreaspis costata*. Dorsal view of head-shield. (After Wängsjö.)

cornua or distinct sinuses, but where fins occur they occupy the position of both the fins and cornua of cephalaspids. *Witaaspis* from the Upper Silurian is tentatively identified as a primitive genus of the group; it does not have the greatly shortened shield of the other members. The kiaeraspids (Fig. 2.10) are a late group from the Lower Devonian of Spitsbergen. The earliest genus, *Kiaeraspis*, has a long shield and small cornua, but in succeeding genera the cornua have been lost, and the pectoral fins become enlarged as the shield is reduced. In *Nectaspis* the shield finally becomes incomplete

22

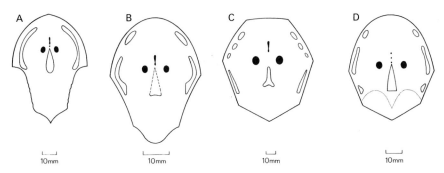

Fig. 2.10. Evolutionary series in the Kiaeraspidida. Head-shields in dorsal view. (After Wängsjö and Westoll.) A. *Kiaeraspis auchenaspidoides*; B. *Axinaspis whitei*; C. *Acrotomaspis instabilis*; D. *Nectaspis peltata*.

behind the floor of the oralobranchial chamber (Fig. 2.5). The anterior part of the shield is sometimes not ossified in *Acrotomaspis*.

There remain only the galeaspids, with the single genus *Galeaspis* from the Lower Devonian of China. This is an odd form with widely separated orbits, a long slit-like nasohypophysial opening and no sensory fields (Liu, 1965). The well-developed shield with distinct cornua leaves little doubt that *Galeaspis* is an osteostracan, but its affinities are obscure (see *Polybranchiaspis*, Chapter 3 §4).

2.4. INFRACLASS 2, ANASPIDA

The anaspids are a group of rather small cephalaspidomorphs, never much more than 150 mm in length, of which most of the genera are found in the Upper Silurian. Two genera, *Endeiolepis* and *Euphanerops* (Stensiö, 1939), are found as late as the Upper Devonian.

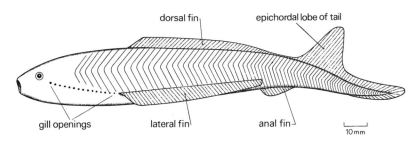

Fig. 2.11. *Jamoytius kerwoodi*. Restoration in lateral view. (After Ritchie.)

23

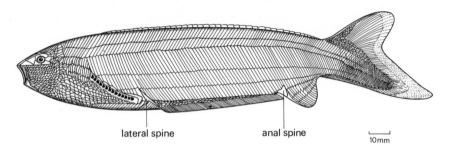

lateral spine   anal spine

10mm

Fig. 2.12. *Pharyngolepis oblongus*. Restoration in lateral view. (After Ritchie.)

2.4.1. Structure

These fishes (Figs. 2.11, 2.12, 2.13) are fusiform and somewhat laterally compressed. The body in armoured genera such as *Birkenia, Pterygolepis*, and *Rhyncholepis* (Kiaer, 1924; Ritchie, 1964) is covered by dorsoventrally elongated scales, which articulate with one another and overlap one another in a manner similar to those of osteostracans, and are arranged in definite dorsoventral and longitudinal rows. The scale rows correspond one to one with the segments of the body and may for the most part have followed the myotomes accurately. If so, the myotomes were in the form of simple, posteriorly-open V's as in Amphioxus, and not W-shaped as in living agnathans and jawed fishes (Stensiö, 1958, 1964).

Microscopically the dermal skeleton consists mainly of laminated bone without included bone cells, as in the inner layer of heterostracans (Chapter 3 §3.1). Superficially it is ornamented with fine tubercles. The pore-canal system is poorly developed, if present at all. In *Lasanius* (Parrington, 1958) the body is naked except for the dorsal row of ridge scales and perhaps small denticles in large individuals; while in *Jamoytius* the scales are so thin and flexible that Ritchie (1968) has questioned whether they are formed of bone.

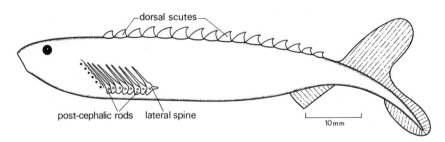

dorsal scutes

post-cephalic rods   lateral spine

10mm

Fig. 2.13. *Lasanius problematicus*. Restoration in lateral view. (After Parrington.)

24

In scaled anaspids the head is covered with numerous small, separate, but symmetrically arranged plates somewhat similar to the scales which cover the body (Smith, 1957); other forms have a naked head. The mouth is terminal and apparently in the form of an oval, vertical split, perhaps surrounded by soft tissues (Stensiö, 1958, 1964; Heintz, 1958; Ritchie, 1964, 1968). In *Jamoytius* it was supported by an annular cartilage (Fig. 2.14). The eyes are lateral but high up on the head with the pineal foramen lying between them. Directly in front of the pineal is situated a single median naso-hypophysial opening. Thus, as in osteostracans, the head has a well-developed prenasal rostral part. There may be as many as fifteen or as few as six laterally placed gill openings, usually arranged in an oblique row in front

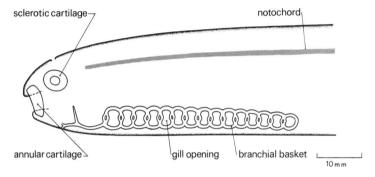

Fig. 2.14. *Jamoytius kerwoodi*. Restoration of head in lateral view. (After Ritchie.)

of the pectoral spine, each independently opening to the outside. *Jamoytius* shows that the gills were in the form of pouches surrounded by a branchial basket of the lamprey kind. The first pair of pouches lay shortly behind the orbits in *Jamoytius*, and although there is no good evidence on the matter they were presumably spiracular pouches innervated by the facial (VII) nerve; but the gill apparatus is much more posteriorly situated in other anaspids (Fig. 2.12, 2.13). The only traces of the endoskeleton are sclerotic ossifications which almost completely surrounded the eye, and badly-defined otic capsules in *Lasanius*.

The lateral-line system is poorly known, but it can be safely presumed to have been largely superficial to the bones. In *Pharyngolepis* short longitudinal and transverse pit-lines have been recorded on the head and branchial region, where the corium was particularly thin (Smith, 1957).

Sometimes there are faint traces of the axial skeleton with an unconstricted notochord; there are never signs of ossified centra.

The tail is hypocercal with the large epichordal or upper lobe usually

25

covered proximally with scales (Fig. 2.12), its distal part being supported by dermal fin-rays. Endoskeletal radials extend to the edges of the lobes (Jarvik, 1959). In *Jamoytius* and *Endeiolepis* a long single dorsal fin extends down the back, but in *Lasanius* and the scaled anaspids it is replaced by a row of dorsal ridge scales. There is a small scale-covered anal fin which usually has an anterior fin-spine. The paired fins are represented by continuous lateral structures which normally extend from just behind the branchial region to the level of the anal fin (Stensiö, 1939; Ritchie, 1964, 1968). These lateral fins are not differentiated into pectoral and pelvic regions, although in *Pharyngolepis heintzi* the exceptionally short fins have almost the position of pectorals. The lateral fins are covered with single rows of dorsal and ventral scales and were probably flexible structures provided with endoskeletal radials and radial muscles. They are supported anteriorly by a stout pectoral spine. In *Lasanius* there are between seven and ten such spines carried by large postcephalic rods on each side, arranged in a longitudinal row (Parrington, 1958), the last of which presumably supported a membranous lateral fin.

The lateral fins of anaspids are homologous with the pelvic fins plus the ventrolateral ridges of osteostracans. These structures in the two groups are of considerable interest for the light they cast on the origin of paired fins, particularly in connection with the restated Lateral Fin-fold Theory: '... there was a paired line of potential skin folding, from which keel-like structures could develop ... The earliest such structures in many groups appear to have been stiff, and became variously modified. In many groups the fully-controlled flexible fin capable of giving the animal a more perfect control of movement is a late development' (Westoll, 1958). Anaspids evidently developed flexible lateral fins with muscles and an internal skeleton, from the stiff keel-like structures, but the differentiation into pectoral and pelvic fins did not take place within the group.

2.4.2. Growth

The discrete scales of anaspids permitted growth by the addition of bone to the margins, unlike the solid shield of osteostracans. As a considerable size range is found in some species, it is unlikely that anaspids had a long larval life followed by metamorphosis and the ossification of the skeleton at maturity; probably the exoskeleton was acquired at an early stage of growth. In *Birkenia* there is clear evidence that the size but not the number of the scales increased with age (Parrington, 1958). It is possible that the youngest growth stages of the scaled anaspids were clothed in the fine denticles that ornament the adult scales.

2.4.3. Diversity

Jamoytius from the Silurian of Scotland is the oldest anaspid, and in some respects is remarkably like the living agnathans (see Relationships of agnathans, Chapter 3 §6), although the branchial basket may also be compared with that of larval Amphioxus (Wickstead, 1969). However, the long dorsal fin suggestive of a median fin-fold, and the long lateral fins, are sometimes regarded as primitive characters, as is the anterior position of the gill openings. One of the last anaspids, *Endeiolepis* from the Upper Devonian, has the same fin development and thin scales as *Jamoytius* (Stensiö, 1939), and together with *Euphanerops* from the same Upper Devonian beds might be closely related to the Silurian genus, in spite of the large gap in the record. These three genera are probably only distantly related to the other anaspids. *Lasanius* is an almost naked genus of isolated position, characterized by the postcephalic rods in front of the lateral fins. The birkeniids are the scaled anaspids. There is no way of telling whether thick scales are primitive or specialized in anaspids. The second alternative is possible in view of the low level of ossification in *Jamoytius*, although *Lasanius* may have been derived from scaled forms by the reduction of the skeleton. *Birkenia* has a characteristic double mid-dorsal ridge scale, and the most dorsal flank scales slope downwards and backwards in the posterior half of the body, instead of downwards and forwards as in other scaled genera. Clearly they do not here reflect the form of the myotomes.

2.5. INFRACLASS 3, PETROMYZONIDA

The only known fossil lamprey is the Upper Carboniferous *Mayomyzon* (Bardack and Zangerl, 1968). These remarkably preserved fossils are so similar to the living *Lampetra* that no doubts can be expressed about their affinities, even though a large gap in the record separates them from the living species. *Mayomyzon* reached a length of about 65 mm and is known from both adult and subadult specimens. Skeletal and 'soft' tissues are preserved as dark stains on the rock.

2.5.1. Structure

The body is eel-like with continuous dorsal, anal and caudal fins. The caudal is separated from the dorsal by a notch, and though its form is not quite clear, obviously it is neither strongly heterocercal nor hypocercal. As in living lampreys, paired fins and girdles are completely absent, as are scales and dermal armour.

No circumoral hood, cirri or horny teeth are found and the mouth appears

27

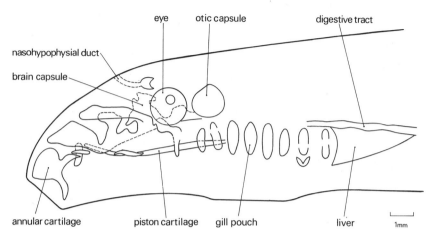

Fig. 2.15. *Mayomyzon pieckoensis.* Restoration of head in lateral view. (After Bardack.)

as a narrow slit, but in other respects the head skeleton is as in living lampreys. The usual cartilages are present (Fig. 2.15), including a large annular cartilage surrounding the mouth and the piston cartilage of the rasping tongue. The eyes are laterally situated, and above them lies the olfactory capsule which has the usual single median opening on the top of the head. There are seven gill sacs in the adult, with the first, which may be the spiracular sac, lying below the otic capsule. In adult *Lampetra* the first sac lies posterior to the otic capsule and is innervated by the glossopharyngeal (IX) nerve, the spiracular sac of the ammocoete having been obliterated at metamorphosis. Only slight traces of the gill basket are preserved. There is a fenestrated pericardial cartilage.

Of the viscera, both the liver and alimentary canal are found although no details of structure can be seen.

2.6. INCERTAE SEDIS *PALAEOSPONDYLUS*

There remains only to be described the small problematic fish *Palaeospondylus gunni* (Moy-Thomas, 1940), known exclusively from the Middle Devonian of Scotland. This species has sometimes been referred to the myxinoids, and although its affinities are still unknown and strictly speaking the hagfishes have no fossil record, it will be convenient to deal with it here. *Palaeospondylus* seldom exceeds 50 mm in length, and consists of a well-calcified skull, vertebral column and caudal fin (Fig. 2.16). There are also traces of the skeleton of the paired fins, probably pelvics. In the vertebral column there are well-formed, ring-like centra, except in the caudal region.

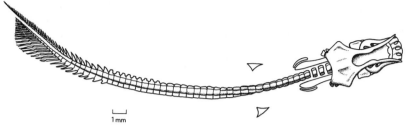

Fig. 2.16. *Palaeospondylus gunni*. Restoration with head and anterior end in dorsal view but posterior part of vertebral column in lateral view. (After Moy-Thomas.)

The dorsal arches are low anteriorly but become lengthened into spines posteriorly. Ventrally there are short haemal ribs which posteriorly become haemal arches with spines, and in the caudal region are articulated with distally bifurcating radials forming a heterocercal tail.

The neurocranium is dorsoventrally compressed and complete ventrally with a depression for the hypophysis, but the larger part of the skull-roof appears to have been uncalcified. The auditory capsules are large and the skull ends anteriorly in a number of rostral processes. Beneath the neurocranium lie several paired rods which have been interpreted as part of the mechanism of a rasping tongue apparatus, although they may be branchial arches. Anterior to them lie structures which have been interpreted as the upper and lower jaws. Unfortunately the nature of the preservation prevents the microscopic structure of the skeleton from being studied.

The majority of workers have related *Palaeospondylus* to the agnathans, and Halstead Tarlo (1967) has recently suggested that it may be a larval hagfish. However, it has also been interpreted as an elasmobranch, a placoderm, a larval *Coccosteus* (Placodermi), a larval lung-fish, a larval amphibian and a member of a new class. The presence of paired fins is hard to reconcile with a position in the myxinoids, but it is quite possible that *Palaeospondylus* is a larva, since the neurocranium is in much the same stage of development as the chondrocranium of many larvae. However, the presence of centra in the vertebral column, and the fact that there is no difference in development between the smallest specimen of about 12 mm and the largest, are opposed to this view. The affinities of this genus are in fact still not known.

2.7. MODE OF LIFE

The osteostracans and anaspids show a marked contrast in body form, and presumably had distinct modes of life, although there are similarities in the feeding mechanism imposed by the limited evolutionary potential of the agnathous condition.

29

Early osteostracans like *Tremataspis* had a shield of almost circular cross-section. The form of the tail is not usually clear and has been variously described as heterocercal and diphycercal. In *Tyriaspis* it is clearly heterocercal. This sort of tail has long been supposed to have produced a depressing force at the anterior end of the body in swimming, which was countered by the flattened anterior region of the shield acting as a gliding plane. However, recent work on living sharks does not entirely support this view, and it is possible that the tail generated lift without the help of paired fins. *Tremataspis* has no well-marked lateral fins or keel-like ridges, and probably swam erratically like a tadpole. There is no doubt that tremataspids were benthic fish, for they have the dorsal eyes and nostril and ventral mouth of other osteostracans. They are mainly Silurian forms and were rapidly replaced in the early Devonian by more typical broad-headed osteostracans. These were more narrowly specialized for bottom-living with the flat undersurface of the shield covering a large area of the substratum, and pectoral fins developed to serve as props. In such osteostracans the shortened shield had released the anterior myotomic musculature for use in swimming, with a resulting increase in propulsive force, and the pectoral fins also gave some control over pitching. The large cornua of finless tremataspids, like *Sclerodus* and *Tyriaspis*, probably functioned as rigid gliding planes, and can be looked upon as experiments in the evolution of lateral stabilizing structures, that were less successful than flexibly mobile fins. The cornua of cephalaspids may have functioned as cutwaters in front of the pectoral fins. Such osteostracans bear a striking resemblance to the present day, stream-living loricariid catfishes (Actinopterygii), and may have been specifically adapted to this environment.

The ventral position of the mouth confirms that osteostracans were bottom feeding forms, and probably they sucked in food using the flexible floor of the oralobranchial chamber and associated ventral branchial muscles as a pump. The shape of the mouth varies from a circle to either a transverse or a longitudinal slit, which indicates some diversity in feeding. One suggestion is that *Ateleaspis* and similar genera with denticles on the roof of the buccal cavity could crush small, shelled invertebrates, although the mechanism involved has not been satisfactorily explained, whilst other forms were unselective mud swallowers. Stensiö has used the shape of the mouth, among other characters, as the basis for a new classification, but his scheme does not appear to be soundly based, and the rasping tongue with which he provides some genera is entirely hypothetical.

The hypocercal tail of anaspids probably raised the anterior end of the body in swimming, and this, together with the more normal fusiform fish shape, in contrast to osteostracans, has given rise to the suggestion that they were surface living forms feeding on plankton. The lateral fins may have been functionally related to the hypocercal tail, although the hydrodynamic significance of this combination has not been explained. In heterostracans (Chapter 3 §3.1) the hypocercal tail exists without lateral fins.

The small mouth and pouched gills make plankton feeding an unlikely mode of life for anaspids, and the absence of jaws rules out biting or nibbling. It is therefore probable that anaspids were suction feeders, like osteostracans. In several species (e.g. *Endeiolepis aneri*) fine sediment in the alimentary canal shows that they swallowed mud, presumably to digest the contained invertebrates and organic detritus. Parrington (1958) has suggested that anaspids fed head down with the body steeply inclined to the bottom, and that the action of the hypocercal tail enabled them to plough through the bottom mud in pursuit of prey. The large, protective exoskeletal 'mandibular plate' on the chin of *Pharyngolepis* can be explained as an adaptation for the ploughing action. Thus although anaspids may have been more free-living than osteostracans they were also largely bottom feeding forms. Nevertheless other suctorial feeding habits may have existed in the group. The large carbonaceous sheets of the problematic organism *Dictyocaris* are irregularly perforated by holes of the same diameter as the annular cartilage of *Jamoytius*, which occurs in the same beds. Assuming that *Jamoytius* was responsible for these wounds, Ritchie (1968) suggests that petromyzonid ancestors initially fed on plants, and scraped algae from rocks and the skin of other fish, and that this led to the peculiar predatory mode of life of the living forms. It is possible that some anaspids had already evolved a rasping tongue like petromyzonids, although concrete evidence of this does not exist. Whatever the case, it is now clear that lampreys with a rasping tongue have existed since the Upper Carboniferous, and although *Mayomyzon* apparently lacked the circumoral hood of living genera, it probably differed only slightly from these forms in its mode of feeding.

REFERENCES

Allis, E. P. (1931) 'Concerning the mouth opening and certain features of the visceral endoskeleton of *Cephalaspis*'. *J. Anat.*, **65**, 509–27.

Bardack, D. and Zangerl, R. (1968) 'First fossil lamprey: a record from the Pennsylvanian of Illinois'. *Science, N.Y.*, **162**, 1265–1267.

Damas, H. (1954) 'La branchie préspiraculaire des Céphalaspides', *Annls. Soc. r. zool. Belg.* **85**, 89–102.

Denison, R. H. (1947) 'The exoskeleton of *Tremataspis*'. *Amer. J. Sci.*, **245**, 337–65

Denison, R. H. (1951a) 'Evolution and classification of the Osteostraci'. *Fieldiana, Geol.* **11**, 157–196.

Denison, R. H. (1951b) 'The exoskeleton of early Osteostraci'. *Fieldiana, Geol.*, **11**, 199–218.

Denison, R. H. (1952) 'Early Devonian fishes from Utah. Pt. 1. Osteostraci'. *Fieldiana, Geol.*, **11**, 265–87.

Denison, R. H. (1961) 'Feeding mechanisms of Agnatha and early gnathostomes'. *Am. Zool.*, **1**, 177–81.

Denison, R. H. (1963) 'The early history of the vertebrate calcified skeleton'. *Clin. Orthop.*, **34**, 141–52.

Dineley, D. L. (1968) 'Osteostraci from Somerset Island'. *Geol. Surv. Can., Bull.*, **165**, 49–63.

Gross, W. (1938) 'Der histologische Aufbau der Anaspiden-Schuppen'. *Norsk geol. Tidsskr.*, **17**, 191–95.

Gross, W. (1961) 'Aufbau des Panzers obersilurischer Heterostraci und Fische'. *Acta zool. Stockh.*, **42**, 73–150.

Halstead, L. B. (1969) *The pattern of vertebrate evolution.* (Oliver & Boyd, Edinburgh).

Heintz, A. (1939) 'Cephalaspida from Downtonian of Norway'. *Skr. norske VidenskAkad. Oslo, Mat.-naturv. Kl.*, (1939) 1–119.

Heintz, A. (1958) 'The head of the anaspid *Birkenia elegans*, Traq.', in *Studies on fossil vertebrates*, ed. Westoll, T. S. (The Athlone Press, London) p. 71.

Heintz, A. (1967a) 'A new tremataspidid from Ringerike, South Norway'. *J. Linn. Soc. (Zool.)* **47**, 55–68.

Heintz, A. (1967b) 'Some remarks about the structure of the tail in cephalaspids'. *Colloques int. Cent. natn. Rech. Scient.*, **163**, 21–35.

Heintz, A. (1969) 'New agnaths from Ringerike Sandstone'. *Skr. norske VidenskAkad. Oslo, Mat-naturv. Kl.* (1969) 1–28.

Jarvik, E. (1959) 'Dermal fin-rays and Holmgren's principle of delamination', *K. svenska VetenskAkad. Handl.*, (4) **6**, 1–51.

Jarvik, E. (1965) 'Die Raspelzunge der Cyclostomen und die pentadactyle Extremität der Tetrapoden als Beweise für monophyletische Herkunft'. *Zool. Anz.*, **175**, 101–43.

Jefferies, R. P. S. (1968) 'The subphylum Calcichordata (Jefferies 1967) primitive fossil chordates with echinoderm affinities'. *Bull. Br. Mus. nat. Hist., (Geol.)*, **16**, 243–339.

Kiaer, J. (1924) 'The Downtonian fauna of Norway. 1. Anaspida'. *Skr. norske VidenskAkad. Oslo, Mat.-naturv, Kl.*, (1924) 1–139.

Lindström, T. (1949) 'On the cranial nerves of the cyclostomes with special reference to N. Trigeminus'. *Acta. zool., Stockh.*, **30**, 315–458.

Liu, Y-H. (1965) 'New Devonian agnathans of Yunnan'. *Vertebr. Palasiat.* **9**, 125–34.

Moy-Thomas, J. A. (1940) 'The Devonian fish *Palaeospondylus gunni* Traquair'. *Phil. Trans. R. Soc.*, (B) **230**, 391–413.

Obruchev, D. V. (1967) 'Class Monorhina (Cephalaspidomorphi)', in *Fundamentals of Palaeontology, 11. Agnatha, Pisces*, ed. Obruchev, D. V. (Israel program for scientific translations, Jerusalem) p. 106.

Ørvig, T. (1965) 'Palaeohistological notes. 2. Certain comments on the phyletic significance of acellular bone tissue in early vertebrates'. *Ark. Zool.*, **16**, 551–56.

Ørvig, T. (1968) 'The dermal skeleton; general considerations'. *Nobel Symposium*, **4**, 373–97.

Pageau, Y. (1969) 'Nouvelle fauna ichthyologique du Dévonien Moyen dans les Grès de Gaspé (Quebec). 2. Morphologie et Systematique'. *Naturaliste can.*, **96**, 399–478, 805–89.

Parrington, F. R. (1958) 'On the nature of the Anaspida', in *Studies on fossil vertebrates*, ed. Westoll, T. S. (The Athlone Press, London) p. 108.

Ritchie, A. (1964) 'New light on the morphology of the Norwegian Anaspida'. *Skr. norske VidenskAkad. Oslo, Mat.-naturv. Kl.* (1964) 1–22.

Ritchie, A. (1967) '*Ateleaspis tessellata* Traquair, a non-cornuate cephalaspid from the Upper Silurian of Scotland'. *J. Linn. Soc. (Zool.)*, **47**, 69–81.

Ritchie, A. (1968) 'New evidence on *Jamoytius kerwoodi* White, an important ostracoderm from the Silurian of Lanarkshire, Scotland'. *Palaeontology*, **11**, 21–39.

Romer, A. S. (1933) 'Eurypterid influence on vertebrate history'. *Science, N.Y.*, **78**, 114–117.

Romer, A. S. (1942) 'Cartilage an embryonic adaptation'. *Amer. Nat.*, **76**, 394–404.

Schaeffer, B. (1961) 'Differential ossification in the fishes'. *Trans. N.Y. Acad. Sci.*, (**2**)**23**, 501–505.

Smith, I. C. (1957) 'New restorations of the heads of *Pharyngolepis oblongus* Kiaer and *Pharyngolepis kiaeri* sp. nov., with a note on their lateral line systems'. *Norsk geol. Tidsskr.*, **37**, 373–402.

Stensiö, E. A. (1927) 'The Downtonian and Devonian vertebrates of Spitsbergen I. Family Cephalaspidae'. *Skr. Svalbard Nordishavet*, **12**, 1–391.

Stensiö, E. A. (1932) *The cephalaspids of Great Britain*. (Br. Mus. (Nat. Hist.), London).

Stensiö, E. A. (1939) 'A new anaspid from the Upper Devonian of Scaumenac Bay in Canada, with remarks on the other anaspids'. *K. svenska VetenskAkad. Handl.*, (3)**18**, 1–25.

Stensiö, E. A. (1958) 'Les cyclostomes fossiles ou ostracodermes', in *Traité de Zoologie*, **13**:1, ed. Grassé, P.-P. (Masson, Paris) p. 173.

Stensiö, E. A. (1963) 'The brain and cranial nerves in fossil, lower craniate vertebrates'. *Skr. norske, VidenskAkad. Oslo, Mat.-naturv. Kl.* (1963) p. 1–120.

Stensiö, E. A. (1964) 'Les cyclostomes fossiles ou ostracodermes', in *Traité de Paléontologie* **4**:1, ed. Piveteau, J. (Masson, Paris) p. 96.

Strahan, R. (1958) 'Speculation on the evolution of the agnathan head'. *Proc. cent. & bicent. Congr. Biol., Singapore*, 83–94.

Tarlo, L. B. H. (= Halstead, L. B.)(1967)'Agnatha' in *The fossil record*, ed. Harland, W. B., *et al.* (Geol. Soc., London) p. 629.

Wängsjö, G. (1952) 'The Downtonian and Devonian vertebrates of Spitsbergen. IX, Morphologic and systematic studies of the Spitsbergen cephalaspids'. *Skr. norsk. Polarinst.*, **97**, 1–611.

Watson, D. M. S. (1954) 'A consideration of ostracoderms'. *Phil. Trans. Roy. Soc.*, (B) **238**, 1–25.

Westoll, T. S. (1945) 'A new cephalaspid fish from the Downtonian of Scotland, with
33

notes on the structure and classification of Ostracoderms'. *Trans. R. Soc. Edinb.*, **61**, 341–357.

Westoll, T. S. (1958) 'The lateral fin-fold theory and the pectoral fins of ostraco-derms and early fishes', in *Studies on fossil vertebrates*, ed. Westoll, T. S. (The Athlone Press, London) p. 180.

White, E. I. (1958) 'On *Cephalaspis lyelli* Agassiz'. *Palaeontology*, **1**, 99–105.

Wickstead, J. H. (1969), 'Some further comments on *Jamoytius kerwoodi* White.' *Zool. J. Linn. Soc.*, **48**, 421–422.

CHAPTER THREE

Class Pteraspidomorphi

3.1. CLASSIFICATION

SUBCLASS 1, Heterostraci
  Order 1, Astraspidida
      e.g. *Astraspis*, M. Ord.
  Order 2, Eriptychiida
      e.g. *Eriptychius*, M. Ord; ?*Tesseraspis*, L. Dev.
  Order 3, Cyathaspidida
      e.g. *Allocryptaspis*, *Anglaspis*, *Ariaspis*, *Corvaspis*, *Ctenaspis*, L. Dev;
          Cyathaspis, U. Sil; *Poraspis*, L. Dev; *Tolypelepis*, U. Sil.
  Order 4, Pteraspidida
      e.g. *Doryaspis*, *Protaspis*, *Psephaspis*, *Pteraspis*, *Rhinopteraspis*, L.
          Dev; *Traquairaspis*, U. Sil.
  Order 5, Psammosteida
      e.g. *Drepanaspis*, L. Dev; *Psammolepis*, M. Dev; *Psammosteus*, M.–U.
          Dev; *Pycnosteus*, M. Dev; *Tartuosteus*, M.–U. Dev.
  Order 6, Cardipeltida
      e.g. *Cardipeltis*, L. Dev.
  Order 7, Amphiaspidida
      e.g. *Angaraspis*, *Amphiaspis*, L. Dev; *Eglonaspis*, L.–M. Dev;
          Gabreyaspis, *Hibernaspis*, *Obliaspis*, *Pelurgaspis*, *Sanidaspis*,
          Siberiaspis, L. Dev.
Incertae sedis *Polybranchiaspis*, L. Dev.
SUBCLASS 2, Thelodonti
  Order 1, Thelodontida
      e.g. *Amaltheolepis*, M. Dev; *Thelodus*, U. Sil–L. Dev; *Turinia*,
          L. Dev.
  Order 2, Phlebolepidida
      e.g. *Katoporus*; ?*Lanarkia*, *Logania*, *Phlebolepis*, U. Sil.

L., Lower; M., Middle; U., Upper; Ord, Ordovician; Sil. Silurian; Dev,
Devonian.

3.2. PTERASPIDOMORPH CHARACTERISTICS

Pteraspidomorphs are much more diverse than their distant agnathan relatives, the cephalaspidomorphs. Whether the heterostracans and thelodonts are correctly brought together in the Pteraspidomorphi is, however, questionable. If the pteraspidomorphs are a natural group, they may best be defined as agnathans with paired nasal sacs and openings, no nasohypophysial duct, and the rostral region formed by the morphologically anterior part of the head. This is hardly a satisfactory definition, and even the paired nature of the nasal organ is disputed by Stensiö (1958, 1963, 1964, 1968). To a large extent our difficulties are due to a lack of information about the internal anatomy. In neither subdivision is there an ossified endocranium, and our understanding of the group comes from the exoskeleton of large plates and scales in heterostracans, and small superficial denticles in thelodonts. Pteraspidomorphs are usually thought to lack bone cells in the skeleton, like anaspids; and there is normally only one pair of branchial openings, although more have been described for thelodonts and *Polybranchiaspis*.

3.3. SUBCLASS 1, HETEROSTRACI

Remains of heterostracans are the earliest securely determined vertebrate fossils, being found as isolated plates, *Astraspis* and *Eriptychius*, in the Middle Ordovician (Ørvig, 1958; Denison, 1967b). The group is best developed in the Upper Silurian and Lower Devonian, but continues into the Upper Devonian. They are not usually much more than 300 mm in length, and the majority are rather smaller, although a few species are as long as 1.5 m.

3.3.1. Structure

The exoskeleton (Fig. 3.1) consists of an outer layer of dentinal tissue, a middle layer of cancellous vascular bone, and an underlying laminated layer (Wills, 1935; Gross, 1961; Denison, 1964; Halstead Tarlo, 1964). The dentinal layer in the majority of forms appears to consist of greatly elongated denticles which have fused to form superficial ridges (Bystrow, 1959). Between the ridges, intercostal grooves open to the surface, either continuously or by separate narrow slits. These grooves seem to be homologous with the pore-canal system of osteostracans, and probably are part of the laterosensory system. In some genera they have been observed to connect with the lateral-lines (White, 1935; Denison, 1964). In other forms there are separate tubercles (or denticles) on the surface of the skeleton instead of ridges. These are frequently rounded and crimped at their edges (e.g. *Psammosteus*), resembling the denticles of the thelodont *Thelodus*.

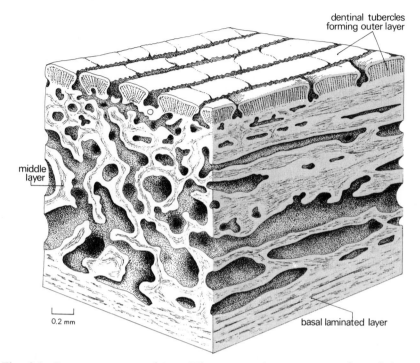

Fig. 3.1. *Psammosteus meandrinus*. Diagram to show structure of exoskeleton. (After Kiaer.)

Heterostracan bone, the so-called aspidin, is usually thought to be acellular. Despite this, Halstead Tarlo (1963, 1964; Halstead, 1969) has described cavities in psammosteid aspidin as cell spaces, which others (e.g. Ørvig, 1967) interpret as collagen fibre spaces. If the acellular nature of aspidin is maintained, the problem remains as to whether this condition is primitive, as the great age of the heterostracans suggests, or secondary, as in the case of acellular bone in higher fishes (Denison, 1963*a*; Ørvig, 1965,

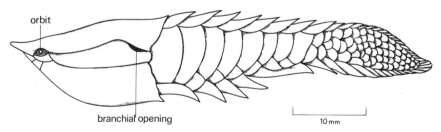

Fig. 3.2. *Anglaspis heintzi*. Restoration in lateral view. (After Kiaer.)

37

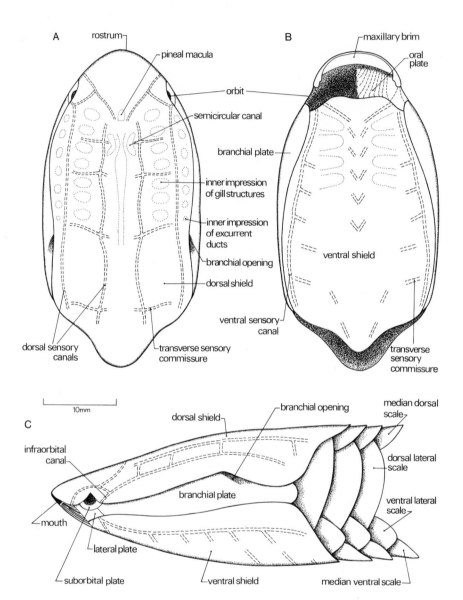

Fig. 3.3. *Poraspis* sp. Restorations of shield in dorsal (A), ventral (B) and lateral (C) views. Impressions on the inner surface of the shield indicated with dotted lines. (After Denison.)

1967). Halstead Tarlo sees aspidin as a primitive tissue ancestral to true bone.

The head and front part of the body are enclosed in a shield formed of a variable number of bony plates. The simplest arrangement is found in cyathaspids (Figs. 3.2, 3.3). The posterior part of the body is covered with scales of similar structure to the head plates, each one overlapping the scale behind and the one below. The orbits are laterally placed. The mouth is usually anterior and ventral, but it is terminal in some amphiaspids and dorsal in psammosteids (Figs. 3.7, 3.11). The mouth is bounded in front by the dorsal shield, which in cyathaspids ends in a simple maxillary brim, but in other forms may include a separate rostral plate. The rostral plate of pteraspids has the maxillary brim region enlarged into an ascending lamina which forms the roof of the mouth, and in front of this there is a distinct preoral field (Fig. 3.4). The mouth is bounded behind by a series of long, relatively narrow oral plates, each bearing a fine tooth lamina. Probably, however, these plates did not bite against the maxillary brim, as was once believed (Kiaer, 1928), but were in a membrane and capable of extrusion to form a shovelling apparatus (White, 1935, 1961; A. Heintz, 1962; Denison, 1964). The gill pouches are enclosed in the cephalic shield. As in the living hagfish *Myxine*, they open posteriorly by right and left common pores, the external gill openings being covered by an elongated branchial plate.

Traces of a calcified endoskeleton are found in the Ordovician *Eriptychius* (Denison, 1967b), but there is no evidence of an endocranium in any other form, and an extensive endoskeleton may not have been present (Denison, 1964; Whiting and Halstead Tarlo, 1965). The internal structure of the head has been inferred from impressions on the inner surface of the dorsal and ventral shields (Fig. 3.3A, B). Unfortunately there is wide disagreement about the exact interpretation of some of these structures (Watson, 1954; Stensiö, 1958, 1964; Denison, 1964; Halstead Tarlo and Whiting, 1965; Whiting and Halstead Tarlo, 1965). The nasal sacs are paired, although the position of the nasal openings is unknown. Since no obvious external openings have been found, it is concluded that the nasal sacs opened into the cavity of the mouth. There is a median pineal organ, and apparently only two semicircular canals. The brain appears to have been primitively organized, with a long, unspecialized medulla, and without the compressed telencephalon of lampreys. Lateral oval impressions on the dorsal and ventral shields are usually thought to have been produced by the gill chambers. Sometimes the impressions bear cross-striations which recall the striations in the gill chambers of some osteostracans (Chapter 2 §3.1). Lateral to these impressions there may be a second series of impressions on the dorsal shield, produced by the excurrent ducts of the gill pouches. Halstead Tarlo and Whiting (1965), however, have interpreted the oval

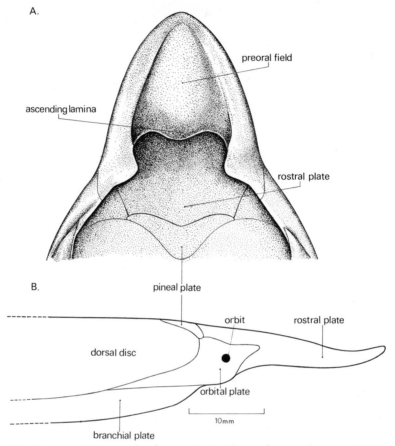

Fig. 3.4. *Pteraspis (Pteraspis) robusta*. Restorations of snout in ventral (A) and lateral (B) views. (After Stensiö.)

impressions as attachment surfaces for a series of muscle blocks, which pumped water through small gill pouches, of which we have no direct evidence. According to either interpretation there were about seven pouches. It has been claimed that the first pouch corresponds to the mandibular or even premandibular somite. But all the attempts to identify the pouches by reference to the position of the semicircular canals fail, if the variable relations of the gills to the ear capsules in osteostracans are taken into consideration. The presence of prespiracular pouches is in any case unlikely, as there was probably a velum (Chapter 2 §3.1) at the back of the oral cavity (Watson, 1954; Stensiö, 1958, 1963). Markings are sometimes found on the ventral shield, indicating the position of salivary glands and perhaps an endostyle.

40

The lateral-line system (White, 1935; Denison, 1964) is well-developed in the form of canals in the middle layer of the exoskeleton, which open to the outside by a series of pores. The arrangement of the canals, particularly in cyathaspids (Figs. 3.3, 3.6), approaches the hypothetical primitive condition from which the patterns in other agnathans, and gnathostomes, can be derived. There are two paired dorsal and two paired ventral longitudinal canals, joined into separate dorsal and ventral networks by transverse commissures. The infraorbital canals connect the dorsal and ventral networks.

The anterior part of the body is dorsoventrally flattened, but the posterior part is laterally compressed. There are no dorsal, anal or paired fins, although some of the functions of paired fins are fulfilled by skeletal outgrowths in the more advanced groups. The tail is hypocercal as in anaspids, but with the larger lobe ventral.

3.3.2. Growth and the evolution of the shield

The study of growth in heterostracans has been largely concerned with the application of the lepidomorial theory in recent years (Stensiö, 1958, 1968; Halstead Tarlo, 1960, 1962a, b, 1964, 1967b). This theory postulates that the primitive element of the exoskeleton is the lepidomorium, initially a simple crown of dentine developing over a vascular loop in the dermis (compare odontode or dermal tooth of Ørvig, 1968). Lepidomoria are individually incapable of growth, but units of lepidomoria are said to grow in one of two basic ways. They may become united at their bases so that their simple pulp cavities remain separate. In this way discrete lepidomoria are continuously

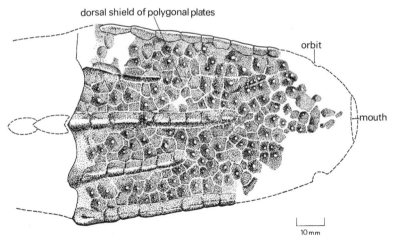

Fig. 3.5. *Astraspis desiderata*. Restoration of head in dorsal view. (After Tarlo.)

41

added around a primordium to give a growing *cyclomorial* unit. Or the developing lepidomoria may fuse before calcification takes place, with the result that a complex *synchronomorial* unit with a compound pulp cavity is formed in one step. More complicated growth patterns are also recognized, with, for example, a synchronomorial primordium growing cyclomorially by the addition of further synchronomorial units (Stensiö, 1961). Whilst there can be little doubt of the importance of the lepidomorial theory, particularly in the description of the elasmobranch scales on which it is based, its rigid application to heterostracans has unfortunately led to both incorrect interpretations of growth and doubtful phylogenetic conclusions (Denison, 1964; Westoll, 1967). For these reasons, the theory is not applied in this chapter (see Chapter 9 §2).

A primitive heterostracan exoskeleton is possessed by the Ordovician genera *Astraspis* and *Eriptychius*, (Fig. 3.5), in which the shield is a mosaic of small polygonal plates (Stensiö, 1958; 1964; Halstead Tarlo, 1962*a*; Denison, 1967*b*). These plates grew in area by marginal addition, and in thickness by the apposition of successive generations of tubercles on the surface. Growth continued throughout life, and was accompanied by a limited amount of resorption and reformation of the bone. The apparently simple shield of cyathaspids, however, offers a rather more complicated picture when growth is considered (Denison, 1964; Westoll, 1967). There is a limited range of size for any one species, which as in osteostracans is evidence of a long, naked larval life, followed by the rapid acquisition of the skeleton at the cessation of growth. Moreover, the most superficial part of the skeleton formed first, and the outer layer seems to some degree to have been morphogenetically independent of the middle and basal layers, again as in osteostracans. In many cyathaspids the dorsal shield is divided into distinct areas, the epitega, by the pattern of the superficial ridges, and in *Tolypelepis* the epitega are further subdivided into scale-like units, which recall the polygonal plates of *Astraspis*. Although this subdivision of the shield is entirely superficial, it has been taken to show that the adult cyathaspid shield developed by the fusion of scale-like units, that first underwent a lengthy period of independent marginal growth in the larva. However, it is more probable that this superficial subdivision of the shield resulted only from the ontogenetic history of the outer layer, which was first laid down as a series of discrete, superficial tubercles in the skin.

The pteraspids and psammosteids have bone patterns similar to that of cyathaspids, and there can be little doubt that these three groups are closely related. Pteraspids and psammosteids differed from cyathaspids in the early appearance of the armour, to protect the early growth stages. Growth was then accompanied by an increase in the size of the bony plates by marginal addition, until the growth of the animal terminated. In pteraspids

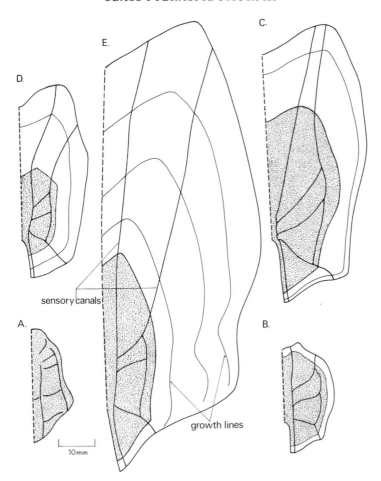

Fig. 3.6. Half dorsal discs showing sensory canals and 'growth-stages'. Stage of completion of armour stippled. (After White). A. *Poraspis polaris*; B. *Pteraspis leathensis*; C. *Pteraspis rostrata*; D. *Pteraspis crouchi*; E. *Rhinopteraspis dunensis*.

the dorsal network of sensory lines became entrapped in the dorsal shield as soon as the armour was formed, and the subsequent growth of the shield took place outside this network (Fig. 3.6). From this we can see that the armour was acquired not long before full growth in early pteraspids, but that in later forms the period of growth after the formation of the armour became progressively longer (White, 1958). Psammosteids differ from pteraspids principally in the separation of the main median and paired plates of the shield by a mosaic of small, scale-like plates (Fig. 3.7). It has been suggested that the small plates were formed to protect the sensory lines in

43

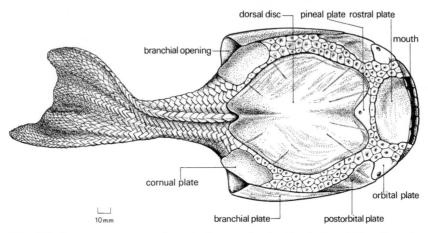

Fig. 3.7. *Drepanaspis gemuendenensis*. Restoration in dorsal view. (After Gross.)

juveniles (Obruchev), but as the mosaic is absent from very small individuals of *Drepanaspis* (Gross, 1963) this is unlikely. Apparently the growth of the large plates by marginal addition, was well-advanced before the mosaic appeared. The dorsal and ventral discs of the later genus *Psammolepis* grew from a thick central area at a deep level in the dermis, to produce flanges on which the superficial mosaic attached. In the still later genus *Psammosteus*, the entire upper surface of all the major plates was situated at a deep level in the dermis, and became covered by the mosaic. These genera thus provide further evidence of the ontogenetic separation of the superficial and deeper layers of the exoskeleton, and with *Drepanaspis* as the starting point form a series showing some remarkable changes in the growth and disposition of the armour. The adaptive significance of these changes is not understood. Besides this, the reappearance of a mosaic of scale-like plates in the shield in psammosteids demonstrates that the evolution of the armour in heterostracans involved both assimilative and regressive phases (see Chapter 5 §3), that is to say, both the fusion of small plates to produce large ones, and the disintegration of large plates into scale-like components.

Cardipeltids have both marginally-growing large plates and small plates in a mosaic (Fig. 3.13), and in these respects are similar to *Drepanaspis* (Denison, 1966). The amphiaspids, however, present new problems. The shield is normally preserved as a sutureless capsule, and might be thought to have ossified only at full growth, as in osteostracans (Figs. 3.11, 3.12). It appears, however, that the young had separate, marginally-growing plates, which then fused in the adults and became covered with a continuous layer of dentinal tissue (Obruchev, 1967a; Novitskaya, 1968). Similar changes are thought to have taken place in some placoderms (Chapter 8 §7.1).

3.3.3. Diversity and interrelationships

The Ordovician genera *Astraspis* and *Eriptychius* are similar in having a primitive shield of separate scale-like units. They are nevertheless classified in different orders because of differences in histological details. The eriptychiids seem to stand nearer to the ancestry of later heterostracans. *Tesseraspis* from the Lower Devonian has been placed in this group (Obruchev, 1967*a*), although there is no means of deciding whether the scale-like shield is primitive or secondarily derived from large plates.

Superficially the cyathaspids have a simple armour, with principally median dorsal and ventral shields and paired branchial plates (Fig. 3.3). There is no dorsal spine, although a large ridge scale in *Ariaspis* foreshadows the spine of pteraspids (Denison, 1963*b*, 1964). On the body the scales are few and very large. *Tolypelepis* is a primitive genus, perhaps retaining vestiges of *Eriptychius*-like ancestors in the superficial division of the dorsal shield. Later forms, such as *Cyathaspis*, lose the superficial scale-like subdivisions of the shield, and ultimately the epitega are also lost, e.g. *Poraspis*, *Allocryptaspis*. *Ctenaspis* is an isolated Lower Devonian genus in which the branchial plates have fused with the dorsal shield.

In pteraspids (Figs. 3.4, 3.8, 3.9) the dorsal shield is divided into a rostral, a pineal, a dorsal disc, a paired orbital enclosing the orbit, branchials and cornuals; the ventral disc is bounded anteriorly by one or two lateral plates; there is also a well-formed dorsal spine. The body is covered by numerous, small rhomboidal scales. The classification of pteraspids has proved troublesome because of a bewildering range of minor variations in ornament and form, and the frequency of parallel evolution. Accordingly at a low taxonomic level, a series of "varieties" have been recognized in *Pteraspis* (White, 1935), which, if biologically valid, must now be recognized as subspecies. At a higher level, many subgenera have been erected (White, 1950, 1956, 1961; Denison, 1967*a*), although other workers now recognize each as a genus in its own right (Stensiö, 1958, 1964; Halstead Tarlo, 1961). The earliest pteraspids are generally small with a narrow, rounded snout, e.g. *Pteraspis* (*Protopteraspis*) spp. Later forms tend to be larger with either a

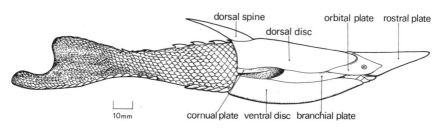

Fig. 3.8. *Pteraspis rostrata*. Restoration in lateral view. (After White.)

broad, blunt snout, e.g. *Protaspis*, or a narrow, long snout, e.g. *Pteraspis* (*Althaspis*) spp. These changes are correlated with the development of the preoral field and differences in the feeding mechanism (see Mode of life §3.4). The long snouted condition seems to have evolved independently in several lines (Halstead Tarlo, 1961; Denison, 1967a). *Doryaspis* (Fig. 3.9) is a highly specialized pteraspid with a dorsally opening mouth and a long "pseudorostrum" reaching forwards from the front margin of the ventral shield (N. Heintz, 1968). Long, curved cornual plates project from the shield to function as gliding planes. This last adaptation is also found in other pteraspids (e.g. *Pteraspis lerichei*).

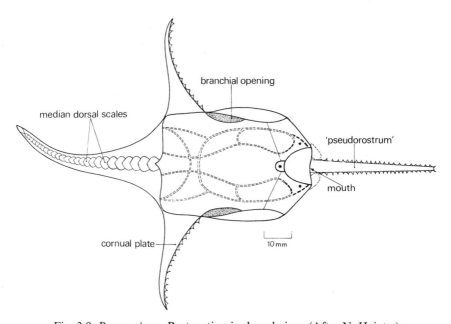

Fig. 3.9. *Doryaspis* sp. Restoration in dorsal view. (After N. Heintz.)

Evidently pteraspids have evolved from cyathaspids by the subdivision of the shield (Denison, 1964). The separate rostral, pineal and dorsal disc of pteraspids are to some extent foreshadowed by the epitega of primitive cyathaspids. *Traquairaspis* (White, 1946) is of interest as possibly a primitive pteraspid in which the branchial and cornual plates have not yet separated, although not all workers agree with this interpretation.

In psammosteids the head-shield is relatively large and much dorso-ventrally flattened. The dorsal part is divided into thirteen large plates. These heterostracans seem to have been derived from pteraspids by the addition of a postorbital plate and the formation of a scale mosaic between the large plates of the shield (Obruchev, 1967a; Westoll, 1967). In *Drepanaspis* the body is covered with numerous, small rhomboid scales (Fig. 3.7). Depressed, early, Lower Devonian pteraspids such as *Protaspis* (*Europrotaspis*) spp. with small cornuals, large branchials and posterior branchial openings, are morphologically suitable as psammosteid ancestors.

We have already noted some of the changes that took place in the growth and form of the psammosteid shield during the evolution of the group, starting with a primitive Lower Devonian form like *Drepanaspis*. In addition, Middle and Upper Devonian genera differ from *Drepanaspis* in the shape and size of the branchial plates. These plates are primitively long and narrow, but develop into a wide variety of broad and long shapes in later forms, to act as gliding planes and props (Halstead Tarlo, 1964; Obruchev and Mark-Kurik, 1965, 1968). *Tartuosteus* and *Pycnosteus* (Fig. 3.10) are

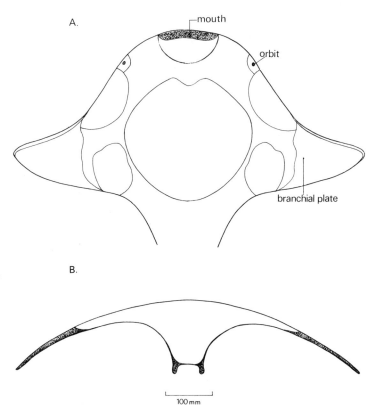

Fig. 3.10. *Pycnosteus tuberculatus*. Restoration of head in dorsal view (A), with thick section through branchial plates (B). (After Obruchev and Mark.)

47

broad genera that reached a length of 1.5 m, whereas *Psammolepis* and *Psammosteus* are smaller, generally narrower forms. A common trend in psammosteid evolution is the narrowing of the ventral shield, to lessen its area of contact with the bottom. In *Pycnosteus* this results in the formation of long ventral runners (Fig. 3.10B).

The cyathaspids, pteraspids and psammosteids are the main groups of heterostracans, and are closely related in the way already shown. They represent successive major radiations of the subclass, the cyathaspids reaching the peak of their evolution in the Upper Silurian and early Devonian, the pteraspids in the Lower Devonian and the psammosteids in the Middle and Upper Devonian. This might appear at first sight to be a simple example of successive replacement by biologically more efficient groups; but the answer is probably more complex, as both different environ-

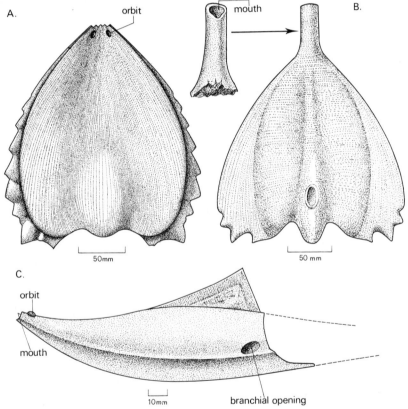

Fig. 3.11. A. *Hibernaspis macrolepis*. Restoration of shield in dorsal view; B. *Eglonaspis rostrata*. Restoration of shield in dorsal view, with ventral view of rostrum; C. *Olbiaspis coalescens*. Restoration of shield in lateral view. (After Obruchev.)

ments (Obruchev, 1967*b*) and the rise of the gnathostomes are involved. Psammosteids were the last large group of heterostracans and they competed successfully with the rapidly radiating gnathostomes by becoming narrowly specialized for bottom living.

There is a fourth major group of heterostracans, the amphiaspids, that underwent an astonishing radiation in Lower and early Middle Devonian times in Siberia (Obruchev, 1967*a, b*; Novitskaya, 1968). This group includes species with a solid, sutureless shield, that are believed to have evolved from a cyathaspid such as *Ctenaspis*, which exhibits incipient fusion of plates. *Hibernaspis* (Fig. 3.11A) has small, anteriorly-situated eyes, and the branchial region produced into large thorn-like outgrowths. *Eglonaspis* (Fig. 3.11B) is closely related, but lacks orbits and was completely blind; it has the mouth at the end of a long, narrow tube. *Olbiaspis* (Fig. 3.11C) has a less compressed shield than these two genera, which is raised into a high dorsal crest; the branchial region extends out as long lateral keels and the branchial openings are dorsal. *Siberiaspis* and *Angaraspis* resemble *Olbiaspis* in having a terminal mouth and lateral keels. These keel-like extensions of the branchial region are an interesting parallel with psammosteids. Several forms have small openings in the shield behind the orbit (Fig. 3.12). These may be spiracles (Halstead), showing that the first gill-pouch was hyoidean in position, as in osteostracans.

The cardipeltids include the single genus *Cardipeltis* (Denison, 1966). It is characterized by its large dorsal disc (Fig. 3.13), orbitals, a series of marginals and a mosaic of scale-like plates. It is a depressed form with a superficial resemblance to psammosteids, although it differs in the position of the branchial openings, which notch the dorsal disc, as well as in the detailed pattern of the plates. The tail is slender, covered with small scales and lacks median fins. *Cardipeltis* has apparently evolved directly from some primitive heterostracans with a shield of small scales, and has no close relationship with the cyathaspids, pteraspids or psammosteids.

3.3.4. Mode of life

The heterostracans were primitively bottom feeding forms, but during the course of their evolution they radiated into a range of nektonic and specialized benthic species far exceeding that found in cephalaspidomorphs.

Cyathaspids have a shield superficially similar to that of tremataspids among osteostracans, although they differ in the possession of a hypocercal tail. A tail of this form elevates the snout during swimming (Kermack, 1943), and whilst this was probably an important factor in the evolution of surface-feeding pteraspids such as *Doryaspis*, it seems to have served initially to push the snout through the bottom mud in the manner described for anaspids

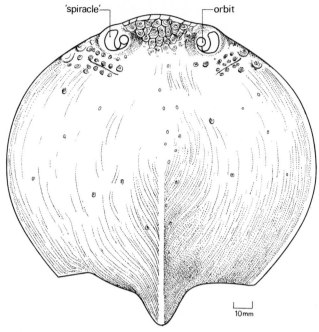

Fig. 3.12. *Gabreyaspis tarda*. Restoration of shield in dorsal view. Note the inclusion of scale-like components in the rostral region. (After Novitskaya.)

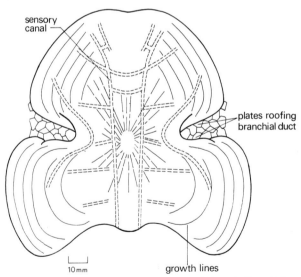

Fig. 3.13. *Cardipeltis richardsoni*. Inner surface of dorsal disc. (After Denison.)

(Chapter 2 §7). The oral plates show no sign of having attached to jaw cartilages or of having had powerful muscle attachments, and accordingly could not have been part of a biting apparatus of gnathostome type. However, they are plausibly interpreted as having been set in a membrane and capable of extrusion. Thus primitive heterostracans probably fed on bottom deposits either by scooping or sucking. If an endostyle was present in cyathaspids, it presumably produced a mucous bag which filtered food particles out of the respiratory stream, as in larval lampreys.

From the unspecialized, bottom feeding cyathaspids evolved the more widely adapted pteraspids, and from these the depressed, benthic psammosteids. Psammosteids were paralleled by the cardipeltids, which evolved from a quite different ancestral group.

In *Pteraspis*, there are species like *P. dairydinglensis* with a strongly vaulted shield, short snout, broad mouth and small preoral field. The preoral field is believed to have been a sensory area connected with food finding, so this species was probably an unselective feeder in food-rich surface waters (White, 1961). *Pteraspis leachi* and *P. dunensis* have even smaller preoral fields, and a long broad snout, and seem to have been mid- or surface-water feeders in strong currents. *Pteraspis crouchi*, on the other hand, has a narrow, rounded snout and a large preoral field, and is interpreted as a bottom feeder in cloudy waters. A highly specialized surface-water feeding pteraspid is found in *Doryaspis* (Fig. 3.9.), in which the oral plates and preoral field have gone, and the mouth opens dorsally (N. Heintz, 1968).

The oral plates were also lost in amphiaspids, which include genera with suctorial mouths in some respects reminiscent of osteostracans, e.g. *Olbiaspis*, *Angaraspis*. The blind, tubular mouthed *Eglonaspis* is adapted for sucking small organisms from the bottom mud. As the shield of heterostracans is a rigid capsule of essentially fixed volume, it is reasonable to suppose that the respiratory current was maintained by a muscular velar pump (Watson, 1954). Presumably this pump was harnessed for feeding, particularly in the more specialized suctorial types, such as *Doryaspis* and the amphiaspids.

The thick, high scales of cyathaspids and lack of fins suggest erratic, tadpole-like swimming. The tail may have been used as a defensive club (Obruchev, 1967a). More advanced heterostracans have smaller scales and were more powerful swimmers; this seems to be particularly true of the pteraspids. Paired fins are absent in the earliest heterostracans, and in contrast to cephalaspidomorphs, flexible pectoral fins were never developed within the group. However, rigid lateral keels were formed by the cornual plates in pteraspids and by the branchial plates in psammosteids and amphiaspids, to function as gliding planes and props. Unlike the pectoral fins of cephalaspidomorphs, these keels did not evolve from ventrolateral ridges

51

of the body, and are only analogous with pectoral fins. The large dorsal spine of pteraspids may have been a stabilizing structure, although it was more probably defensive. The dorsal crest of amphiaspids is more clearly a median keel.

It is not easy to single out characters to explain the success of heterostracans in comparison with osteostracans and anaspids, and their colonization of varied marine and freshwater niches. Of crucial importance, perhaps, was the acquisition by most groups of a mechanism permitting the protective shield to form at an early stage of growth, and then continue to grow throughout the life of the animal.

3.4. INCERTAE SEDIS *POLYBRANCHIASPIS*

Polybranchiaspis (Liu, 1965) is a remarkable agnathan from the Lower Devonian of China, with a sutureless dorsal shield (Fig. 3.14) of similar extent to the fused dorsal and branchial plates of the cyathaspid *Ctenaspis*; and with a ventral shield surrounded by small polygonal scales. It differs from typical heterostracans in that each gill-pouch has a separate opening, as in osteostracans. A somewhat similar arrangement is found, however, in thelodonts, although in these fishes there is no shield. *Polybranchiaspis* has a

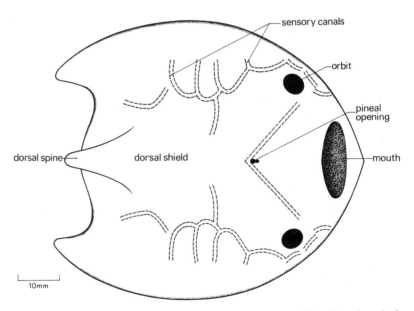

Fig. 3.14. *Polybranchiaspis liaojaoshanensis*. Restoration of head in dorsal view. (After Liu.)

52

dorsal pineal opening, but there is no sign of a nasohypophysial foramen and the nasal openings are assumed to be in the mouth as in typical heterostracans. The mouth is dorsal, and together with the orbits it is completely enclosed in the dorsal shield.

Polybranchiaspis shows similarities to psammosteids in the dorsal position of the mouth and eyes, and in its broad, flat form. These, however, are common adaptations in benthic fish, and hardly evidence of close relationship. Halstead Tarlo (1967a) has allied *Polybranchiaspis* with *Galeaspis*, here considered to be an osteostracan, in a new division of the Cephalaspidomorphi termed the Galeaspidida. This is an interesting suggestion, but for the moment we may accept that *Polybranchiaspis* has evolved from the ancestral stock of the heterostracans, as Liu suggests.

3.5. SUBCLASS 2, THELODONTI

The thelodonts are a group of very unsatisfactorily known fishes, whose entire body in the head, trunk and tail regions is covered with placoid-like denticles (Gross, 1967, 1968a, b; Obruchev, 1967a, b; Ørvig, 1969a, b, c; Ritchie, 1968), which may be conical as in *Lanarkia* or stud-like and interlocking as in *Logania*. These two genera are found in the Upper Silurian, and *Turinia* in the Lower Devonian, but denticles which are attributed to thelodonts are known from the Ordovician. *Amaltheolepis* occurs in the Middle Devonian. Thelodonts usually only measure some 100 to 200 mm in length, but the Lower Devonian *Turinia pagei* is about 400 mm long.

3.5.1. Structure

Thelodonts are dorsoventrally flattened anteriorly (Figs. 3.15, 3.16). The denticles frequently show regional differentiation, so that in *Turinia* they

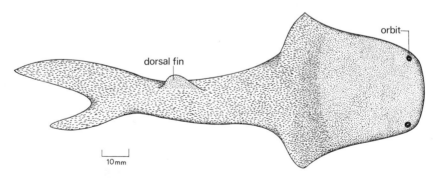

Fig. 3.15. *Longania scotica.* Restoration in dorsal view. (After Traquair.)

53

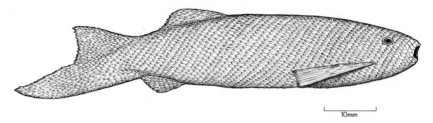

Fig. 3.16. *Phlebolepis elegans*. Restoration in lateral view. (After Ritchie.)

have flat crowns on the head and high crowns on the tail. They are grouped into a "rostral epitegum" on the top of the head in *Phlebolepis*. The orbits are far apart and lateral. The mouth is ventral but nearly terminal. Whether it was in the form of an oval split as in anaspids, or a horizontal fissure as in heterostracans is unfortunately not clear, although the latter interpretation seems the more likely. There are traces of eight branchial chambers (Traquair, 1899; Turner, 1968) which suggest gill-sacs of lamprey type. The chambers open by separate apertures in a short row under the lateral fins (Ritchie, 1968), an arrangement somewhat comparable with that in *Poly-branchiaspis*. These lateral fins are little more than extended posterior lateral angles of the head. That they were flexibly mobile structures comparable with the pectoral fins of osteostracans is doubtful. They seem to be more closely comparable with the laterally extended cornual and branchial plates of advanced heterostracans. The tail is hypocercal, with the upper lobe the larger, and there are single dorsal and anal fins.

The denticles have a crown of dentinal tissue over an open pulp cavity. The basal region is composed of aspidin. Histologically, two types of denticles are recognized. The Thelodontida have the *Thelodus* type of denticle, in which the dentine tubules arise directly from between one and three large pulp cavities and rarely branch (Fig. 3.17A). The Phlebolepidida have the *Katoporus* type of denticle, in which typically there are many

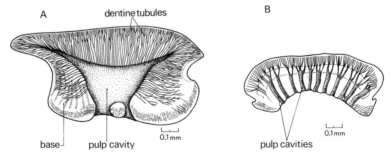

Fig. 3.17. Thin sections of thelodont scales to show structure. (After Gross.) A. *Thelodus parvidens*; B. *Katoporus rhizoides*.

54

posteriorly situated pulp cavities (Fig. 3.17B) which give rise to immediately branching bundles of dentine tubules in the crown of mesodentine (Gross, 1967). Occasionally the pulp cavities merge into one large cavity in this second type. Traces of the lateral-line system have been found in the form of pore-canal scales in *Phlebolepis*. The arrangement of these scales is poorly understood, although they seem to form longitudinal rows (Gross, 1968a).

3.5.2. Diversity and affinities

Thelodonts prove to be a remarkably uniform group where they are known from articulated specimens. Like the anaspids with a hypocercal tail and lateral fins, they seem to have been bottom feeding forms, finding small organisms in the mud. This interpretation is supported by the depressed form of the head. The subclass is divided into two orders on histological grounds, but this division is not reflected in the gross morphology of the fishes.

There are two outstanding questions about thelodonts: are they a natural group, and if so are they more closely related to heterostracans than to other agnathans? The answer to the first question is clearly yes, if we consider only well-known genera such as *Thelodus*, *Logania*, *Turinia*, *Phlebolepis* and *Lanarkia*. In all probability most of the detached denticles that have been described as thelodonts really belong to this group. Nevertheless the suspicion lingers that denticles from early growth stages of other groups have been confused with thelodonts, perhaps because denticle-like teeth (lepidomoria or odontodes) are believed to be the first formed units of the early vertebrate exoskeleton, both in ontogeny and phylogeny (Westoll, 1945; Obruchev, 1967a, b; Ørvig, 1968).

Thelodonts resemble heterostracans in general form, the position of the eyes and gill chambers, the absence of a dorsal nasohypophysial duct, the dentinal tissue of the exoskeleton and in the resemblance of the denticles to the superficial layer of the shield. It seems then that the heterostracans and thelodonts are more closely related to each other than to other groups, and if this is the case they are correctly classified together as pteraspidomorphs. Yet the relationship can at best only be a distant one. The most obvious difference between the two groups lies in the dermal skeleton. Some authors, particularly Stensiö (1932, 1958, 1964), believe that the thelodont skeleton has been derived from the plates of heterostracans by regressive evolution, so that the plates have become broken up into their original denticle-like components. Ørvig (1968) has pointed out, however, that where we can follow the break-up of large bones in later fishes, e.g. in osteichthyans, the head plates and trunk scales do not assume the same form. Thus it is probable that the nearly uniform denticles of thelodonts are primitive units, and not the break-down products of large plates, for their regional differentiation is of a superficial nature.

3.6. RELATIONSHIPS OF AGNATHANS

From the foregoing descriptions of fossil agnathans it will be seen that the osteostracans and anaspids on the one hand, and the heterostracans on the other, have in common the bony exoskeleton, the absence of jaws, the presence of two semicircular canals, and possibly the nature of the gill-pouches. The thelodonts are clearly agnathans as far as the better-known genera are concerned, and they may be related to heterostracans. In the last three of the above characters, the osteostracans, anaspids and heterostracans resemble the living petromyzonids and myxinoids. The petromyzonids and myxinoids differ from one another most obviously in the position of the nasohypophysial opening, which is dorsal in the former due to the hypertrophy of the upper lip during ontogeny, and terminal or slightly ventral in the latter. On account of this, attempts have been made (Stensiö, 1927, 1958, 1964) to prove that on the one hand myxinoids are closely related to heterostracans, in which the nasohypophysial opening is not dorsal, and that on the other, petromyzonids are closely related to osteostracans and anaspids, in which the nasohypophysial opening is dorsal. This is extremely unlikely, because heterostracans have a paired nasal capsule and probably a paired nasal opening, whereas the single capsule and opening in the other groups is an important common specialization (Halstead Tarlo, 1961; A. Heintz, 1962, 1963).

As has been emphasized, the living agnathans, particularly the petromyzonids, have many points in common with osteostracans, but the majority of them are probably primitive agnathan characters and are not necessarily signs of close affinity. In addition to specializations in the feeding mechanism (rasping tongue or transversely biting, horny tooth-plates), the living forms differ from most osteostracans and anaspids in the complete absence of bone and dentine and of paired fins. However, the arrangement of the muco-cartilage in the head of the ammocoete larva of *Petromyzon* is very reminiscent of the head-shield of osteostracans, and it is not impossible that the petromyzonids have lost their bone and paired fins, or evolved from early members in which paired fins were not developed. It is very common to find in all groups of bony fishes that have been in existence for a long time a progressive loss of bone as the group becomes older. Perhaps the anaspids are more likely to be related to the ancestors of the petromyzonids, in view of their mutual possession of long cranial and branchial regions. *Jamoytius* is particularly suggestive of the ancestral condition, with its lightly ossified skeleton, branchial basket, and round, subterminal mouth supported by an annular cartilage. Unfortunately the only fossil lamprey, the Carboniferous *Mayomyzon*, neither confirms nor denies this theory; it only shows us that remarkably "modern" lampreys were in existence shortly after the decline of typical, well-armoured Palaeozoic agnathans.

Whilst it is by no means unbelievable that the petromyzonids shared a common ancestor with the anaspids or osteostracans, the origin of the myxinoids is still a puzzle. A comparison between petromyzonids and myxinoids is beyond the scope of this book, but despite their superficial similarity they differ profoundly in their detailed morphology, and are believed to have had long separate histories (Jarvik, 1965). This view is supported by *Mayomyzon*, which has no myxinoid characters.

The osteostracans, anaspids and petromyzonids seem to be more closely related to one another than to the myxinoids; and all four groups more closely related to one another than they are to any other group of fishes.

The heterostracans, and probably also the thelodonts, stand far apart from other agnathans. Heterostracans resemble gnathostomes in having paired nasal capsules and the snout formed by the front of the cranium, and some amphiaspids appear to have a spiracular opening. Consequently it has been suggested that the heterostracans may be ancestral to the gnathostomes (Halstead, 1969). But such an evolutionary position is impossible if their gills are correctly interpreted as internally-directed structures of the type found in other agnathans (see Halstead Tarlo and Whiting, 1965). Further, the terminally-situated, paired nasal capsules are a primitive vertebrate character, being found in the early developmental stages of the living monorhinal petromyzonids and myxinoids, and are thus not evidence of close heterostracan-gnathostome relations. We can only conclude that the affinities of pteraspidomorphs are still hidden, but the suggestion of gnathostome affinities is important enough to warrant very careful consideration.

REFERENCES

References given in Chapter 2 are not repeated

Bystrow, A. P. (1959) 'The microstructure of the skeletal elements in some vertebrates from Lower Devonian deposits of the URSS'. *Acta. zool. Stockh.*, **40**, 59–83.

Denison, R. H. (1953) 'Early Devonian fishes from Utah. Pt. 2. Heterostraci'. *Fieldiana. Geol.*, **11**, 291–355.

Denison, R. H. (1955) 'Early Devonian vertebrates from the Knoydart Formation of Nova Scotia'. *Fieldiana, Zool.*, **37**, 449–62.

Denison, R. H. (1960) 'Fishes of the Devonian Holland shale of Ohio'. *Fieldiana, Geol.*, **10**, 555–97.

Denison, R. H. (1963a) See Chapter 2.

Denison, R. H. (1963b) 'New Silurian Heterostraci from Southeastern Yukon'.

Fieldiana, Geol., **14**, 105–41.

Denison, R. H. (1964) 'The Cyathaspididae. A family of Silurian and Devonian jawless vertebrates'. *Fieldiana, Geol.*, **13**, 309–473.

Denison, R. H. (1966) '*Cardipeltis* an early Devonian agnathan of the order Heterostraci'. *Fieldiana, Geol.*, **16**, 89–116.

Denison, R. H. (1967a) 'A new *Protaspis* from the Devonian of Utah, with notes on the classification of Pteraspididae'. *J. Linn. Soc. (Zool.)*, **47**, 31–37.

Denison, R. H. (1967b) 'Ordovician vertebrates from western United States'. *Fieldiana, Geol.*, **16**, 131–92.

Denison, R. H. (1968) 'Middle Devonian fishes from the Lemhi Range of Ohio'. *Fieldiana, Geol.*, **16**, 269–88.

Denison, R. H. (1970) 'Revised classification of Pteraspididae with description of new forms from Wyoming'. *Fieldiana, Geol.*, **20**, 1–41.

Dineley, D. L. (1953) 'Notes on the genus *Corvaspis*'. *Proc. R. Soc. Edinb.*, **65**B, 166–81.

Dineley, D. L. (1964) 'New specimens of *Traquairaspis* from Canada'. *Palaeontology*, **7**, 210–19.

Dineley, D. L. (1967) 'The Lower Devonian Knoydart faunas'. *J. Linn. Soc. (Zool.)*., **47**, 15–29.

Fahlbusch, K. (1957) '*Pteraspis dunensis* Roemer. Eine Neubearbeitung der Pteraspidenfunde (Agnathen) von Overath. *Palaeontographica*, **108**A, 1–56.

Gross, W. (1963) '*Drepanaspis gemuendenensis* Schlüter. Neuuntersuchung'. *Palaeontographica*, **121**A, 133–55.

Gross, W. (1967) 'Über Thelodontier-schuppen'. *Palaeontographica*, **127**A, 1–67.

Gross, W. (1968a) 'Porenschuppen und Sinneslinien des Thelodontiers *Phlebolepis elegans* Pander'. *Paläont. Z.*, **42**, 131–46.

Gross, W. (1968b) 'Die Agnathen-fauna der Silurischen Hallaschichten Gotlands'. *Geol. Fören. Stockh. Förh.*, **90**, 369–400

Heintz, A. (1957) 'The dorsal shield of *Psammolepis paradoxa* Agassiz'. *J. Pal. Soc. India, D.N. Wadia Jub. No.*, 153–62.

Heintz, A. (1962) 'Les organes olfactifs des Heterostraci'. *Colloques int. Cent. natn. Rech. Scient.*, **104**, 13–29.

Heintz, A. (1963) 'Phylogenetic aspects of myxinoids', in *The biology of Myxine*, ed. Brodal A. & Fänge, R. (Universitetsforlaget, Oslo) p. 9.

Heintz, N. (1960) 'The Downtonian and Devonian Vertebrates of Spitsbergen. 11. *Gigantaspis*—a new genus of fam. Pteraspidae from Spitsbergen'. *Norsk Polarinst Årb.*, (1960) 22–27.

Heintz, N. (1968) 'The pteraspid *Lyktaspis* n.g. from the Devonian of Vestspitsbergen'. *Nobel Symposium*, **4**, 73–80.

Jarvik, E. (1964) 'Specializations in early vertebrates'. *Annls. Soc. r. zool. Belg.*, **94**, 11–95.

Kermack, K. A. (1943) 'The functional significance of the hypocercal tail in *Pteraspis*'. *J. exp. biol.*, **20**, 23–27.

Kiaer, J. (1928) 'The structure of the mouth of the oldest known vertebrates, pteraspids and cephalaspids'. *Palaeobiologica*, **1**, 117–34.

Lehman, J. P. (1967) 'Quelques remarques concernant *Drepanaspis gemuendenensis* Schluter'. *J. Linn. Soc. (Zool.)*, **47**, 39–43.

Mark-Kurik, E. (1968) 'New finds of psammosteids (Heterostraci) in the Devonian of Estonia and Latvia', *ENSV, TA Toimetised K, Geoloogia*, **4**, 409–24.

Novitskaya, L. I. (1968) 'New amphiaspids (Heterostraci) from the Lower Devonian of Siberia and the classification of the Amphiaspidiformes' in *Outlines of the phylogeny and systematics of fossil fishes and agnathans*, ed. Obruchev, D. V. (Moscow) p. 43. (In Russian.)

Obruchev, D. V. (1967*a*) 'Class Diplorhina (Pteraspidomorphi)', in *Fundamentals of Palaeontology. 11. Agnatha, Pisces*, ed. Obruchev, D. V. (Israel program for scientific translations, Jerusalem.) p. 41.

Obruchev, D. V. (1967*b*) 'On the evolution of the Heterostraci'. *Colloques int. Cent. natn. Rech. Scient.*, **163**, 37–47.

Obruchev, D. V. and Mark-Kurik, E. (1965) 'Devonian psammosteids (Agnatha, Psammosteidae) of the U.S.S.R.' *Geol. Inst. Acad. Sci. Est. SSR*. (In Russian with English summary.)

Obruchev, D. V. and Mark-Kurik, E. (1968) 'On the evolution of the psammosteids (Heterostraci)'. *ENSV, TA Toimetised K. Geoloogia*, **3**, 279–84.

Ørvig, T. (1958) '*Pycnaspis splendens*, new genus, new species, a new ostracoderm from the Upper Ordovician of North America'. *Proc. U.S. Nat. Mus.*, **108**, 1–23.

Ørvig, T. (1961) 'Notes on some early representatives of the Drepanaspida (Pteraspidomorphi, Heterostraci)'. *Ark. Zool.*, (2) **12**, 515–35.

Ørvig, T. (1967) 'Phylogeny of tooth tissues: evolution of some calcified tissues in early vertebrates', in *Structural and chemical organization of teeth*, ed. Miles, A. E. W. (Academic Press, New York and London) p. 45.

Ørvig, T. (1969*a*) 'Thelodont scales from the Grey Hoek formation of Andrée Land, Spitsbergen'. *Norsk geol. Tidsskr.*, **49**, 387–401.

Ørvig, T. (1969*b*) 'The vertebrate fauna of the *primaeva* Beds of the Fraenkelryggen formation of Vestspitsbergen and its biostratigraphical significance'. *Lethaia*, **2**, 219–39.

Ørvig, T. (1969*c*) 'Vertebrates from the Wood Bay group and the position of the Emsian-Eifelian boundary in the Devonian of Vestspitsbergen'. *Lethaia*, **2**, 273–328.

Ritchie, A. (1968) '*Phlebolepis elegans* Pander, an Upper Silurian theolodont from Oesel, with remarks on the morphology of thelodonts'. *Nobel Symposium*, **4**, 81–88.

Stensiö, E. A. (1961) 'Permian vertebrates', in *Geology of the Arctic*, ed. Raasch, G. O. (University of Toronto Press) p. 231.

Stensiö, E. A. (1968) 'The cyclostomes with special reference to the diphyletic origin of the Petromyzontida and Myxinoidea', *Nobel Symposium*, **4**, 13–71.

Tarlo, L. B. Halstead (1960) 'The Downtonian ostracoderm *Corvaspis* Woodward, with notes on the development of dermal plates in the Heterostraci'. *Palaeontology*, **3**, 217–26.

Tarlo, L. B. Halstead (1961) '*Rhinopteraspis cornubica* (McCoy) with notes on the classification and evolution of the pteraspids'. *Acta palaeont. pol.*, **4**, 367–402.

Tarlo, L. B. Halstead (1962a) 'The classification and evolution of the Heterostraci'. *Acta palaeont. pol.*, **7**, 249–290.

Tarlo, L. B. Halstead (1962b) 'Lignées évolutives chez les ostracodermes hetero-stracés'. *Colloques int. Cent. natn. Rech. Scient.*, **104**, 31–37.

Tarlo, L. B. Halstead (1963) 'Aspidin: the precursor of bone'. *Nature, Lond.*, **199**, 46–48.

Tarlo, L. B. Halstead (1964) 'Psammosteiformes (Agnatha). 1. General part'. *Palaeont. pol.*, **13**, 1–135.

Tarlo, L. B. Halstead (1965) 'Psammosteiformes (Agnatha). 2. Systematic part'. *Palaeont. pol.*, **15**, 1–164.

Tarlo, L. B. Halstead (1967a) See Chapter 2.

Tarlo, L. B. Halstead (1967b) 'The tessellated pattern of the dermal armour in the Heterostraci'. *J. Linn. Soc. (Zool.)*, **47**, 45–54.

Tarlo, L. B. Halstead (1969) 'Calcified tissues in the earliest vertebrates'. *Calc. Tiss. Res.*, **3**, 107–24.

Tarlo, L. B. Halstead and Whiting, H. P. (1965) 'A new interpretation of the internal anatomy of the Heterostraci (Agnatha)'. *Nature, Lond.*, **206**, 148–180.

Traquair, R. H. (1899) 'On *Thelodus Pagei* Powrie, sp. from the Old Red Sandstone of Forfarshire'. *Trans. R. Soc. Edinb.*, **39**, 595–602.

Traquair, R. H. (1905) "Supplementary report on fossil fishes collected by the Geological Survey of Scotland in the Upper Silurian rocks of Scotland'. *Trans. R. Edinb.*, **40**, 879–80.

Turner, S. (1968) '*Turinia pagei* (Powrie)' in Allen, J. R. L., Halstead, L. B. and Turner, S. 'Dittonian ostracoderm fauna from the Brownstones of Wilderness quarry, Mitcheldean, Gloucestershire'. *Proc. geol. Soc. Lond.*, **1649**, 141–53.

Westoll, T. S. (1967) '*Radotina* and other tesserate fishes'. *J. Linn. Soc. (Zool.)*, **47**, 83–98.

White, E. I. (1935) 'The ostracoderm *Pteraspis* Kner and the relationships of the agnathous vertebrates'. *Phil. Trans. R. Soc.*, (B) **225**, 381–457.

White, E. I. (1946) 'The genus *Phialaspis* and the 'Psammosteus Limestones''. *Q. Jl. geol. Soc. Lond.*, **101**, 207–42.

White, E. I. (1950) '*Pteraspis leathensis* White, a Dittonian zone-fossil'. *Bull. Br. Mus. nat. Hist.*, (Geol.), **1**, 69–89.

White, E. I. (1956) 'Preliminary note on the range of *Pteraspis* in western Europe'. *Bull. Inst. r. Sci. nat. Belg.*, **32**, 1–10.

White, E. I. (1958) 'Original environment of the craniates', in *Studies on fossil vertebrates*, ed. Westoll, T. S. (The Athlone Press, London) p. 212.

White, E. I. (1961) 'The Old Red Sandstone of Brown Clee Hill and the adjacent area. 2. Palaeontology'. *Bull. Br. Mus. nat. Hist.*, (Geol.), **5**, 243–310.

White, E. I. (1963) 'Notes on *Pteraspis mitchelli* and its associated fauna', *Trans. Edinb. geol. Soc.*, **19**, 306–22.

Wills, L. J. (1935) 'Rare and new ostracoderm fishes from the Downtonian of Shropshire'. *Trans. R. Soc. Edinb.*, **58**, 427–47.

Whiting, H. P. and Tarlo, L. B. Halstead (1956) 'The brain of the Heterostraci (Agnatha)'. *Nature, Lond.*, **207**, 829–31.

CHAPTER FOUR

Subclass Acanthodii

4.1. CLASSIFICATION

Order 1, Climatiida (=Climatiiformes)
    Suborder 1, Climatioidei
        e.g. *Brachyacanthus*, *Climatius*, *Euthacanthus*, *Erriwacanthus*, L. Dev;
          Nostolepis, U. Sil; *Parexus*, L. Dev.
    Incertae sedis *Gyracanthides*, L. Carb; *Gyracanthus*, L.–U. Carb.
    Suborder 2, Diplacanthoidei
        e.g. *Diplacanthus*, M. Dev; *Rhadinacanthus*, M.–U. Dev.
Order 2, Ischnacanthida (=Ischnacanthiformes)
        e.g. *Acanthodopsis*, U. Carb; *Atopacanthus*, M.–U. Dev; *Ischnacanthus*,
          Xylacanthus, L. Dev.
Order 3, Acanthodida (=Acanthodiformes)
        e.g. *Acanthodes*, L. Carb—L. Perm; *Carycinacanthus*, L. Carb;
          Cheiracanthus, M. Dev; *Homalacanthus*, U. Dev; *Mesacanthus*,
          L.—M. Dev; *Protogonacanthus*, U. Dev; *Pseudacanthodes*,
          Traquairichthys, U. Carb; *Triazeugacanthus*, U. Dev.

L., Lower; M., Middle; U., Upper; Sil, Silurian; Dev, Devonian; Carb, Carboniferous, Perm, Permian.

4.2. ACANTHODIAN CHARACTERISTICS

The acanthodians are the earliest gnathostomatous or true jawed fishes. They are first found in the Upper Silurian. All primitive gnathostomes have in common the presence of paired fins, three semicircular canals in the ear, the neurocranium and gill skeleton as distinct units, the gills on the outside of the gill-arches, and biting jaws formed from the skeleton of the mandibular arch.

Living jawed fishes fall readily into two large groups, the chondrichthyans (sharks, rays, rabbit-fishes) and osteichthyans (ray-finned fishes, lung-fishes, the coelacanth). Chondrichthyans are typified by placoid scales, a cartilaginous internal skeleton, male intromittent organs (claspers), and the lack of an airbladder (Chapter 9 §2); osteichthyans are typified by a bony endo-skeleton and scales, an airbladder which functions as a lung or hydrostatic organ, and the lack of pelvic claspers. The study of fossil chondrichthyans and osteichthyans supports the view that this subdivision of lower gnathos-tomes is natural (Säve-Söderbergh, 1934; Nelson, 1969), although doubts are still occasionally expressed about the position of the lung-fishes (Chapter 7 §6). More serious problems arise when one turns to classifying the wholly extinct acanthodians and placoderms. These groups have been assigned to many different positions in the system since they were first described, and there is still not complete agreement about their affinities. In this book acanthodians are considered to be more closely related to osteichthyans than to chondrichthyans (see Relationships of teleostomes, Chapter 7 §6), and the opposite view is maintained for placoderms. Acanthodians and placoderms are apparently not closely related to each other, and a classification which brings them together as a grade of primitive fishes is now without merit (see Watson, 1937; Moy-Thomas, 1939).

The limits of the two clear-cut major divisions of jawed fishes, based on living species, become blurred with the addition of the extinct acanthodians and placoderms. The resulting higher taxa, the Teleostomi and Elasmo-branchiomorphi, have not been satisfactorily defined, although it is possible that an airbladder was present in all members of the first group, unless secondarily reduced, and absent in all members of the second group.

Acanthodians are teleostomes with small, square-crowned scales, stout spines before the dorsal, anal and paired fins, and a heterocercal caudal fin. They are the only Palaeozoic fishes with paired fin-spines. Silurian species are represented by detached bones, but articulated specimens are known from the Lower Devonian to the Lower Permian, where the group termi-nates. Acanthodians are usually small fishes, rarely exceeding 200 mm in length, although sometimes they reached a length of over two metres (Ørvig, 1967a).

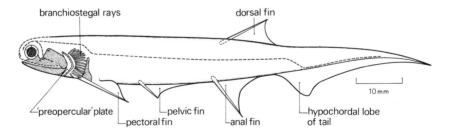

branchiostegal rays   dorsal fin

preopercular plate   pelvic fin   anal fin   hypochordal lobe of tail
pectoral fin   10 mm

Fig. 4.1. *Homalcanthus concinnus.* Restoration in lateral view. (After Miles.)

62

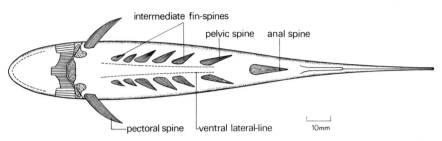

Fig. 4.2. *Euthacanthus macnicoli*. Restoration in ventral view. (After Watson.)

4.2.1. Structure

The body (Figs. 4.1–4.4, 4.13–4.15) is fusiform in shape with one or two dorsal fins, an anal and a heterocercal caudal fin. In addition to paired pectoral and pelvic fin-spines there is primitively a series of intermediate spines, sometimes as many as six pairs (Watson, 1937; Miles, 1966). These additional spines have long been of interest as they appear to support the view that the original paired fins were continuous lateral folds of the body wall (Jarvik, 1965). However, they are more properly interpreted in the light of modern morphogenetic studies as a special development of the ventrolateral body ridges (Chapter 2 §4.1), rather than as vestiges of originally continuous fins (Westoll, 1958; Devillers, 1965). All the fins except the caudal are normally supported by an anterior fin-spine, which in primitive genera like *Climatius* (Fig. 4.3) is restricted to the skin and may be extremely wide from side to side with a large cavity opening on to the fin web, the spine having the appearance of little more than an enlarged scale. In later forms like *Acanthodes* (Fig. 4.4), the spines are much laterally flattened, but the cavity opens only inside the body into which the spine has a considerable area of insertion between the myotomes (Watson, 1937; Westoll, 1945; Miles, 1966). The intermediate spines never have associated fin webs.

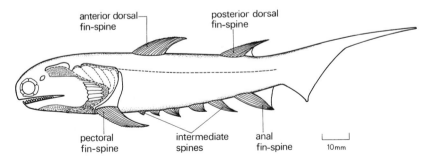

Fig. 4.3. *Climatius reticulatus*. Restoration in lateral view. (After Watson.)

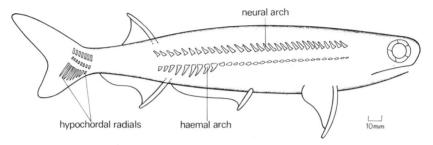

Fig. 4.4. *Acanthodes sulcatus*. Restoration in lateral view. (After Miles.)

In the few cases in which the internal skeleton of the fins is known it consists of much concentrated basals and radials extending a very short way into the web of the fin. The pectoral fin of *Acanthodes* has a concentrated, radially arranged endoskeleton of three stout basals (Jaekel, 1899). The main web of the fin is stiffened internally by a proximal series of bony, unsegmented, unbranched rays. They have a superficial resemblance to the ceratotrichia of chondrichthyans. The pelvic, anal and hypochordal fin webs bear rows of scales which correspond to the hypothetical primitive condition of osteichthyan lepidotrichia (Jarvik, 1959; Miles, 1966). Both branching and intercalated rows of scales occur on the fins. There is no epichordal lobe in the tail, and the short rows of scales that exist in its place have been compared with the dorsal lepidotrichia of palaeoniscoid actinopterygians (Heyler, 1958, 1969a).

The body is covered with a characteristic shagreen of closely fitting scales, which nevertheless do not imbricate. The scales are made up of concentric layers of bone and dentinal tissue. They have no pulp cavity,

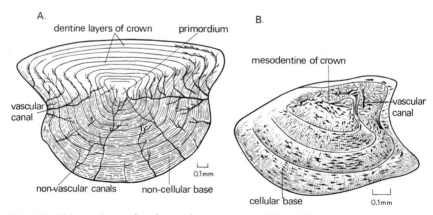

Fig. 4.5. Thin sections of scales to show structure (After Miles). A. *Acanthodes* sp.; B. *Nostolepis* cf. *striata*.

64

which readily separates them from the small scales of thelodonts. Two main sorts of acanthodian scales are recognized on histological grounds (Gross, 1947; Ørvig, 1951, 1967*a*, *b*). The *Nostolepis* type (Fig. 4.5B) has a crown of dentinal tissue (mesodentine) which is penetrated by vascular canals and encloses cell spaces, and a base of cellular bone. The *Acanthodes* type (Fig. 4.5A) has a crown of true dentine (with no cell spaces), and a thick base of acellular bone which is traversed by non-vascular canals. Acanthodian scales grew by the concentric addition of areal zones of growth around a primordial scale. The scales were generally acquired at an early stage of growth, and probably continued to grow throughout the life of the fish. However, the formation of scales in some regions of the body was apparently delayed until growth was well advanced (Watson, 1937).

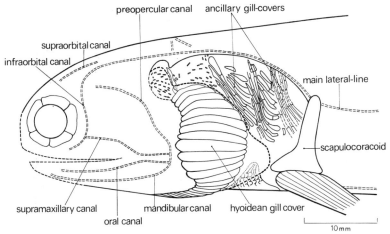

Fig. 4.6. *Euthacanthus macnicoli.* Restoration of head in lateral view. (After (Watson.)

The external nasal openings are always small, lying close together in the middle line, and well above the mouth. In *Triazeugacanthus* they are associated with a large median plate. There is some doubt about the identification of these openings in acanthodians (Miles, 1966). They seem to be too small to represent the common incurrent (anterior) and excurrent (posterior) nostrils. However, if they are only the anterior openings, the problem arises as to the position of the posterior openings. The latter have not been found on the snout, but were possibly situated in the orbit, as in early actinopterygians. The eyes are placed far forward and surrounded by a few bony plates, typically five in number (Fig. 4.6).

The neurocranium is only well known in *Acanthodes* (Watson, 1937; Miles,

1965, 1968) and is remarkably like that of a primitive actinopterygian. It has a short occipital region which is separated from the long otic region by a lateral occipital fissure, incorporating the exit of the vagus (X) nerve (Fig. 4.7). There is a narrow interorbital septum with the brain cavity above. The orbitotemporal region is floored by a median anterior basal bone. This bone has a lateral basipterygoid process for the basal articulation of the upper jaw, and a ventral groove in which lay the spiracular tube, i.e. the dorsal part of the closed spiracular gill-silt. A median basisphenoid pillar carries the hypo-

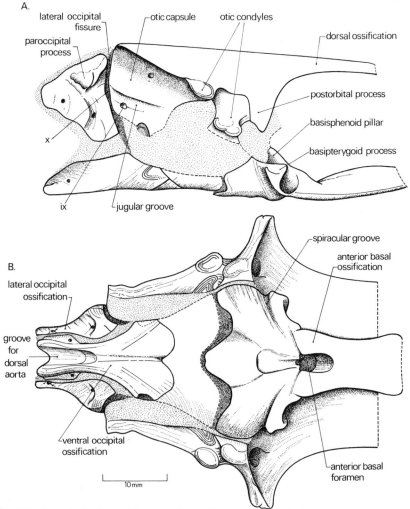

Fig. 4.7. *Acanthodes bronni*. Restorations of neurocranium in lateral (A) and ventral (B) views. (Original.)

66

physial fossa, which opens in the hind wall of the anterior basal foramen, and the cerebral branches of the carotid arteries. There is a large ventral occipital ossification, with a ventral groove for the dorsal aorta and a dorsal groove for the persistent notochord, which ran forward in the basal plate. Paired lateral occipital ossifications have a paroccipital process and foramina for spino-occipital nerves. Dorsally the neurocranium is completed by a large ossification which stretches back from between the orbits to the occipital region. It encloses an anterior fontanelle, probably related to the pineal organ, and ends at a posterior fontanelle. There is a prominent postorbital process, situated slightly in front of a pair of condyles for the otic articulation of the upper jaw. The otic capsules complete the side walls of the dorsal ossification. In life the separate bones of the neurocranium must have been connected by cartilage.

The three semicircular canals of the ear are long and slender (Dean, 1907; Watson, 1937; Heyler, 1969a). The labyrinth is unspecialized in comparison with elasmobranchs, and has an undivided utriculus with the vertical semicircular canals meeting in a sinus superior utriculi. This condition is found in holocephalans and osteichthyans. Large compact otoliths (statoliths) are preserved in some species. In *Carycinacanthus* there appears to be a large otolith in the lagena and a small one in the sacculus, an arrangement which compares well with that of primitive actinopterygians (Berg, 1958).

The palatoquadrates of the two sides do not meet in an anterior symphysis.

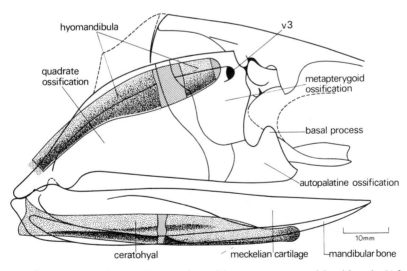

Fig. 4.8. *Acanthodes bronni*. Restoration of jaw apparatus and hyoid arch. (After Miles.)

67

In advanced forms such as *Acanthodes* there is a definite otic process with a pair of fossae articulating on the otic condyles of the neurocranium (Fig. 4.8). The otic process has a large foramen which transmitted the mandibular branch of the trigeminal nerve (V_3). The otic process is absent in primitive forms such as *Climatius*, which lacks the laterally swinging palatoquadrate and wide gape of *Acanthodes* (Miles, 1968). The palatoquadrate and meckelian cartilage either ossify as a single piece as in *Climatius*, or the palatoquadrate as three pieces and the meckelian cartilage as two distinct pieces as in *Acanthodes*. The meckelian cartilage is frequently stiffened by a long, slender dermal bone on its ventral margin (Fig. 4.8). The jaw articulation is double in advanced forms like *Acanthodes*, with both the palatoquadrate and meckelian cartilage carrying an articular process and a fossa (Miles, 1968). This arrangement is strikingly like that found in early sharks. The articulation in primitive acanthodians has not been satisfactorily observed.

Acanthodian teeth are of two sorts (Ørvig, 1957, 1967a; Gross, 1957; Miles, 1966). They may be multicuspid or simple, laterally compressed teeth that are *anchylosed* to the jaw cartilages (Fig. 4.9); or they may be serially forming *whorls* of multicuspid teeth, held in place on the jaw cartilages by connective tissue. In primitive ischnacanthids there is a well-formed sym-

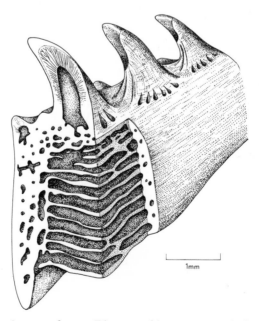

Fig. 4.9. *Atopacanthus* sp. Diagram of jaw structure. (After Ørvig.)

68

physial tooth-whorl in the mandible. In well-preserved specimens of *Ischnacanthus gracilis* there are also numerous small teeth which were situated in the lining of the mouth cavity (Ørvig, 1967*a*).

The hyoid arch is only well known in *Acanthodes* (Miles, 1968). It comprises a dorsal hyomandibula and ventral ceratohyal (Fig. 4.8), both of which ossify in two pieces, and possibly a small interhyal which only rarely ossifies. The lower end of the hyomandibula fits into a groove on the inner surface of the palatoquadrate, and its head meets the side of the neurocranium. In this way the hyomandibula played a part in the jaw mechanism, the jaw suspension being functionally amphistylic as in primitive sharks. The mode of suspension in *Climatius* and other primitive genera in which the palatoquadrate lacked the otic articulation is unknown, but most probably it was hyostylic. The hyoid arch is followed by five gill-arches in *Acanthodes*. Each has a long, slender epibranchial and ceratobranchial,

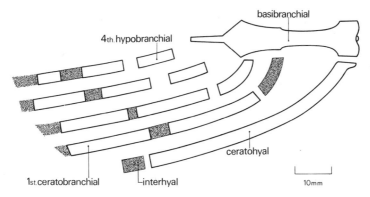

Fig. 4.10. *Acanthodes bronni.* Plan of ventral part of gill-arch skeleton; paired elements shown on one side only; 5th arch not shown. (Original.)

both of which ossify in two pieces, and a short anteriorly-directed hypobranchial. The pharyngobranchials have a short dorsal process, and articulate against pairs of processes on the epibranchials. The orientation of the pharyngobranchials has not been definitely established (Nelson, 1968), although it is possibly posterior as in elasmobranchs. There is a single, large basibranchial element (Fig. 4.10; see Nelson, 1968, 1969). In *Acanthodes*, long gill-rakers are present on the hyomandibula and ceratohyal, and on the epi- and ceratobranchials. In earlier genera there may be teeth (*Ischnacanthus*) or 'denticles' (*Parexus*) on the gill-arches.

In primitive genera such as *Euthacanthus* and *Climatius* (Fig. 4.6) the hyoid and each branchial arch has a small gill-cover closing the gill-slit behind it. Even in these two genera, however, the hyoidean gill-cover is the largest, and in advanced types like *Acanthodes* it comes to cover all the gill-slits, as in osteichthyans, and the ancillary covers disappear. The hyoid arch always carries a long series of branchiostegal rays, but they do not extend on to the throat in a free gular membrane (Miles, 1966).

The head is covered in early forms with numerous small dermal bones similar to the body scales, some of which may form quite large plates, particularly on the gill-cover and branchial arches. *Homalacanthus* is notable for the presence of a long 'preopercular' bone of osteichthyan form (Fig. 4.1). In late genera such as *Acanthodes*, the number of dermal bones is reduced and they are only found surrounding the lateral-line sensory canals of the head, where they may become transformed into rows of short tubes.

The sensory lines otherwise run between the bones and scales of the body, as in elasmobranchs. This arrangement is probably related to the small size of the scales and their lack of overlaps. Large pore-canal scales are associated with some of the head sensory lines in *Ischnacanthus* and its Silurian relatives ('*Poracanthodes*') (Gross, 1956). The pattern of the lines in acanthodians is essentially similar to that of all gnathostomes. The main lateral-line passes down the body, where it may give off a series of dorsal commissures (Dean, 1907), and on to the dorsal surface of the head to a point above the orbit (Fig. 4.6). A ventral branch passes down under the eye as the infraorbital canal. The supraorbital canal is never continuous with the main canal but may meet its fellow anteriorly in rostral and ethmoid commissures. There are also supramaxillary, preopercular, oral and mandibular canals on the cheek and lower jaw. Stensiö (1947) has recognized several configurations of the cheek canals. In *Acanthodes* the preopercular canal joins the main lateral-line in a high posterior position, as in early actinopterygians; but in *Euthacanthus* (Fig. 4.6) the preopercular canal bends forwards dorsally, to run towards the infraorbital canal, as in crossopterygians. In *Acanthodes* there is a specially developed canal on the gill-cover, joining the mandibular and main body canals just in front of the pectoral girdle. A median ventral line on the chin divides in the shoulder region, giving rise to the paired ventrolateral line which passes down the body.

The pectoral girdle always has an endoskeletal scapulocoracoid. In early forms like *Climatius* it is a broad, single ossification, and ventrally there are a variable number of associated dermal bones, some of which form quite large plates (Fig. 4.11). These plates, which cannot be homologized with those of the osteichthyan shoulder-girdle, may be superficially covered with scales. The first intermediate spine has usually become involved in the complex of plates, and other spines may be present in front of the pectoral fin (Ørvig, 1967a). There are never any lateral dermal bones in the shoulder-girdle of acanthodians, although enlarged scales sometimes coat the outside

70

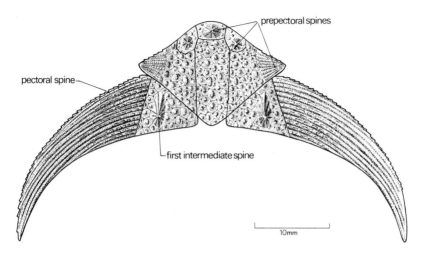

Fig. 4.11. *Climatius reticulatus*. Restoration of shoulder-girdle in ventral view. (Original.)

of the scapulocoracoid (Dean, 1907). In advanced forms the scapulo-coracoid becomes subdivided. In *Acanthodes* (Fig. 4.12) there are separate suprascapular, scapular and procoracoid ossifications, and the fin-spine is received in a deep groove. The articulation of the procoracoid element with the scapula in front of this groove strongly suggests some sort of mechanism for erecting the spine, probably as the fin is spread.

The vertebral column has an unconstricted notochord, and ossified neural and haemal arches (Fig. 4.4). Undivided radials form the skeleton of the hypochordal lobe of the tail, but they end well short of the fin margin. Ossified ribs have never been found.

4.2.2. Diversity and tendencies in evolution

The climatiids range from the Upper Silurian to the Carboniferous and include the most primitive acanthodians (Figs. 4.2, 4.3). Primitive genera have short bodies; thick, high-crowned scales; well-developed ancillary gill-covers; broad and deeply sculptured fin-spines, which are only superficially inserted in the skin; and a long series of intermediate spines. In addition, all members of this order have two dorsal fins, dermal plates on the thorax ventral to the scapulocoracoid and scales of the *Nostolepis* kind. *Climatius* is a typical Lower Devonian climatioid, and the contemporary *Parexus* is similar but has the first dorsal fin-spine greatly elongated. Both genera have tooth-whorls in the lower jaw, but the Upper Silurian *Nostolepis* has both tooth-whorls and dentigerous jaw bones. *Euthacanthus* is a toothless Lower

71

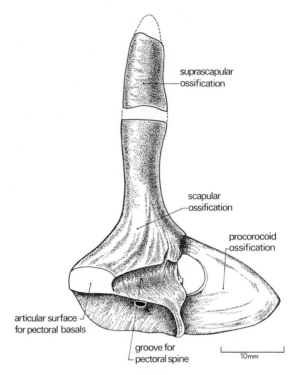

Fig. 4.12. *Acanthodes bronni*. Endoskeletal shoulder-girdle in lateral view. (Original.)

Devonian genus with small, flat-crowned scales and a more elongated body. It exhibits a long series of intermediate spines, normally five pairs.

Gyracanthus is a name given to spines with an ornament of ridges meeting in a chevron pattern, which are widely distributed in the Carboniferous. They are up to 400 mm long, have a deeply inserted basal portion and seem to be pectoral spines of large acanthodians. These spines are often associated with smaller, sparsely tuberculated, triangular spines. *Gyracanthides* (Woodward, 1906) is more completely known. It was apparently a round bodied fish, somewhat depressed dorsoventrally, with large curved pectoral spines. A pair of smaller, nearly straight spines insert between the tips of the pectorals, and have been identified as pelvics, and a pair of ventral bones have been described in the shoulder-girdle region. Although *Gyracanthides* and *Gyracanthus* seem to be closely related, and to be close to climatioids, their affinities are largely unknown.

The diplacanthoids are derived from the more primitive climatioids, and are toothless forms with short jaws and long dorsal and anal spines, deeply

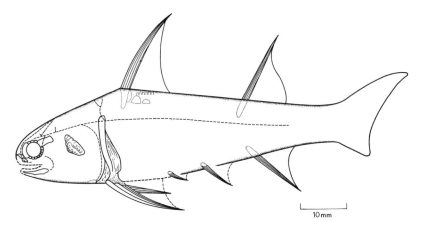

Fig. 4.13. *Diplacanthus striatus*. Restoration in lateral view. (After Watson.)

inserted in the body. *Diplacanthus* (Fig. 4.13) lacks ancillary gill-covers, has one pair of free intermediate spines, and another pair incorporated into the ventral plates of the shoulder-girdle. *Rhadinacanthus* is unusual in that the anterior dorsal fin-spine is shorter than the posterior.

The ischnacanthids are long bodied, lightly armoured species with scales of the *Acanthodes* type, ranging from the Upper Silurian to the Carboniferous. The only known articulated species is *Ischnacanthus gracilis* (Fig. 4.14) from the Lower Devonian. It has two narrow dorsal spines and an anal spine, all deeply inserted in the body; there are neither intermediate spines, nor ancillary gill-covers, nor dermal plates in the shoulder region. *Ischnacanthus* has both multicuspid jaw teeth and symphysial and buccal tooth-whorls, but in the Carboniferous genus *Acanthodopsis* the marginal jaw teeth are large, laterally compressed cones, much developed

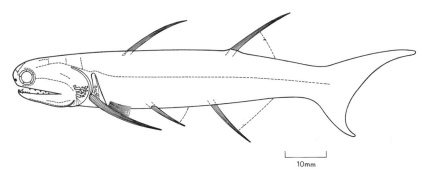

Fig. 4.14. *Ischnacanthus gracilis*. Restoration in lateral view. (After Watson.)

73

at the expense of the buccal teeth. There are cell spaces in the teeth and jaw bones of Silurian ischnacanthids, but in later forms the skeleton is entirely acellular (Ørvig, 1967*a*).

The acanthodids are the last group of acanthodians to appear, and the last to become extinct. They range from the Lower Devonian to the Lower Permian. They are genera without teeth or ventral dermal plates in the shoulder-girdle, with only one dorsal fin, and with *Acanthodes* type scales. In *Mesacanthus* and *Triazeugacanthus* (Fig. 4.15) there is a pair of small intermediate spines lost in more advanced forms. *Mesacanthus* is the most primitive genus with only superficially seated spines and with ancillary gill-covers. As the group evolves the fin-spines become deeply inserted, the pectoral spines increase in size and the pelvics are reduced. At the same time the body becomes elongated and the gill-chamber entirely covered by the large hyoidean cover. In *Acanthodes* the branchial region is notably lengthened.

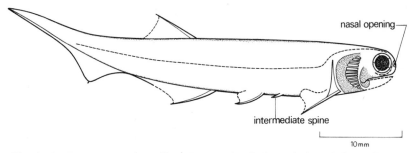

Fig. 4.15. *Triazeugacanthus affinis.* Restoration in lateral view. (After Miles.)

The general evolutionary tendencies in acanthodians may be summarized as reduction of the dermal skeleton, both in thickness and extent; loss of the intermediate spines; deepening of the insertion of the remaining spines; and enlargement of the hyoidean gill-cover as the ancillary gill-covers are lost. These changes are associated with improvements in the swimming, breathing and defence mechanisms. They are best seen in the climatioids, but are probably common to all the orders of acanthodians, although they cannot be demonstrated in ischnacanthids because of the lack of articulated specimens. The reduction of the skeleton was not, however, a straight forward process that proceeded without deviation from heavily armoured early forms to partly naked late forms. At all times the development of bone must have resulted from the interplay of many factors, as noted in Chapter 2 §2 (Schaeffer, 1961, 1968). The development of a large "pre-opercular" bone in diplacanthoids and *Homalacanthus*, and a large bone around the nasal openings in *Triazeugacanthus*, represent reversals of the general trend towards bone reduction in the Middle and Upper Devonian. It is also noteworthy (Denison, 1963) that the most heavily ossified endoskeleton is found in *Acanthodes* in the Carboniferous and Lower Permian, in which perhaps it is developed to compensate for the reduction of the exoskeleton.

4.2.3. Mode of life

Acanthodians have large eyes and small nasal capsules, and throughout their history they were mid- and surface-water feeders. Although some of the heavily-scaled early genera may have rested on the bottom, the group never gave rise to depressed, bottom dwelling forms. This suggests that acanthodians may have had an airbladder which functioned as a hydrostatic organ, as in osteichthyans. Their mode of life perhaps accounts for the early rise of acanthodians in comparison with the first elasmobranchiomorphs, the benthic placoderms. As nektonic fishes, Silurian and Lower Devonian acanthodians were not competing directly to any great extent with the dominant, bottom living agnathans of these times.

The vertebral column of acanthodians retains an unconstricted notochord. This is the primitive condition of the column in gnathostomes, and it may show that swimming was eel-like, with waves of muscular contraction of small amplitude travelling posteriorly down the body. Moreover, *Acanthodes* became elongated and somewhat eel-like in appearance. From the earliest-known articulated acanthodians in the Lower Devonian to the last known members in the Permian, the pectoral fins have a narrow base and a large web stiffened with rows of scales. These fins were flexibly-mobile hydrofoils, showing little sign of an origin from ventrolateral body ridges. On the other hand, the pelvic fins are lengthened in advanced acanthodids, and seem at first sight to have originated from such ridges, although they must have been paedomorphic formations (see Jarvik, 1965). The finspines may have acted as cutwaters, and it has also been suggested that they functioned as hold-fasts in running waters (Gregory and Raven, 1941; Westoll, 1945, 1958). It is likely that they functioned primarily as defensive organs. This suggestion is supported by the changes observed in the spines during their evolution. They are transformed from superficial, broad structures which are little more than enlarged scales, to long slender spines securely fixed in the body musculature. In their advanced form with a long insertion area, they would have been less easily displaced by the jaws of predators, and therefore more efficient defences. As the intermediate spines were lost the remaining spines became more elongated, so that in Carboniferous and Permian species of *Acanthodes* and *Gyracanthides* the pectorals are very much longer than the remaining spines. Acanthodians with long pectoral spines must have been very difficult for the predatory sharks and bony fishes of the time to swallow whole, although the presence of a whole *Acanthodes* in the body cavity of a palaeoniscoid shows that this sometimes happened (Traquair, 1879). A mechanism for erecting the pectoral spines may have been an additional development in *Acanthodes*.

The three orders of acanthodians became divergently specialized in the feeding mechanism, although much about this aspect of their evolution is still hidden. Silurian climatioids and ischnacanthids have a similar dental array of small multicuspid teeth, and were presumably unspecialized microphagous fishes. Subsequently the ischnacanthids became large predators with stout teeth on the jaw margins. From their first appearance the acanthodids are edentulous, and their history is a record of increasing specialization for microphagous feeding. The palatoquadrate gains a moveable joint with the otic region of the neurocranium, and a feeding mechanism is established in which the upper jaw swings laterally to give an exceedingly wide gape (Miles, 1968). A concomitant series of changes include the lengthening of the branchial region and the gill-arches. Gill-rakers are known in *Acanthodes* and *Carycinacanthus*, and may well have been present in many members of the order. In *Acanthodes bronni* the rakers are tooth-like spikes, suggesting that this species could take fairly large food. A specimen of *Acanthodes sulcatus* has a palaeoniscoid fish within the body cavity, but although this is proof of the large gape, it seems unlikely that acanthodids in general were active predators. *Acanthodes gracilis* is probably a more typical species. It has long, slender gill-rakers and gut contents of numerous small invertebrates (probably ostracods) have been found, as they have in the Upper Devonian *Homalacanthus gracilis* (Miles, 1966, 1968). Advanced acanthodids can be pictured swimming slowly through the water with the mouth wide open, straining off small organisms from the continuous stream of water that passes through the oralobranchial chamber.

REFERENCES

Berg, L. S. (1958) 'Lower Carboniferous fishes from the Achinsk's Government'. *Vopr. Iktiol. SSSR.* (1958) ed. Obruchev, D. V. (In Russian.)

Dean, B. (1907) 'Notes on acanthodian sharks' *Am. J. Anat.*, **7**, 209–22.

Denison, R. H. (1960) 'Fishes of the Devonian Holland Quarry Shale of Ohio'. *Fieldiana, Geol.*, **11**, 555–613.

Denison, R. H. (1963) 'The early history of the vertebrate calcified skeleton'. *Clin. Orthop.*, **34**, 141–52.

Devillers, C. (1965) 'The role of morphogenesis in the origin of higher levels of organization'. *Syst. Zool.*, **24**, 259–71.

Gregory, W. K. and Raven, H. C. (1941) 'Studies on the origin and early evolution of paired fins and limbs. 1. Paired fins and girdles in ostracoderms, placoderms, and other primitive fishes'. *Annls. N.Y. Acad. Sci.*, **42**, 273–360.

Gross, W. (1940)'Acanthodier und Placodermen aus Heterostius-Schichten Estlands und Lettlands'. *Annls. Soc. Reb. Nat. invest. Univ. tart.*, **46**, 1–79.

Gross, W. (1947) 'Die Agnathen und Acanthodier des obersilurischen Beyrichien-kalks'. *Palaeontographica*, **96**A, 91–158.

Gross, W. (1956) 'Über Crossopterygier und Dipnoer aus dem baltischen Oberdevon im Zusammenhang einer vergleichenden Untersuchen des Porenkanalsystems paläozoischer Agnathen und Fische'. *K. svenska VetenskAkad. Handl.*, (4) **5**, 1–140.

Gross, W. (1957) 'Mundzähne und Hautzähne der Acanthodier und Arthrodiren'. *Palaeontographica*, **109**A, 1–40.

Gross, W. (1966) 'Kleine Schuppenkunde'. *N. Jb. Geol. Paläont. Abh.*, **125**, 29–48.

Heyler, D. (1958) 'Remarques sur la caudale d'*Acanthodes*'. *C.R. Acad. Sci.*, **247**, 1636–1639.

Heyler, D. (1963) 'Les acanthodiens et le problème de l'aphétohyoidie'. *Colloques int. Cent. natn. Rech. Scient.*, **104**, 39–47.

Heyler, D. (1969a) 'Vertébrés de l'Autunien de France'. *Cahiers Paléont*, (1969) 1–255.

Heyler, D. (1969b) 'Acanthodii', in *Traité de Paléontologie*, 4:2, ed. Piveteau, J. (Masson, Paris) p. 21.

Holmgren, N. (1942) 'Studies on the head of fishes. An embryological, morpho-logical and phylogenetical study. 3. The phylogeny of elasmobranch fishes'. *Acta zool. Stockh.*, **23**, 129–261.

Jaekel, O. (1899) 'Uber die Zusammensetzung des Kiefers und Schultergürtels von *Acanthodes*'. *Z. dt. geol. Ges.*, **51**, 56–60.

Jarvik, E. (1959) 'Dermal fin-rays and Holmgren's principle of delamination'. *K. svenska VetenskAkad. Handl.*, (4) **6**, 1–51.

Jarvik, E. (1965) 'On the origin of girdles and paired fins'. *Israel J. Zool.*, **14**, 141–72.

Krebs, B. (1960) 'Über einen Flossenstachel von *Gyracanthus* (Acanthodii) aus dem Oberkarbon Englands'. *B. schw. pal. Ges.*, **53**, 811–27.

Miles, R. S. (1964) 'A reinterpretation of the visceral skeleton of *Acanthodes*'. *Nature, Lond.*, **204**, 457–59.

Miles, R. S. (1965) 'Some features in the cranial morphology of acanthodians and the relationships of the Acanthodii'. *Acta zool. Stockh.*, **46**, 233–55.

Miles, R. S. (1966) 'The acanthodian fishes of the Devonian Plattenkalk of the Paffrath Trough in the Rhineland, with an appendix containing a classification of the Acanthodii and a revision of the genus *Homalacanthus*. *Ark. Zool.*, (2) **18**, 147–94.

Miles, R. S. (1967) 'Class Acanthodii' in *The fossil record*, ed. Harland, W. B., *et al.* (Geol. Soc., London.) p. 637.

Miles, R. S. (1968) 'Jaw articulation and suspension in *Acanthodes* and their significance'. *Nobel Symposium*, **4**, 109–27.

Miles, R. S. (1971) 'Remarks on the vertebral column and caudal fin of acanthodian fishes'. *Lethaia*, **3**, 343–62.

Moy-Thomas, J. A. (1939) 'The early evolution and relationships of the elasmo-branchs'. *Biol. Rev.*, **14**, 1–26.

Nelson, G. J. (1968) 'Gill-arch structure in *Acanthodes*'. *Nobel Symposium*, **4**, 129–43.

Nelson, G. J. (1969) 'Gill-arches and the phylogeny of fishes, with notes on the classification of vertebrates'. *Bull. Am. Mus. nat. Hist.*, **141**, 475–552.

Novitskaya, L. E. and Obruchev, D. V. (1967) 'Class Acanthodii', in *Fundamentals of palaeontology. 11. Agnatha, Pisces*, ed. Obruchev, D. V. (Israel Program for Scientific Translations, Jerusalem.) p. 263.

Ørvig, T. (1951) 'Histologic studies of placoderms and fossil elasmobranchs. 1. The endoskeleton, with remarks on the hard tissues of lower vertebrates in general'. *Ark. Zool.*, (2) **2**, 321–454.

Ørvig, T. (1957) 'Notes on some Palaeozoic lower vertebrates from Spitsbergen and North America'. *Norsk geol. Tidsskr.*, **37**, 285–353.

Ørvig, T. (1967a) 'Some new acanthodian material from the Lower Devonian of Europe'. *J. Linn. Soc. (Zool.)*, **47**, 131–53.

Ørvig, T. (1967b) 'Phylogeny of tooth tissues: evolution of some calcified tissues in early vertebrates', in *Structural and chemical organization of teeth*, I. ed. Miles, A. E. W. (Academic Press, New York and London.) p. 45.

Säve-Söderbergh, G. (1934) 'Some points of view concerning the evolution of the vertebrates and the classification of this group'. *Ark. Zool.*, **26A**, 1–20.

Schaeffer, B. (1961) 'Differential ossification in the fishes'. *Trans. N.Y. Acad. Sci.*, (2) **23**, 501–505.

Schaeffer, B. (1968) 'The origin and basic radiation of the Osteichthyes'. *Nobel Symposium*, **4**, 202–22.

Stensiö, E. A. (1947) 'The sensory lines and dermal bones of the cheek in fishes and amphibians'. *K. svenska VetenskAkad. Handl.*, (3) **24**, 1–194.

Traquair, R. H. (1879) 'Evidence as to the predaceous habits of the larger Palaeoni-scidae'. *Proc. R. phys. Soc. Edinb.*, **5**, 128–30.

Watson, D. M. S. (1937) 'The acanthodian fishes'. *Phil. Trans. R. Soc.*, (B) **228**, 49–146.

Watson, D. M. S. (1959) 'The myotomes of acanthodians'. *Proc. R. Soc. Lond.*, (B) **151**, 23–25.

Westoll, T. S. (1945) 'The paired fins of placoderms'. *Trans. R. Soc. Edinb.*, **61**, 381–98.

Westoll, T. S. (1958) 'The lateral fin-fold theory and the pectoral fins of ostra-coderms and early fishes', in *Studies on fossil vertebrates*, ed. Westoll, T. S. (The Athlone Press, London.) p. 180.

Woodward, A. S. (1906) 'On a Carboniferous fish fauna from the Mansfield District, Victoria'. *Mem. natn. Mus. Melb.*, **1**, 1–23.

CHAPTER FIVE

Subclass Osteichthyes. Infraclass Actinopterygii

5.1. CLASSIFICATION

Superorder 1, Chondrostei

Order 1, Palaeoniscida

Suborder 1, Palaeoniscoidei

e.g. *Aeduella*, L. Perm; *Australichthys, Canobius, Carboveles*, L. Carb; *Cheirolepis*, M.–U. Dev; *Coccolepis* L. Jur—L. Cret; *Commentrya*, U. Carb; *Cryphyolepis, Cycloptychius*, L. Carb; *Elonichthys*, L. Carb—U. Perm; *Gonatodus, Holurus*, L. Carb; *Kentuckia*, U. Dev—L. Carb; *Moythomasia*, U. Dev; *Nematoptychius*, L. Carb; *Palaeoniscum*, U. Perm; *Paramblypterus*, U. Carb; *Phanerosteon*, L. Carb; *Pteronisculus*, L. Trias; *Pygopterus*, U. Perm; *Rhadinichthys*, L.–U. Carb; *Sphaerolepis*, L. Perm; *Stegotrachelus*, M. Dev; *Styracopterus*, L. Carb; *Tegeolepis*, U. Dev.

Suborder 2, Platysomoidei

e.g. *Adroichthys, Chirodopsis*, L. Carb; *Chirodus*, L.–U. Carb; *Eurynotus*, L.–U. Carb; *Mesolepis*, L. Carb; *Platysomus*, L. Carb—U. Perm; *Proteurynotus, Wardichthys*, L. Carb.

Order 2, Haplolepidida

e.g. *Haplolepis, Pyritocephalus*, U. Carb.

Order 3, Tarrasiida

e.g. *Tarrasius*, L. Carb; ?*Palaeophichthys*, U. Carb.

Order 4, Phanerorhynchida

e.g. *Phanerorhynchus*, U. Carb.

Order 5, Dorypterida

e.g. *Dorypterus*, U. Perm.

Incertae sedis *Andreolepis*, U. Sil; *Dialipina, Ligulalepis*, L. Dev; *Orvikuina*, L. or M. Dev.

Post-Palaeozoic orders not listed.

Superorder 2, Holostei

Order 1, Semionotida
    e.g. *Acentrophorus*, U. Perm.
Other orders not listed.

L., Lower; M., Middle; U., Upper; Sil, Silurian; Dev, Devonian; Carb, Carboniferous; Perm, Permian; Trias, Triassic; Jur, Jurassic; Cret, Cretaceous.

5.2. OSTEICHTHYAN CHARACTERISTICS

The osteichthyans form the large group which includes all living bony fishes, lung-fishes and the coelacanth, and from which tetrapods have diverged. On somewhat unsatisfactory evidence they are first recorded from the Upper Silurian, but it is not till the Lower Devonian that undoubted members of the group are known (Andrews, 1967; Gross, 1968, 1969). Apart from having a skeleton of true bone, osteichthyans have typically the upper biting edge of the mouth formed by dermal bones, the premaxillary and maxillary rather than the palatoquadrate; the teeth are typically fused to the bones; the lateral-line canals primitively run through the dermal bones which at least in part are arranged on a comparable plan in all groups. Among these may be specially noted the dermal parasphenoid forming the roof of the mouth, and the characteristic series of bones formed in relation to the operculum, including the dermal bones of the shoulder-girdle which are attached to the back of the skull and form the hinder margin of the branchial chamber. The neurocranium is perichondrally ossified in primitive forms, and is built up in two main units, one anterior and one posterior, which are usually separated by the cranial fissure. These units represent the regions of the skull developed in relation to the embryonic trabecular-polar bars and parachordal cartilages respectively. The cranial fissure becomes variously modified in the different osteichthyan groups, notably in relation to cranial kinesis in crossopterygians. It is lost in higher bony fishes. Pleural ribs are found in the vertebral column and primitively the fin webs are stiffened by dermal rays, the lepidotrichia. In all members some kind of airbladder is developed, which may serve as a lung, or become modified into a hydrostatic organ.

The osteichthyans fall naturally into three major groups, the actinopterygians (ray-finned fishes), crossopterygians (tassel-finned fishes) and dipnoans (lung-fishes), which are here ranked as infraclasses. Whether dipnoans are more closely related to actinopterygians or crossopterygians is a matter of dispute (see Relationships of teleostomes, Chapter 7; §6), although the consensus favours close affinity with the crossopterygians. The crossopterygians and dipnoans are often classified together as 'sarcopterygians', which is regarded as a group collateral to the actinopterygians. The name sarcopterygians refers to the well-marked fleshy lobe usually possessed by the dorsal, anal and paired fins in crossopterygians and dipnoans; the internal skeleton of the fins is much concentrated. In actinopterygians the fin skeletons are much less concentrated and usually without fleshy lobes. Even at their earliest appearance actinopterygians, crossopterygians and dipnoans are quite distinct, and no intermediate forms have so far been found. In spite of this they resemble one another more closely in anatomy than they do any other group of fishes and it must, therefore, be concluded that they had a common ancestor.

5.3. INFRACLASS ACTINOPTERYGII

The first appearance of undoubted members of this group is in the Lower Devonian (Schultze, 1968), although certain isolated scales from the Upper Silurian may belong to this group, indicating an earlier origin (Gross, 1968, 1969). It is by no means easy to give a comprehensive definition of actinopterygians as the group is a large and diverse one, represented at the present day by the great majority of living fishes. Since their origin a very varied evolution has taken place and many of the later members have lost the essential features of primitive members of the group. However, it can be said that they differ primarily from the majority of crossopterygians in the absence of internal nostrils, both nostrils being relatively high up on the face (see Chapter 7 §2 for the special conditions in dipnoans); and from both crossopterygians and dipnoans in the arrangement of the dermal bones and the course of the lateral-line sensory canals on the head; in the microscopic structure of the dermal bones and scales; in the nature of the internal skeleton of the paired and unpaired fins; in the usual presence of one dorsal fin and ridge scales in place of the epichordal lobe of the tail. The details of these characters will be described below in the various orders. Here it must suffice only to mention the most obvious features which are characteristic of actinopterygians as a whole.

The scales (Fig. 5.1) are never cosmoid (i.e. with the tissue cosmine, Chapter 6 §2) but primitively of the ganoid type (Aldinger, 1937; Gardiner, 1967a) in which the whole scale lies beneath the skin and is periodically added to concentrically both on the outside as well as on the inner surface. The outer shiny layer, the ganoine, thus tends to become relatively very thick, although in some later forms it may be lost (Schultze, 1966). The internal skeleton of the median fins is never concentrated into fused basal plates as in the crossopterygians and dipnoans, but always consists of separate radials. In the paired fins the entire web is supported by the lepidotrichia. These fins are relatively long based and without concentrated radials,

81

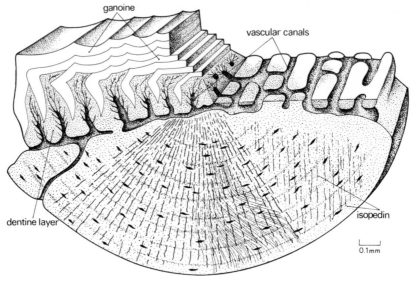

Fig. 5.1. *Cheirolepis* sp. Diagram of scale structure. (After Ørvig.)

and whereas they could be used as organs of balance they were never a means of locomotion.

The lateral-line system is developed as sensory canals in the bones and as pit-lines, forming superficial grooves.

The main lateral-line sensory canal of the body (Fig. 5.2C) continues forward on to the head as the postotic and otic canal, and beneath the orbit as the infraorbital canal, and joins its fellow of the other side posteriorly in the occipital commissure (Gardiner, 1963, 1967a; Jessen, 1968; Heyler, 1969). The supraorbital canal joins the anterior pit-line posteriorly, and is joined to its fellow anteriorly in the ethmoid commissure. There is a preopercular canal which, however, does not unite with the postorbital section of the infraorbital line; it is continued on the lower jaw as the mandibular canal. Supramaxillary and postmaxillary pit-lines are present on the cheek. On the skull-roof there are usually anterior, middle and posterior pit-lines, and on the gular plates median and lateral gular pit-lines.

It has become a recognized fact that the patterns of arrangement of the sensory canals and dermal bones are interrelated through causal factors (Moy-Thomas, 1938; Parrington, 1949, 1967), although other factors which at present are not properly understood must also be responsible for the final architecture of the skull. In order to compare adult structures, the developmental processes which have contributed to their formation must also be compared. In the case of the dermal bones of the skull in fishes these processes are far from being completely understood, nevertheless the little that is known provides a moderately rational means of bone comparison. A short digression into our knowledge of these processes will not be out of place.

It has been observed that the osteoblasts initially aggregate in the vicinity of the sense organs (neuromasts) of the lateral-line canal system (Pehrson, 1922; Devillers, 1947). The small bone rudiments so formed may or may not fuse with neighbouring rudiments to form the adult bones through which the sensory canals pass. On the other hand, those superficial organs which never develop beyond pit-lines seem to play no very important part (Westoll, 1937a). In this way series of small ossifications lying along the canals are produced. The majority of those bones which are not connected with this system develop later, except those which form in connection with the teeth (Moy-Thomas, 1934a) and those of the opercular series which are functional early. This process, however, provides no explanation of the actual limits of

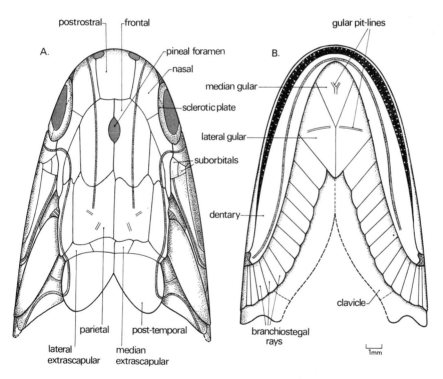

Fig. 5.2. *Moythomasia nitida.* Restorations of the skull in dorsal (A), ventral (B) and lateral (C) views. Spiracular opening shown in too posterior a position and is not labelled. (After Jessen.)

83

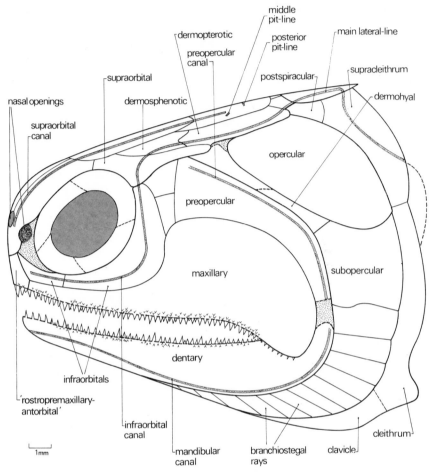

Fig. 5.2. (*C*) see previous page for Legend.

the bones in any series, either with one another or with those unconnected with the sensory canal system. There is evidence that in certain cases the limits are connected with the relative importance of the bone in the skull architecture and its relation to the underlying endocranial elements, but in other cases this is not so (Moy-Thomas, 1941; Parrington, 1967).

In tetrapods experimental evidence indicates that the development of bones is determined much earlier in ontogeny than in fishes, and that they are in consequence much more constant in their final arrangement. In fishes, on the other hand, the bones seem to be in a much more 'fluid' state and the arrangement and number of bones in the different groups, and even in individuals of the same species is subject to con-

84

siderable variation. The number of bones ossifying along the canal may be variable; for example, the infraorbital series of ossifications in the Recent holostean *Amia* vary in different individuals and on different sides of the same individual; and in the Devonian lung-fish *Dipterus* the series of bones related to the postotic and supraorbital sensory-lines behave in a similar way (Moy-Thomas, 1938; Westoll, 1949; White, 1965).

A crucial point is whether the neuromasts act as induction centres for the formation of canal bones, or whether it is the precursors of the bones that influence the courses of the developing lateral-lines. Whilst the first has often been assumed to be the case, so that bones developing in relation to a particular part of the lateral-line system in different fishes are always taken as homologous (Stensiö, 1947; Jarvik, 1948, 1967), there is much evidence in favour of the second view (Moy-Thomas, 1941; Parrington, 1949; Lekander, 1949). Whichever it proves to be in fishes, it is obvious that dermal bones form in amniotes in the absence of neuromasts. Regardless of these considerations, the general principle of constancy of morphological relations makes it convenient for practical purposes to compare series of bones developed in connection with sensory canals in different fishes, although the individual ossifications on them may not really be directly comparable.

A controversial related topic concerns the loss of dermal bones in the evolution of a group, and whether this is because they fuse with neighbouring bones (Stensiö, 1947; Jarvik, 1948; Westoll, 1949), or because they fail to develop and their place is occupied by other, enlarged bones (Parrington, 1949, 1956, 1967; White, 1965; Jardine, 1969). If, however, the problem is examined from both an ontogenetic and phylogenetic point of view, the differences between the two schools of thought are mainly of a semantic nature. Ørvig (1968) has therefore coined the term *assimilative phase of development*, to describe changes in the dermal skeleton during phylogeny in which one bone comes to occupy a position formerly held by two or more bones. The converse process ('fragmentation') is termed by Ørvig the *regressive phase of development*.

The following lateral-line series of bones are found in primitive actinopterygians (Fig. 5.2); an extrascapular series on the occipital commissure, a supratemporal series, usually the dermopterotic (or intertemporo-supratemporal) and dermosphenotic on the postotic and otic regions of the main canal; the fronto-nasal series forms on the supraorbital canal, and the infraorbital series and antorbital on the infraorbital canal; the preopercular, angular and dentary are formed on the preopercular and mandibular canals; the premaxillaries are not differentiated from the rostrals which form on the ethmoid commissure. Lying between the series are areas occupied by a varying number of bones. Between the supratemporal series are the parietals and between the fronto-nasal series, the postrostral(s). In the cheek region there are the suborbital series behind the most dorsal infraorbitals, and a supraorbital lateral to the fronto-nasal series; the tooth-bearing maxillaries, which with the rostro-premaxillaries form the upper margin of the jaws; and there may be a dermohyal series along the posterodorsal margin of the preopercular. The lower jaw, in addition to the tooth-bearing dentary and the angular, includes a very small surangular, and internally an articular, a large prearticular, and a row of tooth-bearing coronoids. There is also an opercular, a subopercular, a series of branchiostegal rays, a pair of lateral gulars and a median gular. A further feature of actinopterygians is the small number of sclerotic plates, typically four, found in the orbit.

Since the main evolutionary tendencies of the actinopterygians are well known, their phylogeny can be reconstructed in general terms. It is possible to trace back all the later forms to the primitive basic type, the palaeoniscids. The most successful line of evolution from this type was that which culminated in the teleosts, the dominant group of bony fishes of the present day. Even as early as the Carboniferous the primitive palaeoniscid type showed a tendency to evolve in this direction, and by the Permian the first holostean, a form very similar to the living *Amia*, had appeared, and from fishes such as these the teleosts evolved. During the Palaeozoic the evolution of actinopterygians consisted of modifications of the original palaeoniscid theme, most of which represent trends towards the holostean grade of structure. The multiplicity of these lines makes classification rather difficult. Here the Palaeozoic actinopterygians are considered to belong to the superorders Chondrostei and Holostei. This classification is discussed below (see Tendencies in evolution §12).

5.4. SUPERORDER 1, CHONDROSTEI

This division includes as orders all the early lines of evolution, and consequent on the great diversity of structure it is not easy to provide a comprehensive definition of the group. However, since each of the orders resembles the primitive basic order Palaeoniscida in either head or body structure more closely than it resembles the typical holostean, the palaeoniscids will be described in detail. The group appears to survive least modified at the present day in the African *Polypterus* and *Erpetoichthys* (Goodrich, 1928; Stensiö, 1947), although the affinities of these genera are still disputed (Jarvik, 1968; Nelson, 1969).

5.5. ORDER 1, PALAEONISCIDA

The palaeoniscids are a very long-lived group and range from the Lower

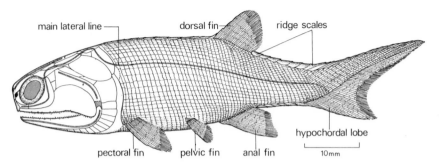

Fig. 5.3. *Moythomasia nitida*. Restoration in lateral view. (After Jessen.)

Devonian to the Cretaceous. This long time range is particularly significant, because during it numerous side lines have acquired the holostean type of organization, while a 'central' line has remained in which the basal type of structure has stayed unaltered except for a few relatively unimportant details, such as the degree of ossification of the neurocranium, the form of the squamation, the shape of the body and the relative position of the fins. Devonian forms like *Stegotrachelus* and *Moythomasia* (Woodward and White, 1926; Gardiner, 1963; Jessen, 1968) are essentially similar in structure to the Lower Cretaceous *Coccolepis* (Gardiner, 1960).

5.5.1. Structure

Typical palaeoniscids are in general carnivorous in habit, having jaws armed with sharp conical teeth and with a wide gape. The body (Fig. 5.3) is usually fusiform or elongate fusiform in shape, and although normally fishes of small or moderate size they may reach a length of one metre or more. There is always a single dorsal and an anal fin, both of which are typically triangular

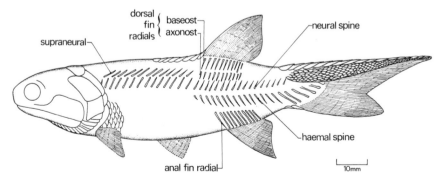

Fig. 5.4. *Phanerosteon mirabile*. Restoration in lateral view. (After White.)

and acuminate, and the tail is strongly heterocercal, and deeply cleft poster-iorly without an epichordal lobe or with only minute traces of one (Watson, 1928; Blot, 1966; Heyler, 1969). The dorsal fin (Fig. 5.4) is typically supported by two rows and the anal fin by one row of radials, and although the number of these radials may be greater than the neural and haemal spines they are never fused together. The notochord was persistent (see Vaughn, 1967). The pectoral fins may be slightly lobed as in *Cheirolepis*, but they are always long based, their internal skeleton (Fig. 5.5) consisting of a row of radials articulating with the scapulocoracoid in a more or less fan-like manner (White, 1939; Jessen, 1968). The scapulocoracoid is very similar to that of sturgeons in shape, and in the position of the muscle attachment areas and the form of the articular crest (Fig. 5.5). It has a mesial mesocoracoid arch. The dermal shoulder-girdle is similar to that of other osteichthyans (Jarvik, 1944), and includes a supracleithrum, a cleithrum and a clavicle. The pelvic fins are also long based with an internal row of radials. The right and left halves of the pelvic girdle are distinct, small, triangular ossifications and do not fuse with one another (Aldinger, 1937). The radials articulate directly with the girdles, which are little more than enlarged basals. The fin-rays or lepidotrichia are of the same structure as the scales (Jarvik, 1959) and are

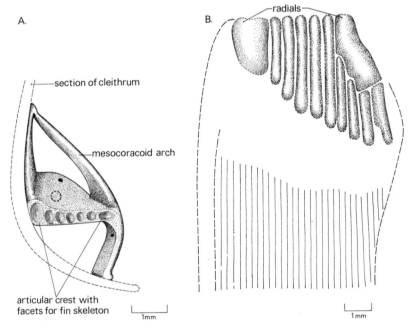

Fig. 5.5. *Moythomasia* cf. *striata*. Restorations of scapulocoracoid in posterior view (A), and pectoral fin skeleton (B). (After Jessen.)

88

very numerous, bifurcating distally and set closely together, far outnumbering the endoskeletal radials. There is typically a row of small fringing fulcral scales along the leading edge of all the fins.

The dermal bones, lepidotrichia and scales are of the type known as 'ganoid', and differ from 'cosmoid' scales as has been pointed out above, in the absence of cosmine and in that they grow not only on the inner, but also on the outer surface. The typical palaeoniscid scale (Fig. 5.1) consists of three layers; the superficial enamel-like layer, the middle dentine layer with a prominent vascular canal system, and the inner layer of lamellated bone or isopedin (Aldinger, 1937). The inner layer is traversed by numerous vascular (Williamson's) canals. As growth occurs on the outer surface as well as the inner, the enamel-like surface of the scale develops into a thick transparent layer known as ganoine, the entire scale increasing in size concentrically. Certain Upper Silurian and Lower Devonian scales have a slightly different structure and mode of growth (Gross, 1968; Schultze, 1968), and may lack or have only a very thin layer of ganoine.

The scales are usually thick, rhomboid and overlapping, articulating with one another by a dorsal peg fitting into a socket on the bottom of the scale above it. In some genera like *Cryphiolepis* (Fig. 5.9) and *Sphaerolepis* (Gardiner, 1967a) the scales are cycloid. Dorsal and ventral rows of ridge scales are usually present in front of the median fins, especially along the dorsal surface of the axial lobe of the tail, forming effective cutwaters. A striking peculiarity of the squamation is found in the caudal region where the normal forward slope of the dorsoventral scale rows is reversed. This appears to be connected with the fact that the tail does not at first during development turn upwards (see Smith, 1956; Patterson, 1968, for functional explanation). Further scales are added from before backwards, and by the time the scales develop near the tail end the axial lobe has become turned upwards, producing an apparent change in the direction of the tail scales relative to those on the rest of the body and giving an appearance of discontinuity where the anterior scales meet those of the caudal pedicle.

In the skull, the neurocranium (Watson, 1925; Eaton, 1939; Rayner, 1951) functionally forms a single piece and there was no dorsoventral flexure (Fig. 5.6). In general appearance it is very like that of *Acanthodes*, which suggests that this type of neurocranium is close to that of the primitive teleostome stock. The lateral occipital fissure meets its antimere in the posterior dorsal fontanelle. From here it passes down to the more anteriorly situated vestibular fontanelle. Further forwards in the floor of the neurocranium there is a transverse ventral fissure, immediately behind the basisphenoid region covered by the dermal parasphenoid. The ventral fissure separates the trabecular-polar region of the neurocranium from the parachordal region. The neurocranium is tropibasic, with large orbital cavities and a thin inter-

89

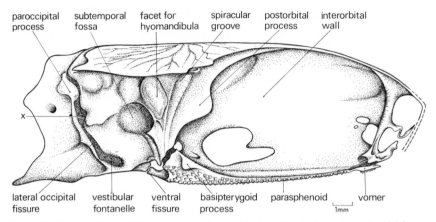

Fig. 5.6. Restoration of the neurocranium of a stegotrachelid palaeoniscoid from the Upper Devonian of Australia, in lateral view. The fossa bridgei is covered by the dermal skull-roof. (After an unpublished drawing provided by Dr. B. G. Gardiner.)

orbital wall. There are large postorbital processes, behind which the spiracular groove runs up the side wall of the otic region. All early palaeoniscids seem to have had an open spiracle (Jessen, 1968). Other features of the otic region include the well-developed articular surface for the hyomandibula, the subtemporal fossa for the insertion of hyomandibular and opercular muscles and the dorsally situated fossa bridgei. In all but the most primitive forms there is a well-formed posterior myodome or eye-muscle canal in the posterior wall of the orbit. Endocasts suggest that the brain was organized essentially as in later actinopterygians (Stensiö, 1963). A primitive feature retained by a few Devonian genera is the presence of a pineal opening in the dermal skull-roof, (Fig. 5.2), and there is sometimes a buccohypophysial foramen in the parasphenoid. Primitively the parasphenoid ends just behind the hypophysial region, but in later forms it extends back to bridge over the ventral fissure in the floor of the neurocranium. Dermal vomers lie under the nasal capsules, closely associated with the anterior region of the parasphenoid.

The palatoquadrate is attached to the neurocranium by the hyomandibula, a basal process articulating with the basipterygoid process of the neurocranium and an ethmoid articulation. Although an otic process is present it never seems actually to form a connection with the neurocranium. The basal and otic processes are ossified as the metapterygoid, in addition to which the palatoquadrate has tooth-bearing ecto- and endopterygoids, a varying number of tooth-bearing dermal palatines, an autopalatine and a quadrate. The hyomandibula articulates with the otic region of the neurocranium and usually slopes at a very oblique angle, the ventral end pointing backwards (see Tendencies in evolution §12). There is an interhyal bone between the hyomandibula and ceratohyal, and a well-developed hypohyal. The gill-skeleton is not known in Palaeozoic species, but in the early Triassic *Pteronisculus* the arches are very similar to those of higher actinopterygians, except that the first two include both infra- and suprapharyngobranchials (Nielsen, 1942). There is a short ventral series of copulae.

The typical arrangements of the sensory lines and dermal bones of the head have already been described, but there is a certain amount of variation in the different families. The shape of the maxillary is very characteristic. Posteriorly it has a greatly expanded portion, which forms a large part of the covering of the cheek, but it is continued anteriorly under the orbit only as a narrow strip of bone. In typical forms teeth are borne along its entire ventral margin. The varying conditions of the snout bones can be explained by assuming the primitive presence of a compound 'rostropremaxillary-antorbital', which 'fragmented' in different ways to give at least three different bone patterns (Gardiner, 1963; see Westoll, 1937*b*, 1944).

5.5.2. *Suborder 1, Palaeoniscoidei*

Much diversity of form exists in the primitive palaeoniscids, but so far they have not been very satisfactorily grouped together in superfamilial taxa. This is largely because many species are known only from squashed dermal bones and scales. The families which will be mentioned here are not intended to be a complete list and must be considered to be of a very tentative nature. They are only intended to illustrate the chief variations in the fundamental palaeoniscid scheme. Some recent classifications recognize up to 42 families (Gardiner, 1967*a*, 1969). Further research will undoubtedly show that many of the genera here grouped together are not really very closely related.

The palaeoniscoids are palaeoniscids of normal habit, with from elongated to short fusiform bodies.

The family Palaeoniscidae includes the majority of fishes belonging to this suborder, all of which have the characteristic rhomboid scales, triangular and acuminate median fins with fulcral scales, typically deeply cleft heterocercal tail and an oblique jaw suspension. The family is represented by such forms as the Devonian *Stegotrachelus* and *Moythomasia* (Fig. 5.3), the Carboniferous *Rhadinichthys* (Fig. 5.7) (Moy-Thomas and Bradley Dyne, 1938), *Nematoptychius*, *Elonichthys* (Gardiner, 1963), *Gonatodus*, *Cycloptychius*, *Commentrya* (Blot, 1966) and *Paramblypterus* (Blot, 1966; Heyler, 1969), and the Permian *Palaeoniscum* and *Pygopterus* (Aldinger, 1937). The Lower Carboniferous *Phanerosteon* (Fig. 5.4) (White, 1927) is peculiar in having lost most of its body scales as in sturgeons, a few scales remaining

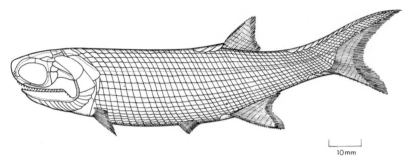

Fig. 5.7. *Rhadinichthys canobiensis.* Restoration in lateral view. (After Moy-Thomas and Bradley Dyne.)

just behind the pectoral fin and on the caudal prolongation of the body. This genus is often placed with the Lower Carboniferous *Carboveles* (White, 1927), in the family Carbovelidae.

The family Cheirolepididae contains only the Devonian genus *Cheirolepis* (Fig. 5.8) which is similar to the Palaeoniscidae except for the form and size of its scales (Watson, 1925; Lehman, 1947), which are minute and square, closely resembling those of acanthodians. The Tegeolepididae are another Devonian family, although they survive to the Triassic (Gardiner, 1963). *Tegeolepis* has small thin scales, no fulcral scales and unjointed lepidotrichia in the pectoral fins.

The family Cryphiolepididae, including the Lower Carboniferous *Cryphiolepis* (Traquair, 1877–1914), is also similar in general form to the Palaeoniscidae but has cycloid deeply overlapping scales (Fig. 5.9). Similar scales are found in the Permian *Sphaerolepis* (Gardiner, 1967a). This, however, is a quite distinct genus with a more or less vertical jaw suspension. On the skull-roof there is a large foramen partly separating the frontals, parietals and dermopterotics. So far no explanation of this fossa has been put forward. *Sphaerolepis* is placed in the family Trissolepididae.

The family Canobiidae is of particular interest as it includes the earliest palaeoniscids to approach the holostean grade of structure in any one

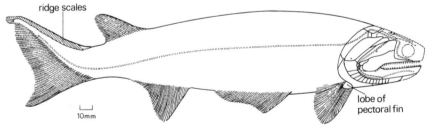

Fig. 5.8. *Cheirolepis canadensis.* Restoration in lateral view. (After Lehman.)

92

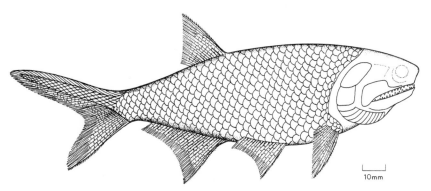

Fig. 5.9. *Cryphiolepis striatus*. Restoration in lateral view. (After Traquair.)

character. The Lower Carboniferous *Canobius* is similar to the Palaeoniscidae in body and scale structure but has an almost vertical jaw suspension (Fig. 5.21B) and not the typical oblique suspension found in other families (Moy-Thomas and Bradley Dyne, 1938). Similar changes have taken place in the Permian Aeduellidae (Westoll, 1937*b*; Heyler, 1967). In *Aeduella* (Fig. 5.10) an interesting modification is found in the upper jaw; the maxillary having grown down to sheath the bases of the teeth (Blot and Heyler, 1963). More significant changes are found in the large number of postorbital bones and small preopercular.

The family Holuridae, for example the Lower Carboniferous *Holurus* and *Australichthys* (Gardiner, 1969), have an exceedingly long based dorsal fin, and both the dorsal and anal fins are rounded and low, not acuminate (Fig. 5.11). The tail is heterocercal but not deeply cleft, and there are no fulcral scales and none of the epidotrichia bifurcate distally. It is from this type of palaeoniscid that a form like *Tarrasius* (§7; Fig. 5.16) with continuous median fins might have been derived.

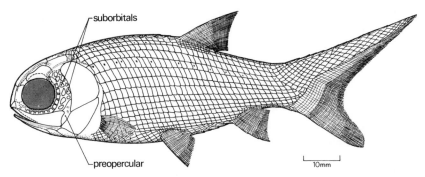

Fig. 5.10. *Aeduella blainvillei*. Restoration in lateral view. (After Heyler.)

93

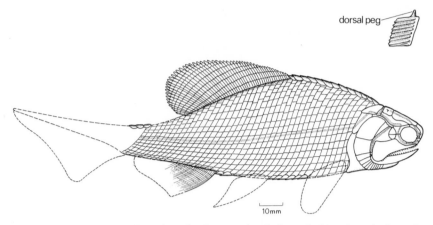

Fig. 5.11. *Australichthys longidorsalis*. Restoration in lateral view. A scale from the anterior part of the flank is shown at a higher magnification. (After Gardiner.)

The family Styracopteridae includes the Lower Carboniferous fish *Styracopterus* (Moy-Thomas, 1937), whose most notable characteristics are the not very oblique jaw suspension, the very large size of the fulcral scales and the inequilobate and not very deeply cleft caudal fin. These characters are also found in the Willmorichthyidae (Gardiner, 1969), which, however, have a deeply fusiform body.

5.5.3. Suborder 2, Platysomoidei

The platysomoids (Figs. 5.12–5.14) are in all essential features similar in structure to the palaeoniscoids, but are much dorsoventrally deepened and laterally compressed, being similar in body shape to the living John Dory. Consequently the main features of the group are really little more than modifications due to the change in body shape by differential growth. The dorsal fin is usually very much elongated and in very deep-bodied forms like *Chirodus* (Fig. 5.12), the anal fin is also long based. The body scales are much elongated dorsoventrally; the jaw suspension is upright; the length of the skull is short in relation to its height, as a consequence of which the maxillary is almost triangular; and the nostrils are high up on the face far removed from the mouth.

Two families, the Chirodontidae and Platysomidae, can be recognized in this suborder, and in each there are forms in which the body is little more than deeply fusiform (Fig. 5.13) ranging to far more specialized fishes in which the body is almost as deep as long (Fig. 5.14).

The Chirodontidae include both Carboniferous and Permian genera, of which the chief characteristic is a dentition modified for crushing. The primi-

94

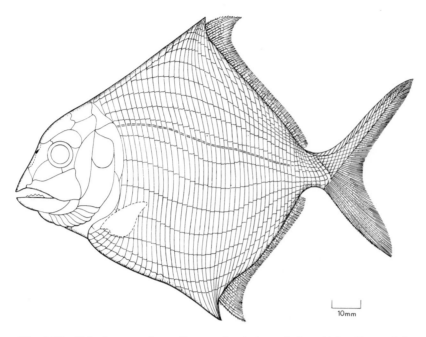

Fig. 5.12. *Chirodus granulosus*. Restoration in lateral view. (After Traquair.)

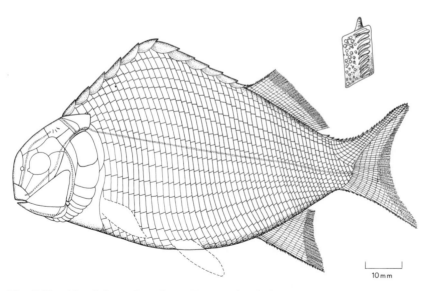

Fig. 5.13. *Adroichthys tuberculatus*. Restoration in lateral view. A scale from the outerior part of the flank is shown at a higher magnification. (After Gardiner.)

95

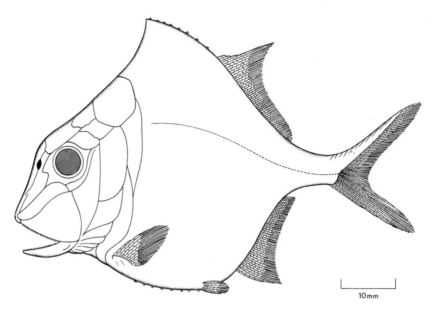

Fig. 5.14. *Platysomus parvulus*. Restoration in lateral view. Pattern of bones in skull known to be incorrect. (After Traquair.)

tive member *Proteurynotus* (Moy-Thomas and Bradley Dyne, 1938) is only deeply fusiform, and *Eurynotus* (Traquair, 1879) is similar in shape but has a much elongated dorsal fin. *Adroichthys* (Fig. 5.13) has a short dorsal fin, but in front of it there is a series of greatly enlarged dorsal ridge scales (Gardiner, 1969). The teeth of *Eurynotus* are short, obtuse and spherical. In *Cheirodopsis* the body is deep and rounded, and both the dorsal and anal fins are much elongated. There are no teeth on the maxillary and dentary, but large pterygoid and coronoid tooth-plates. *Chirodus* (Fig. 5.12) is at the climax of the evolutionary series. It has a very deep body, which is rhombic and drawn out dorsally and ventrally into peaks in front of the long dorsal and anal fins and there are no pelvic fins. The dentition is similar to that of *Cheirodopsis*, but the premaxillary is drawn out into a beak (Bradley Dyne, 1939).

The members of the family Platysomidae do not have a crushing dentition, the teeth being conical and often pointed. There are forms like the Carboniferous *Mesolepis* (Traquair, 1879) in which the body is only deeply fusiform with an elongated dorsal fin, whereas in *Platysomus* (Fig. 5.14) which is found in both the Carboniferous and Permian, the modifications are carried further and the body is very deep, and the unpaired fins much elongated. The Upper Carboniferous *Platysomus parvulus* is an interesting form in which the body is drawn out dorsally into a peak and in which the preopercular ossi-

96

fies as two bones along the preopercular canal. The Lower Carboniferous *Wardichthys* (Traquair, 1907) is a somewhat similar type of fish to *Platysomus*, but its body is very deep and rounded, and the dorsal fin is relatively rather short, arising well behind the dorsal hump of the body.

5.6. ORDER 2, HAPLOLEPIDIDA

This is an Upper Carboniferous group of fusiform fishes (Fig. 5.15), which are the earliest forms to show any significant departure in structure from the basic palaeoniscid type (Westoll, 1944; Baird, 1962). The head lacks a prominent rostrum, and is broad and short, with a small opercular apparatus, reduced number of branchiostegal rays and enlarged gular plates. The suspensorium is almost vertical and there is a tendency for the preopercular to break up into several small ossifications. The fin-rays are large although few in number, and they do not bifurcate distally. The caudal fin is obliquely truncated and hardly cleft posteriorly at all. The fins are fringed anteriorly by large fulcral scales, and the cleithrum is greatly expanded ventrally. The scales are thin and tend to be deep on the flank of *Haplolepis*. A feature of *Pyritocephalus* (Fig. 5.15) is the presence of a pair of large fossae in the skull-roof between the frontals, parietals and more lateral bones, as in *Sphaerolepis*. In this case it is possible that the fossae were connected with the large size of the eyeball (Westoll, 1944).

5.7. ORDER 3, TARRASIIDA

This order is known from the Lower Carboniferous fish *Tarrasius* (Moy-Thomas, 1934*b*; Moy-Thomas and Bradley Dyne, 1938), although the Upper Carboniferous *Palaeophichthys* may also belong here. The head is essentially palaeoniscid in structure, but the body is elongated and superficially re-

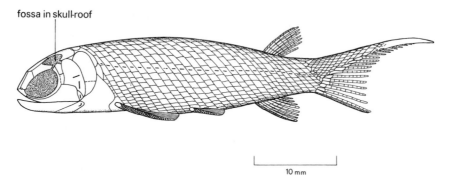

fossa in skull-roof

10 mm

Fig. 5.15. *Pyritocephalus lineatus*. Restoration in lateral view. (After Westoll.)

97

sembles the modern *Polypterus* (Fig. 5.16). The dorsal and anal fins are continuous with the caudal, which is diphycercal and the general eel-like appearance produced by this is accentuated by the absence of pelvic fins. As in the holurids, the sort of forms from which it has been pointed out *Tarrasius* might have been derived, the fins are without fringing fulcral scales and the lepidotrichia do not bifurcate distally. The pectoral fins, although typically actinopterygian in internal structure, have a rounded fleshy lobe as in *Polypterus*, a character which originally led to both *Tarrasius* and *Polypterus* being included in the crossopterygians.

The general appearance of *Tarrasius* is rendered more remarkable by the absence of scales from the greater part of the body. Scales are only present on the caudal region and these are very numerous, small and square like those in *Cheirolepis*. The axial skeleton is similar to that of other actinopterygians with two rows of radials below the dorsal and one row above the anal fin, both more numerous than the neural and haemal spines.

5.8. ORDER 4, PHANERORHYNCHIDA

This order is known from a single Upper Carboniferous genus, *Phanerorhynchus* (Gardiner, 1967a). The skull (Fig. 5.17) appears to be of much the same structure as that of typical haplolepids, but it has small orbits and a greatly elongated rostrum which gives the head a very strong likeness to that of a sturgeon. The suspensorium is almost vertical and there is a small, oval opercular bone. The body scales are relatively large and rather few, and there are prominently developed ridge scales both dorsally and ventrally, which grade into stout fulcra on the anterior edges of the fins. However, the most striking feature of *Phanerorhynchus* is the reduction in the number of the fin-rays, which are well spaced and probably correspond in number

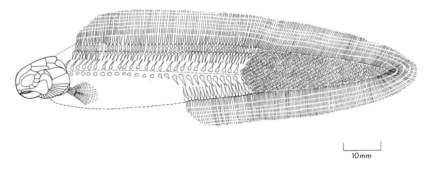

10mm

Fig. 5.16. *Tarrasius problematicus.* Restoration in lateral view. (After Moy-Thomas.)

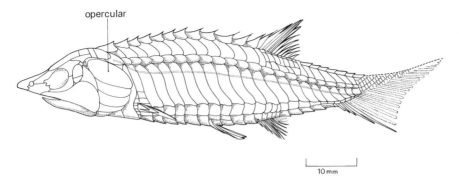

opercular

10 mm

Fig. 5.17. *Phanerorhynchus armatus*. Restoration in lateral view. (After Gardiner.)

to the internal radials. In this last character *Phanerorhynchus* approaches the holostean condition.

5.9. ORDER 5, DORYPTERIDA

The peculiar deep-bodied fish *Dorypterus* (Gill, 1925; Westoll, 1941) from the Upper Permian has many characters resembling the platysomids, but in other ways is extremely specialized and approaches the holostean type in structure (Fig. 5.18). The body is scaleless except for the caudal prolongation, there is a great reduction in most of the dermal bones of the head, and there are no teeth. The internal skeleton of the paired and unpaired fins is essentially similar to that of palaeoniscids. The dorsal fin has very long anterior lepidotrichia lying close together, but its posterior lepidotrichia and all those of the anal fin are slightly more widely spaced, and the pelvic fin is far forward and in front of the pectoral. The caudal fin has the axial lobe of the tail very much narrowed and reduced to two rows of scales, its central rays being widely spaced as in holosteans.

5.10. SUPERORDER 2, HOLOSTEI

In the Palaeozoic only a single true holostean is known, the Upper Permian fish *Acentrophorus* (Gill, 1923; Gardiner, 1960). It must be emphasized that this early holostean makes its appearance while the palaeoniscids are still the dominant group of actinopterygians. During the succeeding Triassic Period more and more lines of evolution from the palaeoniscids approach the holostean condition in certain characters, but more markedly than those described above. For all these families the name subholosteans has been proposed by Brough (1936).

99

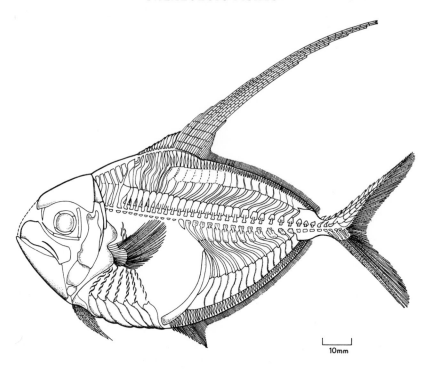

Fig. 5.18. *Dorypterus hoffmanni*. Restoration in lateral view. (After Westoll.)

5.11. ORDER 1, SEMIONOTIDA

Acentrophorus (Fig. 5.19) is a small fish covered in more or less cycloid overlapping ganoid scales. Although it has not yet been described, there is every reason to believe that their microscopical structure is a modification of the palaeoniscoid type known as the lepidosteoid, as in later holosteans (Goodrich, 1908; Brough, 1936). In the lepidosteoid type of scale the dentine

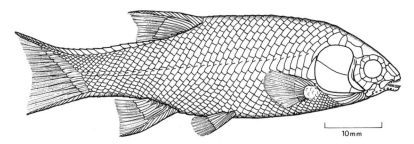

Fig. 5.19. *Acentrophorus varians*. Restoration in lateral view. (After Gill.)

100

and vascular layers of the scales have disappeared leaving only the outer ganoine and the underlying layer of isopedin. In later actinopterygians, such as the teleosts, a further modification occurs, the ganoine layer being lost and only the layer of lamellated bone remaining.

All the fin-rays are reduced in number, and as in other holosteans must have corresponded numerically with the internal radials. The tail is still heterocercal, but the axial lobe is reduced to a single row of scales. In later holosteans it becomes reduced altogether, producing the condition known as homocercal, in which the tail fin is supported only by lepidotrichia.

The skull (Fig. 5.20) has many very characteristic modifications. The

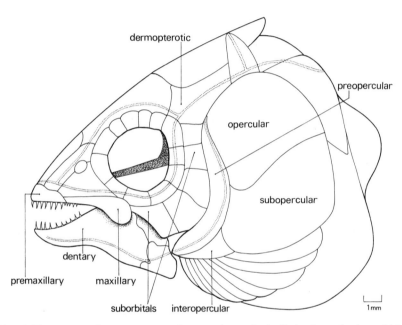

Fig. 5.20. *Acentrophorus varians*. Restoration of skull in lateral view. (After Gardiner.)

jaw suspension is upright, and the maxillary has become freed at its hinder end and no longer plays an important part in the structure of the cheek, and teeth are only found on the front end of the jaws. On the cheek the position usually occupied by the posterior part of the maxillary is filled by a row of numerous suborbitals. A further modification in connection with the reduction of the maxillary and upright jaw suspension is found in the opercular apparatus. In the gular region there is an extra bone, the interoperculum, which appears to be formed by the displacement of the most dorsal branch-

101

iostegal ray. The premaxillary is a tooth-bearing bone unconnected with the sensory canal, comparable with the similar bone found in some palaeoniscids. In living holosteans the lateral-line canal system differs from that of palaeoniscids in that the supraorbital canal is no longer continued back on to the parietals, but joins the infraorbital canal in the dermopterotic. *Acentrophorus* appears already to show the holostean condition (Gardiner, 1960). The neurocranium of 'typical' holosteans is formed of several pairs of cartilage bones (Rayner, 1941).

5.12. TENDENCIES IN EVOLUTION

The taxa Chondrostei, Holostei and Teleostei were erected in the first place for three groups of quite distinct Recent fishes. However, when they were expanded to include numerous imperfectly known fossil actinopterygians, particularly Palaeozoic and Mesozoic genera, they lost their original significance, and also to some extent their phylogenetic validity. Although the teleosts still appear to be a monophyletic group, the chondrosteans and holosteans include many distinct lines of descent, with considerable parallel evolution. As they are now used, these last two categories represent successive levels of organization. In an alternative classification to the one used here, the holosteans and teleosts are grouped together as the Neopterygii (Nelson, 1969), because the living holosteans (*Amia, Lepisosteus*) are more closely related to teleosts than they are to chondrosteans (Sturgeons, *Polyodon.*) This is at best a partial solution to the problem, for it makes it no easier to classify the many fossil species that have to be handled, and it is far from clear that the living holosteans form a natural group (Westoll, 1944).

It must be recognized that the classification of chondrosteans employed here is in no sense a phylogenetic arrangement. The bulk of the Palaeozoic forms are placed in the order Palaeoniscida, and in this group the deep bodied types are separated off as the platysomoids, leaving the remaining forms in the markedly heterogeneous group, palaeoniscoids. It is not clear even that the platysomoids are a natural group. The remaining orders of Palaeozoic chondrosteans represent groups that have diverged sufficiently from the basic palaeoniscid plan to be readily separable, regardless of their true affinities. This story is repeated at a lower level in the palaeoniscoids, where the family Palaeoniscidae is used as a 'hold-all' for a host of 'normal' forms, the divergent types being placed in separate families.

It is against this background that the evolutionary tendencies of Palaeozoic chondrosteans have to be considered. The ways in which they approach the holostean level of organization, particularly in the feeding and locomotor mechanisms, are of interest. The attainment of the holostean level involved changes that ultimately led to the teleost level and the great adaptive radiation which made actinopterygians the dominant vertebrates of the hydrosphere.

In many early palaeoniscids such as *Rhadinichthys* and *Nematoptychius*, the cheek bones form a solid unit, with the maxillary, preopercular and suborbitals firmly united with each other and with the palatoquadrate (Fig. 5.21A). The hyomandibula is obliquely placed, the long mandible functioned as a simple straight lever and the adductor mandibulae muscles inserted in a chamber between the cheek bones and the palatoquadrate. These fishes had a deep gape and were predators, seizing prey, which they must have swallowed whole or bitten into smaller pieces. In both feeding and gill ventilation, the expansion of the oralobranchial chamber depended upon movements of the hyomandibula and palatoquadrate-maxillary complex, as well as of the hyoid bars, neurocranium and shoulder-girdle (Schaeffer and Rosen, 1961). As long as the hyomandibula had an oblique position the lateral expansion of the oralobranchial chamber was very limited. At the same time the bony plated cheek presented only limited possibilities for adaptive change. In more advanced forms the suspensorium became more upright and the hyomandibula came to swing in the vertical plane, giving greater lateral expansion of the oralobranchial chamber. Various other modifications are associated with this change (Gardiner, 1967*b*). Thus in many genera, such as *Canobius* (Fig. 5.21B) and *Holurus*, the palatoquadrate-maxillary chamber became open dorsally and the adductor muscles extended their area of origin up on to the hyoid and neurocranium and became more

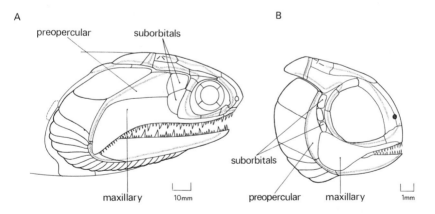

Fig. 5.21. Restorations of the skulls in lateral view of two palaeoniscoids to contrast an oblique (A) with an upright (B) jaw suspension. A. *Nematoptychius greenocki* (After Gardiner.); B. *Canobius elegantulus*. (After Moy-Thomas and Bradley Dyne.)

powerful. Further changes included the break up of the connections between the maxillary, suborbital and preopercular bones, as the palatoquadrate-maxillary chamber was eliminated. The 'fragmentation' of the top of the preoperculum took place in some forms, such as the haplolepids and *Aeduella*. The loosening up of the cheek region can be correlated with the elaboration of the adductor mandibulae musculature, and the development of a more efficient mechanism for the expansion of the oralobranchial chamber (Schaeffer and Rosen, 1961). Some advanced palaeoniscids such as *Aeduella* approached the holostean condition very closely in the structure of the head, even to the extent of having a coronoid process in the lower jaw, comparable with that of *Acentrophorus*. This process converted the straight mandibular lever of primitive forms into a bent lever, with an increase in torque about the mandibular joint. At the holostean level, actinopterygians underwent an extensive radiation in the feeding mechanism in the Mesozoic (Rayner, 1941).

The tail of palaeoniscids is characteristically strongly heterocercal, as it is in the living sturgeons and *Polyodon*. This type of tail is usually said to have produced a downward movement at the anterior end of the body, which was countered by the pectoral fins functioning as hydrofoils. However, in certain Triassic palaeoniscids which have been grouped as subholosteans (Brough, 1936), there is a reduction of the scaled dorsal lobe of the tail, to give a hemiheterocercal tail. This type of tail is also found in holosteans (*Acentrophorus*, Fig. 5.19). Further reduction of the lobe gives rise to the externally symmetrical homocercal tail of advanced holosteans and teleosts. The above changes in the tail can be correlated with the development of the airbladder as a hydrostatic organ. As the fishes attained neutral buoyancy with the development of the swimbladder, the tail was no longer required to produce a lifting force, and it became modified into the most efficient form for forward locomotion. Concomitant changes are found in the attitudes and structure of the pectoral fins (Westoll, 1944; Schaeffer, 1956), which are free to take on new functions in swimming. These changes in the tail in Triassic forms are not foreshadowed in Palaeozoic chondrosteans, although there is a reduction in the number of scale rows in the caudal lobe of *Haplolepis* and *Pyritocephalus*. This is surprising as a correlation might be expected between improvements in the feeding and locomotor mechanisms (Schaeffer, 1956).

Although the mainstream of chondrostean evolution is concerned with fusiform, predatory fishes, there are several notable early exceptions. *Tarrasius* has an almost larval type of body and its habit is perhaps intelligible as an example of paedomorphosis. At least twice, in the platysomoids and dorypterids, very deep bodied fishes have been evolved. In the chirodontid platysomoids the dentition is modified for crushing, while *Dorypterus* has no teeth and probably fed on soft plant food (Westoll, 1941). Such deep bodied, small mouthed fishes have arisen independently several times in actinopterygian history, in chondrosteans, holosteans and teleosts, and are often adapted for life in coral reefs. The jugular position of the pelvic fins in *Dorypterus* is a strikingly modern adaptation.

REFERENCES

Aldinger, H. (1937) 'Permische Ganoidfische aus Ostgrönland'. *Medd. Grønland*, **102**, 1–392.

Andrews, S. M. (1967) 'Class Crossopterygii' and 'Class Dipnoi' in *The fossil record*, ed. Harland, W. B., *et al.* (Geol. Soc., London.) p. 641.

Baird, D. (1962) 'A haplolepid fish fauna in the early Pennsylvanian of Nova Scotia'. *Palaeontology*, **5**, 22–29.

Berg, L. S., Kazantseva, A. A. and Obruchev, D. V. (1967) 'Superorder Palaeonisci' in *Fundamentals of palaeontology. 11. Agnatha, Pisces*, ed. Obruchev, D. V. (Israel program for scientific translations, Jerusalem.) p. 336.

Blot, J. (1966) 'Étude des palaeonisciformes du Bassin de Commentry'. *Cahiers Paleont.*, (1966) 1–90.

Blot, J. and Heyler, D. (1963) 'Sur une particularité anatomique de certains Poissons du Permo-Carbonifère des bassins de Commentry et Autun'. *Bull. Soc. géol. Fr.*, (7) **5**, 64–69.

Bradley Dyne, M. (1939) 'The skull of *Amphicentrum granulosum*'. *Proc. zool. Soc. Lond.*, **109** (B), 195–210.

Brough, J. (1936) 'On the evolution of bony fishes during the Triassic period'. *Biol. Rev.*, **11**, 385–405.

Currey, J. D. (1961) 'The histology of the scales of *Orvikuina* (Palaeoniscoidea)'. *Paläont. Z.*, **35**, 187–90.

Daget, J. (1950) 'Révision des affinités phylogénétiques des Polyptérides'. *Mém. Inst. franc. Afr. noire*, **11**, 1–178.

Devillers, C. (1947) 'Rechèrches sur la crâne dermique des téléostéens'. *Annls. Paléont.*, **33**, 1–94.

Dunkle, D. H. (1946) 'A new palaeoniscoid fish from the Lower Permian of Texas'. *J. Wash. Acad. Sci.*, **36**, 402–09.

Dunkle, D. H. (1964) 'Preliminary description of a palaeoniscoid fish from the Upper Devonian of Ohio'. *Scient. publs Cleveland Mus. nat. Hist.*, N.S. 3, 1–16.

Eaton, T. H. Jr. (1939) 'A paleoniscid brain case'. *J. Wash. Acad. Sci.*, **29**, 441–51.

Gardiner, B. G. (1960) 'A revision of certain actinopterygian and coelacanth fishes, chiefly from the Lower Lias'. *Bull. Br. Mus. nat. Hist., (Geol.)*, **4**, 239–384.

Gardiner, B. G. (1962) '*Namaichthys schroederi* Gurich and other Palaeozoic fishes from South Africa'. *Palaeontology*, **5**, 9–21.

Gardiner, B. G. (1963) 'Certain palaeoniscoid fishes and the evolution of the snout in actinopterygians'. *Bull. Br. Mus. nat. Hist., (Geol.)*, **8**, 255–325.

Gardiner, B. G. (1967a) 'Further notes on palaeoniscoid fishes with a classification of the Chondrostei'. *Bull. Br. Mus. nat. Hist., (Geol.)*, **14**, 143–206.

Gardiner, B. G. (1967b) 'The significance of the preoperculum in actinopterygian evolution'. *J. Linn. Soc. (Zool)*, **47**, 197–209.

Gardiner, B. G. (1967c) 'Class Actinopterygii. Subclass Chondrostei' in *The fossil record*, ed. Harland, W. B. *et al.* (Geol. Soc., London) p. 644.

Gardiner, B. G. (1969) 'New palaeoniscoid fish from the Witteberg series of South Africa'. *Zool. J. Linn. Soc.*, **48**, 423–452.

Gill, E. L. (1923) 'The Permian fishes of the genus *Acentrophorus*'. *Proc. zool. Soc. Lond.*, (1923) 19–40.

Gill, E. L. (1925) 'The Permian fish *Dorypterus*' *Trans. R. Soc. Edinb.*, **53**, 643–61.

Goodrich, E. S. (1908) 'On the scales of fish, living and extinct, and their importance in classification'. *Proc. zool. Soc. Lond.*, (1908) 751–74.

Goodrich, E. S. (1928) '*Polypterus* a palaeoniscid?'. *Palaeobiologica*, **1**, 87–91.

Gross, W. (1953) 'Devonische Palaeonisciden-Reste in Mittel—und Osteuropa'. *Paläont. Z.*, **27**, 85–112.

Gross, W. (1966) 'Kleine Schuppenkunde'. *N. Jb. Geol. Paläont. Abh.*, **125** 29–48.

Gross, W. (1968) 'Fragliche Actinopterygier-Schuppen aus dem Silur Gotlands' *Lethaia*, **1**, 184–218.

Gross, W. (1969) '*Lophosteus superbus* Pander, ein Teleostome aus dem Silur Oesels'. *Lethaia*, **2**, 15–47.

Heyler, D. (1967) 'Quelques points nouveaux au sujet d'*Aeduella* Westoll'. *Colloques int. Cent. natn. Rech. scient.*, **163**, 81–88.

Heyler, D. (1969) 'Vertébrés de l'Autunien de France', *Cahiers Paleont.*, (1969) 1–255.

Jardine, N. (1969) 'The observational and theoretical components of homology; a study based on the morphology of the dermal skull-roofs of rhipidistian fishes'. *Biol. J. Linn. Soc.*, **1**, 327–61.

Jarvik, E. (1944) 'On the exoskeletal shoulder-girdle of teleostomian fishes, with special reference to *Eusthenopteron foordi* Whiteaves'. *K. svenska VetenskAkad. Handl.*, (3) **21** 3–32.

Jarvik, E. (1948) 'On the morphology and taxonomy of the Middle Devonian osteolepid fishes of Scotland'. *K. svenska VetenskAkad. Handl.*, (3) **25**, 1–301.

Jarvik, E. (1959) 'Dermal fin-rays and Holmgren's principle of delamination'. *K. svenska VetenskAkad. Handl.*, (4) **6**, 1–51.

Jarvik, E. (1967) 'The homologies of frontal and parietal bones in fishes and tetrapods'. *Colloques int. Cent. natn. Rech. Scient.*, **163**, 181–213.

Jarvik, E. (1968), 'Aspects of vertebrate phylogeny'. *Nobel Symposium*, **4**, 497–527.

Jessen, H. (1968), '*Moythomasia nitida* Gross und *M.* cf. *striata* Gross, Devonische Palaeonisciden aus dem Oberen Plattenkalk der Bergisch–Gladbach–Paffrather Mulde (Rheinisches Schiefergebirge)'. *Palaeontographica*, **128A**, 87–114.

Jollie, M. (1960) 'Sensory canals of the snout of actinopterygian fishes'. *Trans. Ill. St. Acad. Sci.*, **62**, 61–69.

Lehman, J. P. (1947) 'Description de quelques exemplaires de *Cheirolepis canadensis* (Whiteaves)'. *K. svenska VetenskAkad. Handl.*, (3) **24**, 1–40.

Lehman, J. P. (1966) 'Actinopterygii', in *Traité de Paléontologie*, 4.3, ed. Lehman, J. P. (Masson, Paris) p. 1.

Lekander, B. (1949) 'The sensory-line system and the canal bones in the head of some Ostariophysi'. *Acta zool. Stockh.*, **30**, 1–131.

Moy-Thomas, J. A. (1934*a*) 'On the teeth of the larval *Belone vulgaris* and the attachment of teeth in fishes', *Q. Jl. microsc. Sci.*, **76**, 481–98.

Moy-Thomas, J. A. (1934*b*) 'The structure and affinities of *Tarrasius problematicus*, Traquair'. *Proc. zool. Soc. Lond.*, (1934) 367–76.

Moy-Thomas, J. A. (1937) 'The palaeoniscids from the Cement Stones of Tarras Waterfoot'. *Ann. Mag. nat. Hist.*, (10) **20**, 345–56.

Moy-Thomas, J. A. (1938) 'The problem of the evolution of the dermal bones in fishes' in *Evolution, Essays on aspects of evolutionary biology*, ed. de Beer, G. R. (Oxford University Press.) p. 305.

Moy-Thomas, J. A. (1941) 'Development of the frontal bones of the Rainbow Trout'. *Nature, Lond.*, **147**, 681.

Moy-Thomas, J. A. and Bradley Dyne, M. (1938). 'Actinopterygian fishes from the Lower Carboniferous of Glencartholm, Eskdale, Dumfriesshire'. *Trans. R. Soc. Edinb.*, **59**, 437–80.

Nelson, G. J. (1969) 'Gill-arches and the phylogeny of fishes, with notes on the classification of vertebrates'. *Bull. Am. Mus. nat. Hist.*, **141**, 475–552.

Nielsen, E. (1942) 'Studies on Triassic fishes from East-Greenland, I. *Glaucolepis* and *Boreosomus*'. *Medd. Grønland*, **138**, 1–403.

Ørvig, T. (1957) 'Palaeohistological notes. I. On the structure of the bone tissue in the scales of certain Palaeonisciformes'. *Ark. Zool*, (2) **10**, 481–90.

Ørvig, T. (1968) 'The dermal skeleton: general considerations'. *Nobel Symposium*, **4**, 373–97.

Ørvig, T. (1969) 'Cosmine and cosmine growth', *Lethaia*, **2**, 241–60.

Parrington, F. R. (1949) 'A theory of the relation of lateral lines to dermal bones'. *Proc. zool. Soc. Lond.*, **119**, 65–78.

Parrington, F. R. (1956) 'The patterns of dermal bones in primitive vertebrates'. *Proc. zool. Soc. Lond.*, **127**, 389–411.

Parrington, F. R. (1967) 'The identification of the dermal bones of the head'. *J. Linn. Soc. (Zool.)*, **47**, 231–39.

Patterson, C. (1968) 'The caudal skeleton in Lower Liassic pholidophorid fishes'. *Bull. Br. Mus. nat. Hist., (Geol.)*, **16**, 201–39.

Pehrson, T. (1922) 'Some points in the cranial development of teleostomian fishes'. *Acta zool., Stockh.*, **3**, 1–63.

Rayner, D. M. (1941) 'The structure and evolution of the holostean fishes'. *Biol. Rev.*, **16**, 218–237.

Rayner, D. H. (1951) 'On the cranial structure of an early palaeoniscid, *Kentuckia*, gen, nov. *Trans. R. Soc. Edinb.*, **62**, 53–83.

Schaeffer, B. (1956) 'Evolution in the subholostean fishes'. *Evolution, N.Y.*, **10**, 201–12.

Schaeffer, B. (1968) 'The origin and basic radiation of the Osteichthyes'. *Nobel Symposium*, **4**, 207–22.

Schaeffer, B., and Rosen, D. E. (1961) 'Major adaptive levels in the evolution of the actinopterygian feeding mechanism'. *Am. Zool.*, **1**, 187–204.

Schultze, H. P. (1966) 'Morphologische und histologische Untersuchungen an Schuppen mesozoischer Actinopterygier (Übergang von Ganoid-zur Rundschuppen)'. *N. Jb. Geol. Paläont. Abh.*, **126**, 232–314.

Schultze, H. P. (1968) 'Palaeoniscoidea-Schuppen aus dem Unterdevon Australiens und Kanadas und aus dem Mitteldevon Spitzbergens'. *Bull. Br. Mus. nat. Hist.*, *(Geol)*, **16**, 341–68.

Schultze, H. P. (1970) '*Indaginilepis rhombifera* n.gen. et n.sp., ein altertümlicher Palaeoniscoide (Pisces, Actinopterygii) aus dem Wealden von Norddeutschland'. *Paläont. Z.*, **44**, 10–24.

Smith, I. C. (1956) 'The structure of the skin and dermal scales in the tail of *Acipenser ruthensis* L.' *Trans. R. Soc. Edinb.*, **63**, 1–14.

Stensiö, E. A. (1947) 'The sensory lines and dermal bones of the cheek in fishes and amphibians'. *K. svenska VetenskAkad. Handl.*, (3) **24**, 1–194.

Stensiö, E. A. (1963) 'The brain and cranial nerves in fossil, lower craniate vertebrates'. *Skr. norske VidenskAkad. Oslo, Mat.-naturv. Kl.* (1963) 1–120.

Traquair, R. H. (1877–1914) 'The ganoid fishes of the British Carboniferous formations. Part I. Palaeoniscidae'. *Palaeontogr. Soc. (Monogr.)*, London, **31**, 1–186.

Traquair, R. H. (1879) 'On the structure and affinities of the Platysomidae', *Trans. R. Soc. Edinb.*, **29**, 343–91.

Traquair, R. H. (1907) 'Report on fossil fishes collected by the Geological Survey from the shales exposed on the shore near Gullane, East Lothian'. *Trans. R. Soc. Edinb.*, **46**, 103–17.

Vaughn, P. P. (1967) 'Evidence of ossified vertebrae in actinopterygian fish of Early Permian age, from southeastern Utah'. *J. Paleont.*, **41**, 151–60.

Watson, D. M. S. (1925) 'The structure of certain palaeoniscids and the relationships of that group with other bony fish'. *Proc. zool. Soc. Lond.*, (1925) 815–70.

Watson, D. M. S. (1928) 'On some points in the structure of palaeoniscid and other allied fish'. *Proc. zool. Soc. Lond.*, (1928) 49–70.

Westoll, T. S. (1937a) 'On the cheek-bones in teleostome fishes'. *J. Anat.*, **71**, 362–82.

Westoll, T. S. (1937b) 'On a remarkable fish from the Permian of Autun, France'. *Ann. Mag. nat. Hist.*, (10) **19**, 553–78.

Westoll, T. S. (1941) 'The Permian fishes *Dorypterus* and *Lekanichthys*', *Proc. zool. Soc. Lond.*, **111**(B) 39–58.

Westoll, T. S. (1944) 'The Haplolepidae, a new family of Late Carboniferous bony fishes. A study in taxonomy and evolution'. *Bull. Am. Mus. nat. Hist.*, **83**, 1–122.

Westoll, T. S. (1949) 'On the evolution of the Dipnoi', in *Genetics, palaeontology, and evolution*, ed. Jepson, G. L., Mayr. E. and Simpson, G. G. (Princeton University Press.) p. 121.

White, E. I. (1927) 'The fish-fauna of the Cementstones of Foulden, Berwickshire'. *Trans. R. Soc. Edinb.*, **55**, 257–87.

White, E. I. (1939) 'A new type of palaeoniscoid fish, with remarks on the evolution of the actinopterygian pectoral fin'. *Proc. zool. Soc. Lond.*, **109**(B) 41–61.

White, E. I. (1965) 'The head of *Dipterus valenciennesi* Sedgwick & Murchison'. *Bull. Br. Mus. nat. Hist., (Geol.)*, **11**, 1–45.

Woodward, A. S. and White, E. I. (1926) 'The fossil fishes of the Old Red Sandstone of the Shetland Islands'. *Trans. R. Soc. Edinb.*, **54**, 567–72.

CHAPTER SIX

Subclass Osteichthyes.
Infraclass Crossopterygii

6.1. CLASSIFICATION

Superorder 1, Rhipidistia
  Order 1, Holoptychiida (=Porolepiformes)
    e.g. *Glyptolepis*, M.–U. Dev; *Holoptychius*, U. Dev—? L. Carb; *Porolepis*, L.–M. Dev.
  Order 2, Osteolepidida (=Osteolepiformes)
    Suborder 1, Osteolepidoidei
      e.g. *Glyptopomus*, U. Dev; *Gyroptychius*, M. Dev; *Latvius*, U. Dev; *Osteolepis*, M. Dev; *Panderichthys*, M.–U. Dev; *Thursius*, M. Dev; *Megalichthys*, L.–U. Carb; *Ectosteorhachis*, *Lohsania*, L. Perm.
    Suborder 2, Eusthenopteroidei
      e.g. *Eusthenodon*, *Eusthenopteron*, *Platycephalichthys*, U. Dev; *Tristichopterus*, M. Dev.
    Suborder 3, Rhizodopsidoidei
      e.g. *Rhizodopsis*, L.–U. Carb; ?*Callistiopterus*, U. Dev.
  Order 3, Rhizodontida
    e.g. *Rhizodus*, *Strepsodus*, L.–U. Carb; *Sauripterus*, U. Dev.
Superorder 2, Actinistia (=Coelacanthiformes)
  Order 1, Coelacanthida
    e.g. *Chagrinia*, U. Dev; *Coelacanthus*, U. Carb—L. Trias; *Dictyonosteus*, *Diplocercides*, U. Dev; *Euporosteus*, M. Dev; *Nesides*, U. Dev; *Rhabdoderma*, L.–U. Carb; *Spermatodus*, L. Perm; *Synaptotylus*, U. Carb; *Latimeria*, Extant.
  Order 2, Laugiida
    e.g. *Laugia*, L. Trias.
Incertae sedis Onychodontidae (=Struniiformes)
    e.g. *Onychodus*, M.–U. Dev; *Strunius*, U. Dev.

L., Lower; M., Middle; U., Upper; Dev, Devonian; Carb, Carboniferous; Perm, Permian; Trias, Triassic.

6.2. CROSSOPTERYGIAN CHARACTERISTICS

As we have noted in the previous chapter, there seems to be no doubt that crossopterygians and actinopterygians are derived from a common ancestor. But as is the case in all big divisions of the fishes, the first appearance of crossopterygians in the Lower Devonian is in a disconcertingly fully evolved condition, and in structure they are quite distinct from actinopterygians. The crossopterygians contain at least two very distinct types of fishes, the rhipidistians and actinistians (coelacanths); the onychodontids may represent a third equally distinct type. It is from the first of these groups that the tetrapods have diverged, and as the relationship of crossopterygians with amphibians is so much closer than with actinopterygians, some authors include crossopterygians and tetrapods in a single group the Choanata, in order to emphasize their affinity (Säve-Söderbergh, 1934; Nelson, 1969).

Primitive crossopterygians had certain characteristic features which are often lost in the later more specialized forms, although they may be shared by primitive dipnoans (Chapter 7 §3.1). There are always primitively two dorsal fins and an anal (Fig. 6.1), in which the internal supports are very much concentrated, usually forming a proximal basal plate with which a varying number of radials articulate. The paired fins have well-formed fleshy lobes with an internal skeleton which is also much concentrated so that a single element only articulates with the girdles. The caudal fin was either heterocercal or diphycercal and had characteristically an epichordal as well as a hypochordal lobe. Crossopterygians were basically predatory fishes with a well-developed sense of smell and small eyes. The possession of internal nostrils (choana), once thought to characterize all crossopterygians, is apparently restricted to rhipidistians, and this group and actinistians are divergently specialized in the snout. Possibly the primitive members of both groups had separate anterior and posterior external nasal openings on the side of the snout, as in actinopterygians.

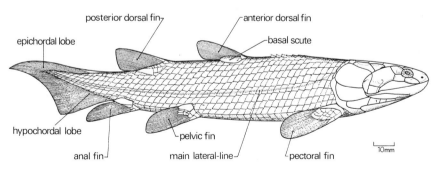

Fig. 6.1. *Osteolepis macrolepidotus*. Restoration in lateral view. (After Jarvik.)

Many early crossopterygians and dipnoans had dermal bones, scales and lepidotrichia of the cosmoid type (Fig. 6.2), which consist of an outer layer of cosmine underlain by a layer of vascular bone, which is underlain in its turn by a layer of laminated bone or isopedin. Cosmine is a tissue (Gross, 1966; Ørvig, 1969) of odontodes or dermal denticles which have fused to form a continuous sheet, and may even be continuous over several bones, ignoring the suture-lines. It comprises a layer of dentine, with a well-developed pore-canal system comparable to that of osteostracans (Gross, 1956), and a more superficial layer of enameloid substance which may be compared with actinopterygian ganoine. The pore-canal system opens on to the shiny surface of the enameloid layer giving the bones and scales a punctate appearance. The pore-canal system is probably part of the acustico-lateral system (Chapter 2 §3.1). Somewhat larger pits on the surface of the head may have been for cutaneous sensory organs of a different type (Jarvik, 1948; Ørvig, 1961). The cosmine layer is periodically resorbed to allow for growth to take place in the bony layer (see Chapter 7 §5). This periodic loss of cosmine has led to the erection of genera and species based on animals which are merely phases in the life-history of a single species.

The most characteristic feature of crossopterygians is the division of the neurocranium into two parts (Fig. 6.3), an anterior ethmo-sphenoid portion and a posterior otico-occipital portion (Jarvik, 1937, 1954; Romer, 1937; Thomson, 1965, 1967a, 1969; Bjerring, 1967; Schaeffer, 1968). This feature clearly separates crossopterygians from actinopterygians and dipnoans. The

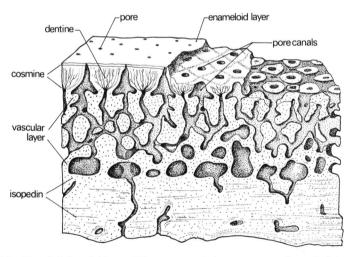

Fig. 6.2. *Megalichthys hibberti.* Diagram to show structure of exoskeleton. (After Goodrich.)

112

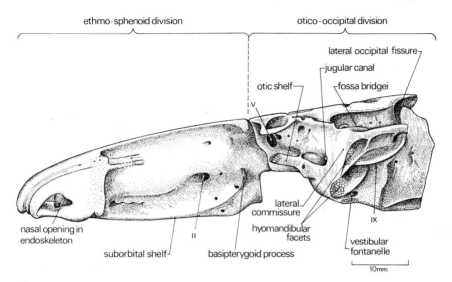

Fig. 6.3. *Eusthenopteron foordi.* Restoration of neurocranium in lateral view. (After Jarvik.)

division not only affects the neurocranium but also separates the dermal bones of the skull-roof (Figs. 6.6, 6.13, 6.19) into an anterior and posterior shield. This subdivision allows a certain amount of dorsoventral flexure between the two parts of the skull, although this movement may be lost in some adult forms (Jarvik, 1937, 1944*a*). The anterior moiety of the neurocarnium consists of the nasal capsules and sphenoid regions with the pituitary fossa. The posterior part is formed of the auditory capsules and the occipital region. These two parts of the neurocranium correspond to the parts formed in relation to the trabecular-polar bars and parachordals in the embryo. With respect to the primitive osteichthyan condition, it seems that the ventral fissure has become extended up to the roof of the neurocranium, taking in, in the process, the foramen of the trigeminal nerve (V).

6.3. SUPERORDER 1, RHIPIDISTIA

Rhipidistians are fairly large and voracious fishes, reaching to over four metres in length, which existed from the Middle Devonian to the Lower Permian (Andrews, 1967). They differ from actinistians, their specialized relatives, principally in the arrangement and number of the dermal bones of the head, in having branched lepidotrichia and many more lepidotrichia in the caudal fin than radials, and in having internal nostrils. In the case of the

113

dermal bones the most notable distinctions between rhipidistians and actinistians are the presence in the former of a maxillary, quadratojugal and a submandibular series of lateral gular plates.

6.3.1. Structure

In a typical unspecialized rhipidistian, such as the Middle Devonian *Osteolepis* (Fig. 6.1), the body is slender and the tail strongly hetercercal with a small epichordal and a large hypochordal lobe; but in some like *Gyroptychius* (Fig. 6.4) the tail is diphycercal with a large epichordal lobe (Jarvik, 1948). A third condition is shown by *Eusthenopteron* (Fig. 6.5), in which the tail is almost symmetrical (hetero-diphycercal) with large epichordal and hypochordal lobes, but has also a prominent axial lobe (Jarvik, 1959, 1960; Thomson and Hahn, 1968; Andrews and Westoll, 1970). The axial lobe is relatively larger in small individuals. The pectoral and pelvic fins may be

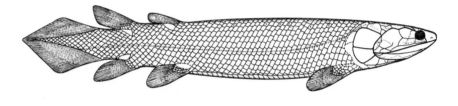

10mm

Fig. 6.4. *Gyroptychius agassizi*. Restoration in lateral view. (After Jarvik.)

obtusely lobate or with long and slender lobes, the internal skeleton of radials being concentrated (Fig. 6.5). The dorsal and anal fins are also lobed and have a concentrated internal skeleton. In *Osteolepis* (Fig. 6.1) the scales are rhomboidal and fairly thick, and as in the case of the dermal bones are covered with a smooth layer of cosmine. In others like *Glyptolepis* the scales may be round with the dentine restricted to tubercles or a few fine ridges, and with no sign of the pore-canal system that characterizes cosmine. Finally, in forms like *Eusthenopteron* the superficial layers are completely reduced, and the round scales consist only of bone (Ørvig, 1957).

Rhipidistian anatomy has been made known in extraordinary detail in a long series of papers on *Eusthenopteron* by Jarvik (1937, 1942, 1944a, b; 1952, 1954, 1959, 1963, 1965a, 1966) and Andrews and Westoll (1970). Consequently *Eusthenopteron* is one of the best known of all fossil fishes, and the following account may be based on this genus.

The lateral-line system is developed as sensory canals in the bones with

114

many much-branched tubes, and as pit-lines forming superficial grooves. The dermal bones (Fig. 6.6) of the skull-roof and cheek are on the whole developed in much the same way as those of actinopterygians. Since the main differences in the arrangement of the external dermal bones are associated with the course of the lateral-line sensory canals of the head, the latter will be described at the same time. First, however, brief mention must be made of a serious problem of bone terminology in the skull-roof. Jarvik, and many other workers in the older literature, have employed names that can be compared directly with those of the same series in actinopterygians, although the common usage of some of the bone names is slightly different. It might seem logical to follow this system here, as we are using a partly horizontal classification in which crossopterygians are grouped with other bony fishes as osteichthyans, and distinctly separated from the phylogenetically more closely related tetrapods. Nevertheless, Westoll (1938, 1940,

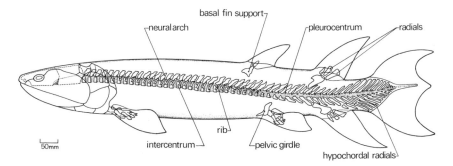

Fig. 6.5. *Eusthenopteron foordi*. Restoration in lateral view, with scales omitted to show postcranial skeleton. (After Andrews and Westoll.)

1943*a*; see Jarvik, 1967) has revised the nomenclature of the crossopterygian skull-roof to bring it into line with that used for primitive tetrapods. The homologies between these two groups are particularly clear (Parrington, 1967), whereas those between crossopterygians and actinopterygians are still partly speculative. Accordingly Westoll's identifications of the bones are to be preferred. As many of the bone names were first applied to the human skull, and as it is desirable that topographically homologous bones should as far as possible bear the same name throughout the system, the nomenclature usually applied to the bones of the skull-roof in actinopterygians should probably now be changed to correspond with the revised nomenclature of crossopterygians.

The main lateral-line canal of the body continues forward on to the head and joins its fellow of the other side in the supraoccipital cross-commissure on

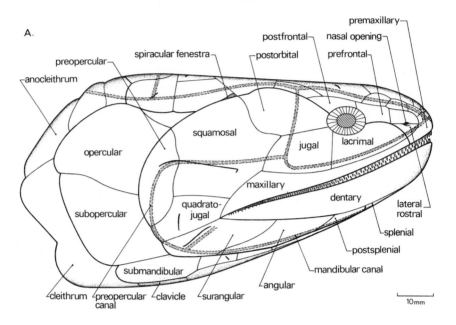

A.

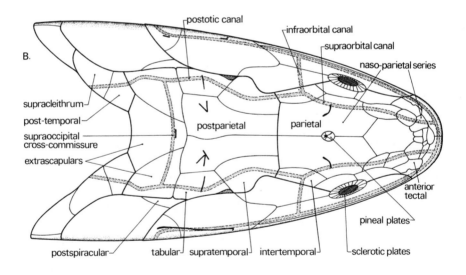

B.

Fig. 6.6. *Eusthenopteron foordi.* Restorations of skull in lateral (A) and dorsal (B) views. (After Jarvik.)

116

which ossify the extrascapular series of bones, whence it passes as the postotic canal through the tabular and supratemporal bones in the otic region. It continues through the intertemporal and down through the infraorbital series, the postorbital, jugal and lacrimal bones, as the infraorbital canal. The intertemporal contains the connection between the supraorbital and infraorbital canals, and the naso-parietal series forms on the supraorbital canal. The preopercular canal joins the infraorbital canal in the jugal, and ventrally continues round on to the lower jaw as the mandibular canal. The preopercular and infradentary series, the squamosal, preopercular, surangular, angular, postsplenial and splenial, are formed on the preopercular and mandibular canals. The premaxillaries are formed on the ethmoid commissure. A varying number of bones lie between the lateral-line series. Between the supratemporal and tabular are the postparietals (cf. actinopterygian parietals) and between the naso-parietal series, the internasals and interfrontals. The bones of the snout are very variable. The pineal opening lies between the parietals (cf. actinopterygian frontals) and is encircled by six or so small pineal plates. In the cheek region there are the supraorbital series lateral to the naso-parietal series, including the pre- and postfrontals, and the tooth-bearing maxillaries, which with the quadratojugals form the upper margin of the jaws. The lower margin is formed by the tooth-bearing dentaries, internally by a large prearticular, a row of tooth-bearing coronoids, on which the teeth show alternate replacement, and posteriorly a small articular. There is also an opercular, a subopercular, a series of numerous submandibulars (or lateral gulars), a pair of principal gulars and a small median gular (Fig. 6.7). Up to 30 sclerotic plates are found in the orbit. There is a single external nasal opening on the snout, margined above by the anterior tectal and below by the lateral rostral bone. This opening is probably equivalent to the anterior nostril of actinopterygians. The posterior nostril may be represented by a foramen in the posterior wall of the nasal capsule, which Jarvik (1942; Panchen, 1967) believes to be an incipient nasolachrymal duct.

Apart from the ethmo-sphenoid and otico-occipital portions, the neurocranium has no separate ossification, although the occipital region may be partly delimited by a cartilaginous band in the position of the actinopterygian lateral occipital fissure, which ends ventrally in a small vestibular fontanelle. There is a tooth-bearing parasphenoid (Fig. 6.8) with a buccohypophysial canal, and paired vomers beneath the ethmo-sphenoid part. A stout internasal septum separates the nasal cavities. An anterior depression in the floor of the ethmo-sphenoid portion is bounded by the premaxillaries and the vomers to form the anterior palatal recess (Thomson, 1967b, 1968b). This recess received the large anterior teeth of the lower dentition. The ethmo-sphenoid part also has a narrow suborbital shelf and a prominent basi-

117

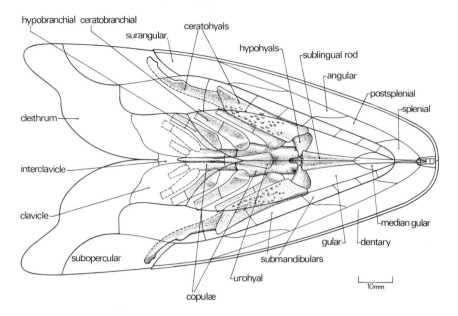

Fig. 6.7. *Eusthenopteron foordi*. Restoration of skull in ventral view to show the position of the hypobranchial skeleton. (After Jarvik.)

pterygoid process for articulation with the epipterygoid region of the palatoquadrate. Other articulation areas are found above the basipterygoid process for the ascending process, and on the nasal capsule for the autopalatine region of the palatoquadrate. The otico-occipital part has well-marked surface on the hind edge of the lateral commissure for the double-headed articulation of the hyomandibula. Above these surfaces lies a deep fossa bridgei, and in front of them the otic shelf. The surface of the otic region is invested with a number of small tooth-plates, some of which were situated in the spiracular tube, and ventrally there are large parotic and subotic dental plates. The palatoquadrate articulates with the otic shelf in *Eusthenopteron*, though like the articulation of the ascending process, this is apparently lacking in other genera (Thomson, 1967*b*). The big unconstricted notochord extends forwards through the otico-occipital portion to articulate against a well-defined fossa on the hind end of the ethmo-sphenoid. A complicated series of joints hinge the two portions of the cranium, involving both the neurocranium and dermal bones (Bjerring, 1967). Ventrally there were basicranial muscles spanning the joint, as in the living coelacanth, *Latimeria*.

The brain cavity is known in some detail (Stensiö, 1963). The ethmo-sphenoid portion contained the nasal capsules with well-developed olfactory bulbs, the diencephalon, pineal and pituitary organs and the mesencephalon.

118

The otico-occipital portion contained the metencephalon, myelencephalon and ear structures. The metencephalon was apparently little developed in comparison with the long myelencephalon.

The dermal ossifications of the palatoquadrate (Fig. 6.9) consist of a tooth-bearing dermopalatine, ectopterygoid and entopterygoid. The teeth are fused to the jaw-bones, and those on the palate frequently show alternate replacement as in early amphibians. Their dentine walls are folded into a pattern (Fig. 6.10) which resembles that of the teeth of labyrinthodont amphibians (Schultze, 1969, 1970).

In addition to the hyomandibula, the hyoid arch includes a stylohyal (interhyal), two long ceratohyal ossifications and a small hypohyal (Fig. 6.7, 6.9). There are four or five gill-arches. The first two are attached dorsally to the neurocranium, and include both infra- and suprapharyngeals. Cerato-branchials, hypobranchials and two large ventral copulae are also present. In front of the copulae is a long sublingual rod which projects anteriorly to the symphysis of the lower jaw. The internal faces of the gill-arch

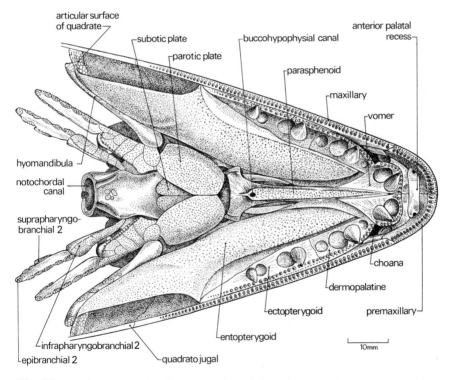

Fig. 6.8. *Eusthenopteron foordi*. Restoration of the palate and the upper parts of the anterior gill-arches. (After Jarvik.)

119

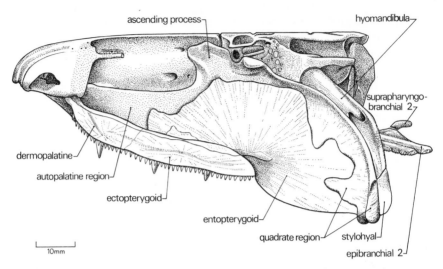

Fig. 6.9. *Eusthenopteron foordi*. Restoration of the neurocranium, upper jaw apparatus and upper parts of the anterior gill-arches. (After Jarvik.)

elements are thickly invested with tooth-plates. Below the copulae there is a large urohyal which gave attachment to some of the hypobranchial muscles.

The shoulder-girdle (Fig. 6.6) consists of the following dermal bones: a post-temporal articulating with the extrascapular series at the back of the skull, a supracleithrum, an anocleithrum, a cleithrum and a clavicle; and

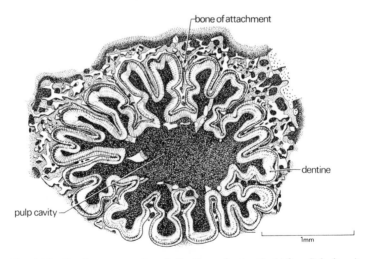

Fig. 6.10. *Eusthenopteron foordi*. Section of a tooth. (After Schultze.)

120

ventrally an interclavicle connecting this series with its fellow in the middle line. A small endoskeletal scapulocoracoid is attached to the inner surface of the cleithrum (Fig. 6.11). As in the case of the bones of the skull-roof, tetrapod names may conveniently be used for the postcranial skeleton, where the nature of homologous elements is absolutely clear. Thus the scapulocoracoid can be regarded as a three-legged bone with a glenoid fossa for the articulation of the member, and a supporting supraglenoid buttress (cf. actinopterygian mesocoracoid arch). The remaining 'leg' of the bone is the infraglenoid buttress. The pelvic girdle consists of a small triangular ossification with pubic and iliac rami (Fig. 6.5). The pubic ramus was pro-

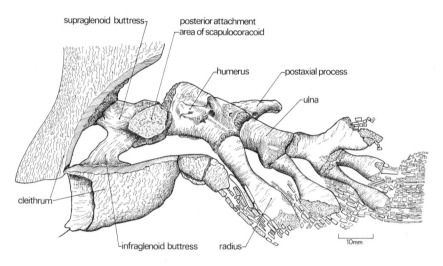

Fig. 6.11. *Eusthenopteron foordi*. Left pectoral fin skeleton, scapulocoracoid and part of cleithrum in dorsal view. Part of cleithrum over scapulocoracoid removed. (After Andrews and Westoll.)

bably connected to its fellow in the middle line by cartilage, and the iliac ramus connected dorsally to the vertebral column by a cartilaginous sacral rib. There is a large acetabulum for the articulation of the pelvic fin.

A single basal element in the pectoral and pelvic fins (Figs. 6.5, 6.11), the humerus or femur, articulates with the limb girdle; and two more distal elements, the radius and ulna, or tibia and fibula, articulate with this basal element. Distally to these latter two bones a varying number of other radial elements are found in different crossopterygians, and *Eusthenopteron* itself is subject to some variation. Although many detailed comparisons of each element have been made with those of tetrapods, it is hardly safe to go

121

further than a comparison of the three basal elements (Westoll, 1943b; Jarvik, 1964, 1965a; Thomson, 1968b; Andrews and Westoll, 1970). The humerus in particular shows striking resemblances to that of early tetrapods, so that a close comparison is possible between foramina and muscle attachment areas.

The axial skeleton (Fig. 6.5) consists of a large unconstricted notochord with vertebrae that closely resemble the rhachitomous type found in some early tetrapods. The ventral vertebral arch includes a pair of wedge-shaped intercentra around the notochord, which have distinct parapophyses for the articulation of the short dorsal ribs. The dorsal elements comprise a paired neural arch and short neural spine situated above the intercentrum, and more posteriorly a small paired pleurocentrum. The basal fin supports of the dorsal and anal fins carry from one to three unjointed radials, and there is a long series of unjointed hypochordal radials in the tail which articulate with the haemal arches.

6.3.2. Order 1, Holoptychiida

Rhipidistians fall into two main distinct subdivisions (Jarvik, 1942, 1966, 1968b; Jardine, 1969; cf. Thomson, 1964b, 1967b), here termed the holoptychiids and osteolepidids and ranked as orders. Although these groups are surprisingly different in some respects, there can be no real doubt their community of origin (see Stensiö, 1963). A third order, the rhizodontids in a limited sense, is used here for some poorly known forms, but the correct delimitation of this group is still problematical.

The holoptychiids appear earlier than the osteolepidids. Typical occurrences are *Porolepis* is the Lower Devonian with thick, rhombic cosmoid scales; *Glyptolepis* in the Middle Devonian with thin, cycloid scales, no cosmine and the dentine restricted in its development, occurring only as fine ridges or tubercles on the scales and dermal bones; and *Holoptychius* in the Upper Devonian (Fig. 6.12) with cycloid scales and showing further reduction of the dentine layer (Ørvig, 1957). Holoptychiids are not known to have survived Upper Old Red Sandstone times.

In contrast to osteolepidids, such as *Eusthenopteron*, holoptychiids (Fig. 6.12) are plump, fat-bodied fishes with the paired fins acutely lobed. The fins have no basal scutes and the pectorals are inserted in a high position on the flank. This has affected the shape of the cleithrum, and this bone may occasionally be subdivided into dorsal and ventral ossifications (Jarvik, 1950a). There is no pineal foramen and the eyes are particularly small. The dermal bones of the head (Fig. 6.13) differ considerably from those of osteolepidids (Jarvik, 1950a). There are two squamosal ossifications on the preopercular canal in the cheek and the quadratojugal region is formed of

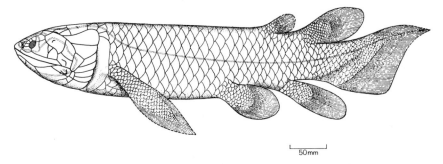

Fig. 6.12. *Holoptychius* sp. Restoration in lateral view. (After Jarvik.)

several small bones. The 'preoperculum' (Thomson, 1966) is a bone situated in the gill-cover, and there are several slender subopercular bones (cf. actinopterygian branchiostegal rays). The ossifications of the posterior shield of the skull-roof have been variously interpreted, according to the different views individual workers have held on the probability of bone fusions and the relationship of sensory lines to bones (Jardine, 1969). According to

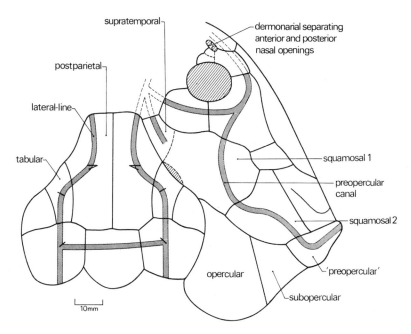

Fig. 6.13. *Holoptychius flemingi*. Dermal bones of head with the cheek bones drawn in the same plane as the roofing bones. (After Jarvik.) The bones of the postparietal shield are labelled according to the interpretation of Parrington.

123

Parrington (1956, 1967) the large median pair of bones are postparietals, through which the lateral-line canal passes from the tabular and on to the intertemporal. Correlated with this arrangement the supratemporal has crossed the intracranial joint to become one of the bones of the cheek. In the snout there are both anterior and posterior external nasal openings (Jarvik, 1942, 1964, 1966). They are far apart in *Porolepis* and *Glyptolepis*, but much closer together in *Holoptychius*, where they are only separated by the dermo-narial bone, possibly the homologue of the osteolepidid lateral rostral (Panchen, 1967). On the lower surface of the neurocranium (Fig. 6.14), the parasphenoid is broad and the anterior palatal recess is represented by a

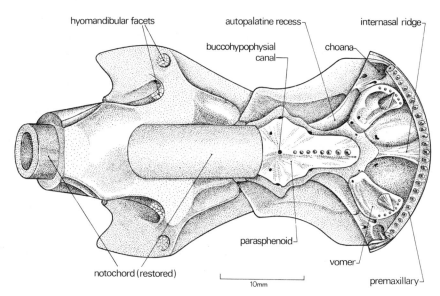

Fig. 6.14. *Porolepis brevis*. Restoration of neurocranium in ventral view. (After Bjerring.)

pair of deep depressions separated by a median internasal ridge. The vomers are small, laterally situated and not contiguous in the middle line. On the side wall of the ethmo-sphenoid portion there is a long recess for the ethmoid articulation of the palatoquadrate (Jarvik, 1966), which is not found in osteolepidids. The teeth are of particular interest as their dentine walls are folded into a more complicated pattern than in osteolepidids and rhizo-dontids (Schultze, 1969, 1970). At the symphysis of the lower jaw there is a pair of large tooth-whorls, each with a row of large sigmoid teeth and several rows of smaller teeth (Fig. 6.22B).

The hypobranchial skeleton is known in *Glyptolepis* (Jarvik, 1963), where

124

it includes a single copula and no sublingual rod. The urohyal is long and slender in comparison with *Eusthenopteron*.

The postcranial skeleton is poorly known. There are no ring-centra in the vertebral column (Watson and Day, 1916; Thomson and Vaughn, 1968), as in some osteolepidids, and the tail is always heterocercal. The internal structure of the pectoral fin is not yet known.

6.3.3. Order 2, Osteolepidida

The basic structure of the members of this order is well shown by *Eusthenopteron*. The osteolepidoids (Romer, 1937, 1941; Jarvik, 1948, 1950*a*, 1950*b*, 1966; Thomson, 1964*a*, 1964*b*, 1965; Jessen, 1966*a*) are the most primitive as well as the longest lived of the three suborders. They range from the early Middle Devonian (*Thursius*) to the Permian (*Ectosteorhachis*), and have slender bodies, thick rhombic scales, obtusely lobate paired fins, basal scutes and sometimes develop ring-like centra (Schaeffer, 1967; Thomson and Vaughn, 1968). Although generally small fishes, *Megalichthys* reached a length of almost two metres. The tail is heterocercal in the Devonian *Osteolepis* (Fig. 6.1) and *Thursius*; hetero-diphycercal in the Carboniferous *Megalichthys* and probably also in the Permian *Ectosteorhachis*; and diphycercal in the Devonian *Gyroptychius* (Fig. 6.4) and *Glyptopomus*. The snout tends to be broad, as in holoptychiids, but nevertheless the vomers touch each other in the middle line (Fig. 6.15), and the snout is built up much as in *Eusthenopteron* (Jarvik, 1950*b*, 1966). In *Megalichthys* and *Ectosteorhachis* (Thomson, 1964*b*; Jarvik, 1966) a tooth-bearing median ridge divides the anterior palatal recess into a pair of chambers. These genera have folded teeth, but in *Osteolepis* and other Middle Devonian genera the teeth are unfolded (Schultze, 1969, 1970). There is typically a single external nasal opening as in *Eusthenopteron*, although separate anterior and posterior nostrils have been described for *Panderichthys* (Vorobjeva, 1960, 1962). The pineal opening is lost in *Megalichthys* and *Ectosteorhachis*, although it is present in older genera. The palatoquadrate of *Megalichthys* is notable for the presence of a series of suprapterygoid ossifications (Watson, 1926).

The eusthenopteroids are all very similar to *Eusthenopteron* in structure, having a diphycercal or hetero-diphycercal tail and cycloid scales without cosmine. *Tristichopterus* is a Middle Devonian genus with a length of about 300 mm. *Eusthenodon* (Jarvik, 1952) and *Platycephalichthys* (Vorobjeva, 1959) are large Upper Devonian genera reaching a length of 2.5 and four metres respectively.

The rhizodopsidoids only certainly include the Carboniferous genus *Rhizodopsis* (Fig. 6.16), although the Upper Devonian *Callistiopterus* may be related (Thomson and Hahn, 1968). These fishes have the same scale struc-

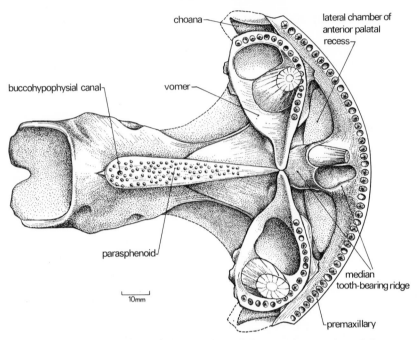

choana

lateral chamber of
anterior palatal
recess

buccohypophysial canal

vomer

parasphenoid

median
tooth-bearing ridge

10mm

premaxillary

Fig. 6.15. *Megalichthys hibberti*. Restoration of the anterior portion of the neuro-cranium in palatal view. (After Jarvik.)

ture as eusthenopteroids, but with a heterocercal tail in which the epichordal lobe is only slightly enlarged. *Rhizodopsis* has ring-vertebrae, and the neuro-cranium is of the expected rhipidistian type (Säve-Söderbergh, 1936).

6.3.4. Order 3, Rhizodontida

The rhizodontids are Upper Devonian and Carboniferous fishes known from very incomplete remains, and include the genera *Rhizodus*, *Strepsodus* and

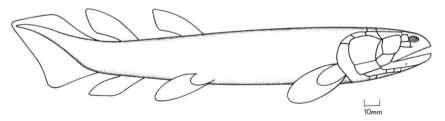

Fig.6.16. *Rhizodopsis sauroides*. Restoration in lateral view. (After Thomson and Hahn.)

126

Sauripterus. They resemble the eusthenopteroids and rhizodopsidoids in scale and bone structure, but differ in the detailed structure of the shoulder-girdle, fins and vertebrae. *Rhizodus* must have been of very considerable size as the lower jaw may be one metre long and the largest teeth 200 mm long. The teeth of *Rhizodus* are laterally compressed, whilst those of *Strepsodus* are round. The pectoral fin of *Sauripterus* has the same three basal elements as in *Eusthenopteron*, but differs considerably in the more distal regions of the skeleton (Jarvik, 1964; Thomson, 1968*b*).

6.3.5. *Tendencies in evolution*

Rhipidistians are usually studied in relation to the problem of the origin of tetrapods, and little progress has been made in unravelling the lines of evolution within the group itself. The holoptychiids and osteolepidids must represent a major division of the group into two diverging lines. The rhizodontids are still too poorly known for their relationships to be seriously considered. There has been a considerable amount of parallel evolution within the rhipidistians. General evolutionary tendencies include the loss of the superficial layers of the bones and scales, the change from rhombic to cycloid scales, the acquisition of a symmetrical tail, the development of ring-vertebrae and the loss of the pineal foramen, all of which parallel changes in actinopterygians. The development of a symmetrical tail probably means that the airbladder was functional as a hydrostatic organ. An unusual fact about scale and bone structure is that the osteolepidids retain a primitive, fully-developed cosmine layer throughout their history, and outlive other rhipidistians with a more advanced scale and bone structure by surviving into the Permian.

6.4. SUPERORDER 2, ACTINISTIA

The actinistians or coelacanths are a specialized group of crossopterygians, usually of small size but sometimes reaching 1.5 m or more in length. They have a remarkably long range in time, starting in the Middle Devonian and continuing to the present day (Andrews, 1967), but with a very limited range of evolutionary changes. So conservative is the composition of these fishes that the earliest and latest species differ essentially only in the degree of ossification of the skull (Jarvik, 1964).

6.4.1. *Structure*

Actinistians (Fig. 6.17) are usually rather slender-bodied fusiform fishes (Stensiö, 1921; Moy-Thomas and Westoll, 1935; Schaeffer, 1952) characteristically with two external nostrils (Jarvik, 1942), no choana, and with two

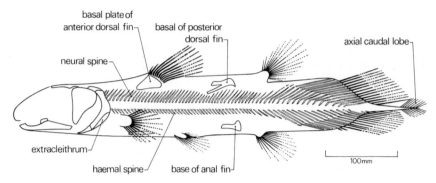

Fig. 6.17. *Coelacanthus granulatus*. Restoration in lateral view. (After Moy-Thomas and Westoll.)

dorsal fins, the anterior of which is situated in front of the centre of the body. Only the posterior of the two dorsal fins is lobed, the lepidotrichia of the anterior articulating directly with an internal plate-like skeletal element. The posterior dorsal and the anal fins are lobed and have a concentrated internal skeleton similar to that of the paired fins. The complete internal ossifications of the paired and median fins is not known in a Palaeozoic species. In the Triassic genus *Laugia* (Stensiö, 1932) the radials of the fins are much concentrated and form an axis of short, jointed elements distally and a large, unjointed proximal portion, much as in the living *Latimeria*. A similar internal skeleton is known for the pectoral fin of the Carboniferous *Rhabdoderma* (Moy-Thomas, 1937). The pelvic girdle is formed of two plates articulating with one another in the middle line.

The tail is one of the most characteristic features of actinistians and is diphycercal and three-lobed. In post-Devonian species the lepidotrichia correspond in number with the radials, each lepidotrichium articulating with a single radial. However, in the Upper Devonian genera *Diplocercides* and *Chagrinia* the lepidotrichia are more numerous than the radials (Jarvik, 1959; Schaeffer, 1962), though they are still fewer in number than in rhipidistians. These fin-rays also differ from those of rhipidistians in never branching.

The notochord is persistent, and the neural and haemal arches have long slender spines. In some species there are ossified pleural ribs. The airbladder is calcified and forms one of the most distinctive features of the fossils. The body scales are cycloid, overlapping and thin. The scales and dermal bones lack cosmine, but they have a surface ornament of fine ridges or tubercles, made up of dentine (Ørvig, 1957; Gross, 1966).

In the primitive Devonian genera *Euporosteus, Nesides* and *Diplocercides* (Stensiö, 1932, 1937; Jarvik, 1954) the neurocranium is ossified in two halves,

128

similar to those of rhipidistians (Fig. 6.18). In the Carboniferous *Rhabdoderma* and *Synaptotylus*, the Permian *Coelacanthus* and *Spermatodus* and later forms (Stensiö, 1921; Moy-Thomas and Westoll, 1935; Moy-Thomas, 1937; Westoll, 1939; Echols, 1963), however, the ossified parts of the neurocranium are more restricted, and there are separate paired ethmoid, a median basisphenoid and paired otic and occipital ossifications. In all these forms there is an intracranial joint allowing a certain amount of dorsoventral flexure, as in rhipidistians. In Devonian species the palatoquadrate meets the ethmo-sphenoid portion of the neurocranium in an anterior articulation with the nasal capsule, a basal articulation with the basipterygoid process and a dorsal articulation with the antotic process (Jarvik, 1954). In later forms the basipterygoid process is reduced and the basal articulation lost, as the antotic process increases in size and its articulation with the palatoquadrate increases in importance (Schaeffer and Gregory, 1961; Echols, 1963). The palatoquadrate (Fig. 6.18) is posteriorly very deep, and includes distinct autopalatine, entopterygoid, metapterygoid and quadrate ossifications. It appears that the brain almost filled the cranial cavity and extended into the ethmo-sphenoid portion in Devonian species (Stensiö, 1963). This is in marked contrast to conditions in *Latimeria*, in which the brain is situated behind the intracranial joint, and occupies less than 1/100 of the volume of the cranial cavity. The hyomandibula is large and has a double-headed

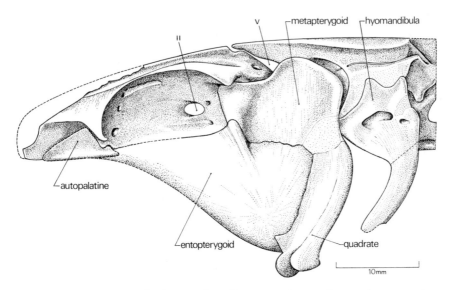

Fig. 6.18. *Nesides schmidti*. Restoration of neurocranium and upper jaw apparatus in lateral view. (After Jarvik.)

articulation with the neurocranium as in rhipidistians. The hyoid arch typically includes additional elements in its dorsal half (Thomson, 1967a), and
plays no direct role in the suspension of the palatoquadrate.

The course of the lateral-line sensory canals of the head is typical of crossopterygians, but the dermal bones of the head are rather peculiar (Fig. 6.19)
and there is no general agreement about the homology of these bones with
those of rhipidistians. This and the variable pattern of the bones have made
for an unstable nomenclature (Schaeffer, 1952). The eye is relatively large
and the dermal bones of the cheek do not appear to articulate with one
another very closely. There is no maxillary nor quadratojugal, the biting
elements of the upper jaw being the pterygoids and dermopalatines. As in

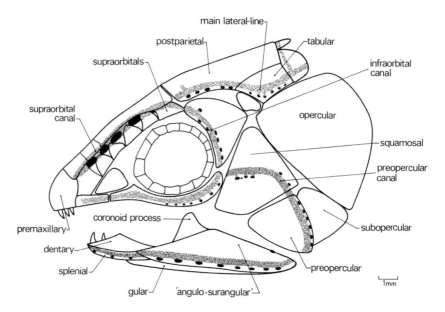

Fig. 6.19. *Rhabdoderma elegans*. Restoration of skull in lateral view. (After Moy-
Thomas.)

holoptychiids the main lateral-line continues forwards through the tabular,
to pass on through the middle pair of bones of the otic region, which may be
identified as postparietals. The remainder of the bones of the skull-roof are
similar to those of rhipidistians, but the supraorbitals are more numerous.
The supraorbital sensory canal lies between the supraorbital and postrostral-
parietal series of bones, and may open to the surface through very large
pores. The opercular is large and typically has a triangular shape; the subopercular is small, and there is only a single pair of large gulars. A pineal

130

foramen is not developed. The roof of the mouth is completed by paired vomers and a long, spatulate parasphenoid, which in Devonian species has an open buccohypophysial canal. The number of ossifications in the lower jaw is reduced. There is a coronoid process, paralleling that evolved in holostean actinopterygians, a short dentary, a single splenial and an elongated 'angulo-surangular'; the prearticular covers most of the inner surface. In *Nesides* there is a urohyal closely similar to that of *Latimeria* (Jarvik, 1963).

The exoskeletal shoulder-girdle is not completely known in any one Palaeozoic species, but nevertheless it is clearly constructed to the usual osteichthyan pattern with a post-temporal, supracleithrum, anocleithrum, cleithrum and clavicle (Jarvik, 1944*b*). A small additional bone, the extra-cleithrum, is peculiar to actinistians.

6.4.2. Diversity

As has already been pointed out, remarkably little adaptive radiation takes place during the long existence of this group, except to a small extent in the Mesozoic in the position of the fins and in the dentition. General phyletic changes include the gradual loss of ossification in the neurocranium, changes in the method of articulation of the palatoquadrate and a reduction in the number of fin-rays. Starting from the primitive Devonian genera, there is a rapid 'modernization' of the character complex of the group, followed by a long steady evolution (Schaeffer, 1952; cf. dipnoans, Chapter 7 §4). It is rather unfortunate that *Laugia*, the earliest form in which the internal skeleton of all the fins is known, should be specialized in the extremely anterior position of the pelvic fins, the pelvic girdle articulating ventrally with the pectoral girdle.

6.5. INCERTAE SEDIS ONYCHODONTIDAE

The onychodontids are a group of Devonian crossopterygians of uncertain relationships, with a somewhat peculiar complex of characters (Gross, 1965; Jessen, 1966*a, b*, 1967). *Strunius*, the best known form, reached a length of at least 100 mm, but *Onychodus* was probably much larger, perhaps up to 1.5m in length, although articulated specimens have not been found. The body of *Strunius* is short and deep (Fig. 6.20) with two posteriorly situated dorsal fins and an anal fin, all short and lacking a fleshy lobe, as in the anterior dorsal of actinistians. The caudal fin is symmetrical with large epichordal and hypochordal lobes and a very long axial lobe. The axial lobe resembles that of actinistians, but as in rhipidistians, its great length may be a juvenile character that was to some extent lost in adults (Thomson and

131

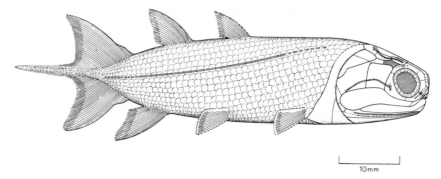

10mm

Fig. 6.20. *Strunius walteri*. Restoration in lateral view. (After Jessen.)

Hahn, 1968). The lepidotrichia are unjointed and numerous, although relatively fewer in number than in rhipidistians. Thin, cycloid scales cover the body. They lack cosmine and ornamentation, although small patches of cosmine occur on some of the head bones of *Onychodus* species.

The head (Fig. 6.21) is broad and deep, with the large eyes and blunt snout of a palaeoniscoid. However, the presence of numerous sclerotic plates, about 18 in *Strunius*, and the pattern of the dermal bones, show that these

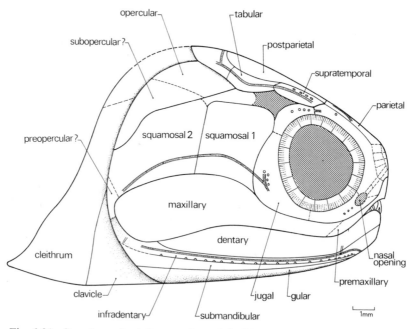

Fig. 6.21. *Strunius walteri*. Restoration of skull in lateral view. (After Jessen.)

fishes are in no way closely related to actinopterygians. The parietal and postparietal shields in the skull-roof are separated by a transverse suture, which probably reflects the division of the neurocranium into ethmosphenoid and otico-occipital portions. The main lateral-line sensory canal runs forwards through the tabular and supertemporal bones in the normal way. The most unusual features of the dermal bone pattern are found in the cheek. All of the circumorbital series are elongated in connection with the large size of the orbit. Behind the jugal there are two large squamosals developed in relation to the preopercular line, somewhat as in holoptychiids. The preopercular sensory line continues down on to the lower jaw, whence it runs forward in a single, very long infradentary bone. The dorsal opercular

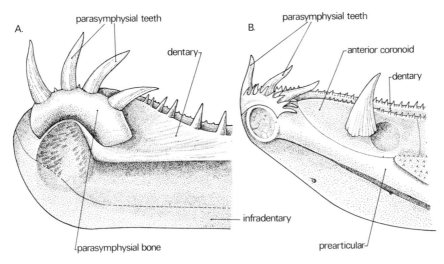

Fig. 6.22. Anterior region of the lower jaw of an onychodontid (A) and a holoptychiid (B) to contrast the parasymphysial dentitions; in mesial view. (After Jessen.); A. *Onychodus sigmoides*; B. *Holoptychius* sp.

bones are small and placed above the squamosals, and the ventral members of the opercular-gular series are represented by one or two long, slender submandibulars, situated laterally to the principal gular plates. There are no branchiostegal rays. The margins of the jaws are formed by the slender premaxillary, maxillary and dentary bones. The maxillary has an expanded postorbital lamella, somewhat as in palaeoniscoids. There appears to be only a single external nasal opening. The marginal dentition is made up of singularly shaped teeth with swollen bases and acutely pointed tips. At the symphysis of the lower jaw there is a large pair of tooth-whorls, each with a main row of long, sigmoid teeth (Fig. 6.22A). There may be a few subsidiary teeth, but there are never as many rows as in holoptychiids. None of the teeth show the infoldings of the dentine wall that characterize advanced rhipidistians.

The dermal shoulder-girdle is anteroposteriorly extensive in its lower part, which is composed of the cleithrum and clavicle. There is apparently no interclavicle, and the supracleithral bones are unknown.

The onychodontids show a strange mosaic of characters. The palaeoniscoid characters are of a quite superficial nature, and many other features demonstrate the crossopterygian affinities of these fishes. However, to which crossopterygian group they should be allied is uncertain. It would be interesting to know whether or not they had choana. The pair of lower symphysial tooth-whorls, the structure of the cheek and the lack of basal scutes for the fins suggest holoptychiid affinities, but these characters are countered by the pattern of bones in the skull-roof and gill-cover, and the form of the fins and tail. On the other hand there are no compelling reasons for grouping them with osteolepidids or rhizodontids. The form of the tail and unlobed condition of the median fins might suggest actinistian affinities, but this suggestion is countered by the posterior position of the anterior dorsal fin and the pattern of bones in the skull, which includes a large tooth-bearing maxillary. The onychodontids are not assigned a place in our classification, and their relationships remain in question.

6.6. MODE OF LIFE

Crossopterygians are fusiform fishes adapted for a free-swimming life, basically in shallow waters. We may assume, therefore, that they were equipped with an airbladder which functioned as a hydrostatic organ, and the tendency to evolve from a heterocercal to a diphycercal tail was probably associated with the development of neutral buoyancy. In contrast to actinopterygians, laterally compressed forms were not evolved within this group, nor were depressed bottom-living types evolved, as they were in elasmobranchiomorphs. It is an interesting fact that strongly depressed fishes were not evolved in any Palaeozoic group of teleostomes, although the condition was simulated much later in the history of actinopterygians by the laterally compressed pleuronectiforms, which came to lie on their side. This difference in the adaptive radiations of the groups was probably correlated with the presence of an airbladder in teleostomes and its absence in elasmobranchiomorphs.

The long body of crossopterygians suggests that swimming was essentially eel-like. There is much variation in the structure of the vertebral column, and ring-vertebrae appear to have evolved more than once within the group. However, the structure of the vertebral column has not yet been satisfactorily related to the mode of life. Primitive rhipidistians such as *Osteolepis* have a heterocercal tail and the anterior dorsal fin situated about mid-way along the body. More advanced forms tend to have the median fins posteriorly situated, and they were probably more powerful swimmers, with considerable directional stability. This is true of both the heterocercal holoptychiids and diphycercal eusthenopteroids. *Eusthenopteron* itself is adaptively similar to the pike, and may have been a lurking predator, adapted for lunging after prey (Andrews and Westoll, 1970). The forward position of the anterior dorsal fin in actinistians has not been satisfactorily explained, although it is one of the most characteristic features of the group. The paired fins of crossopterygians probably functioned as gliding planes, much as those of primitive actinopterygians, and played a part in braking. Although they have a narrow articulation with the girdle in rhipidistians and were clearly highly mobile, they were not capable of the same degree of pronation and supination as in the living *Latimeria*, in which the pectorals can turn through 180°. The pectoral fins probably served as props when the fishes rested on the bottom. It is possible that this function was particularly important in providing support for the body in shallow water (Thomson, 1969). In the case of *Eusthenopteron*, the similarity between the structure and range of movements of the proximal elements of the paired fins and those of tetrapod appendages, has led to the suggestion that rhipidistians could walk short distances over mudbanks. However, whilst it is possible that some rhipidistians could walk on the bottom of the water, it is not clear that they could have made extensive excursions on land. The skeleton was not well-adapted for the stresses of terrestrial locomotion and the viscera would have been liable to crushing under the weight of the animal (Thomson, 1969; Andrews and Westoll, 1970). The well-developed gill-skeleton of genera like *Eusthenopteron* shows that aquatic respiration was of paramount importance. If the airbladder was used in breathing, it can only have been as an accessory respiratory organ, as in the living lung-fish *Neoceratodus*. Nevertheless, in poorly-oxygenated waters or on land, air may have been gulped through the mouth for respiratory purposes.

Rhipidistians were predatory fishes with a well-developed dentition. In contrast to actinopterygians they have small eyes and well-developed nasal capsules, and must have tracked down prey by their sense of smell. Prey was probably enclosed by the fish swimming on to it with widely open jaws, then orientated by mouthing and finally swallowed whole. Crushing dentitions were not evolved by rhipidistians or Palaeozoic actinistians, although this is not unexpected in these wholly fusiform groups, as durophagy is commonly associated with the compression of the body in actinopterygians, and dorsoventral flattening in elasmobranchiomorphs. The intracranial joint means that crossopterygians had a highly kinetic skull. Unfortunately the significance of this joint is obscure, although it was probably important in feeding (Thomson, 1967a, 1969). The joint would have enabled the open mouth to be orientated with respect to the prey, but presumably its significance goes deeper than this. It could not have served either to increase the force of the bite, or as an effective shock-absorbing mechanism.

REFERENCES

References given in Chapter 5 are not repeated

Andrews, S. M. and Westoll, T. S. (1970) 'The postcranial skeleton of *Eusthenopteron foordi* Whiteaves'. *Trans. R. Soc. Edinb.*, **68**, 207–329.

Andrews, S. M. and Westoll, T. S. (1970) 'The postcranial skeleton of rhipidistian fishes excluding *Eusthenopteron*'. *Trans. R. Soc. Edinb.*, **68**, 391–489.

Bjerring, H. C. (1967) 'Does a homology exist between the basicranial muscle and the polar cartilage?'. *Colloques int. Cent. natn. Rech. Scient.*, **163**, 223–67.

Bjerring, H. C. (1968) 'The second somite with special reference to the evolution of its myotomic derivatives'. *Nobel Symposium*, **4**, 341–57.

Bystrow, A. P. (1939) 'Zahnstruktur der Crossopterygier'. *Acta zool. Stockh.*, **20**, 283–338.

Bystrow, A. P. (1942) 'Deckknochen und Zähne der *Osteolepis* und *Dipterus*'. *Acta zool. Stockh.*, **23**, 263–89.

Cruickshank, A. R. I. (1968) 'Tooth structure in *Rhizodus hiberti* Ag., a rhipidistian fish'. *Palaeont. Africana*, **11**, 3–13.

Denison, R. H. (1951) 'Late Devonian fresh-water fishes from the Western United States'. *Fieldiana, Geol.*, **11**, 221–61.

Echols, J. (1963) 'A new genus of Pennsylvanian fish (Crossopterygii, Coelacanthiformes) from Kansas'. *Univ. Kans. Publs. Mus. nat. Hist.*, **12**, 475–501.

Gross, W. (1956) 'Über Crossopterygier und Dipnoer aus dem baltischen Oberdevon im Zusammenhang einer vergleichenden Untersuchung des Porenkanalsystems paläozoischer Agnathen und Fishe'. *K. svenska VetenskAkad. Handl.*, (4) **5**, 1–140.

Gross, W. (1965) '*Onychodus jaekeli* (Crossopterygii, Oberdevon), Bau des Symphysenknochens und seiner Zähne'. *Senck. leth.* **46a**, 123–31.

Jarvik, E. (1937) 'On the species of *Eusthenopteron* found in Russia and the Baltic states'. *Bull. geol. Inst.*, Uppsala, **27**, 63–127.

Jarvik, E. (1942) 'On the structure of the snout of crossopterygians and lower gnathostomes in general'. *Zool. Bidr.*, Uppsala, **21**, 235–675.

Jarvik, E. (1944a) 'On the dermal bones, sensory canals and pit-lines of the skull in *Eusthenopteron foordi* Whiteaves, with some remarks on *E. säve-söderberghi* Jarvik'. *K. svenska VetenskAkad. Handl.*, (3) **21**, 1–48.

Jarvik, E. (1944b) See Chapter 5.

Jarvik, E. (1949) 'On the Middle Devonian crossopterygians from the Hornelan Field in Western Norway'. *Univ. Arsbok Bergen, naturv,-r.*, (1949) 1–48.

Jarvik, E. (1950a) 'Middle Devonian vertebrates from Canning Land and Wegeners

Halvø (East Greenland). 2. Crossopterygii'. *Medd. Grønland*, **96**, 1–132.

Jarvik, E. (1950*b*) 'On some osteolepiform crossopterygians from the Upper Old Red Sandstone of Scotland'. *K. svenska VetenskAkad., Handl.*, (3) **2**, 1–35.

Jarvik, E. (1952) 'On the fish-like tail in the ichthyostegid stegocephalians with descriptions of a new stegocephalian and a new crossopterygian from the Upper Devonian of East Greenland'. *Medd. Grønland*, **114**, 1–90.

Jarvik, E. (1954) 'On the visceral skeleton in *Eusthenopteron* with a discussion of the parasphenoid and palatoquadrate in fishes'. *K. svenska VetenskAkad. Handl.*, (4) **5**, 1–104.

Jarvik, E. (1955) 'The oldest tetrapods and their forerunners'. *Sci. Monthly*, **80**, 141–54.

Jarvik, E. (1960) '*Théories de l'évolution des vertébrés*'. (Masson, Paris).

Jarvik, E. (1962) 'Les porolépiformes et l'origine des urodèles'. *Colloques int. Cent. natn. Rech. Scient.*, **104**, 87–101.

Jarvik, E. (1963) 'The composition of the intermandibular division of the head in fish and tetrapods and the diphyletic origin of the tetrapod tongue'. *K. svenska VetenskAkad. Handl.*, (4) **9**, 1–74.

Jarvik, E. (1964) 'Specializations in early vertebrates'. *Annls Soc. R. zool. Belg.*, **94**, 11–95.

Jarvik, E. (1965*a*) 'Die Raspelzunge der Cyclostomen und die pentadactyle Extremität der Tetrapoden als Beweise für monophyletische Herkunft'. *Zool. Ant.*, **175**, 101–43.

Jarvik, E. (1965*b*) 'On the origin of girdles and paired fins'. *Israel J. Zool.*, **14**, 141–72.

Jarvik, E. (1966) 'Remarks on the structure of the snout in *Megalichthys* and certain other rhipidistid crossopterygians'. *Ark. Zool.*, (2) **19**, 41–98.

Jarvik, E. (1968*a*) 'The systematic position of the Dipnoi'. *Nobel Symposium*, **4**, 223–45.

Jarvik, E. (1968*b*) See Chapter 5.

Jessen, H. (1966*a*) 'Die Crossopterygier des Oberen Plattenkalkes (Devon) der Bergisch-Gladbach-Paffrather Mulde (Rheinisches Schiefergebirge) under Berücksichtigung von amerikanischem und europäischem *Onychodus*-Material'. *Ark. Zool.*, (2) **18**, 305–89.

Jessen, H. (1966*b*) 'Struniiformes'. in *Traité de Paléontologie*, 4.3, ed. Lehman, J. P. (Masson, Paris) p. 387.

Jessen H. (1967) 'The position of the Struniiformes (*Stunius* and *Onychodus*) among crossopterygians'. *Colloques int. Cent. natn. Rech. Scient.*, **163**, 173–80.

Kulcyzcki, J. (1960) '*Porolepis* (Crossopterygii) from the Lower Devonian of the Holy Cross Mountains'. *Acta palaeont. pol.*, **5**, 65–106.

Lehman, J. P. (1966) 'Dipnoi et Crossopterygii', in *Traité de Paléontologie*, 4.3, ed. Lehman, J. P. (Masson, Paris) p. 398.

Moy-Thomas, J. A. (1937) 'The Carboniferous coelacanth fishes of Great Britain and Ireland'. *Proc. zool. Soc. Lond.*, **107** (B), 385–415.

Moy-Thomas, J. A. and Westoll, T. S. (1935) 'On the Permian coelacanth, *Coelacanthus granulatus*, Ag.' *Geol. Mag.*, **72**, 446–57.

Nelson, J. (1970) 'Subcephalic muscles and intracranial joints of sarcopterygian and other fishes'. *Copeia* (1970), 468–471.

Olson, E. C. (1961) 'Jaw mechanisms: rhipidistians, amphibians, reptiles'. *Am. Zool.*, **1**, 205–15.

Ørvig, T. (1957) 'Remarks on the vertebrate fauna of the Lower Devonian of Escuminac Bay, P. Q., Canada, with special reference to the porolepiform crossopterygians'. *Ark. Zool.*, (2) **10**, 367–426.

Ørvig, T. (1961) 'New finds of acanthodians, arthrodires, crossopterygians, ganoids and dipnoans in the Upper Devonian calcareous flags (Oberer Plattenkalk) of the Bergisch Gladbach-Paffrath trough. 2'. *Paläont. Z.*, **35**, 10–27.

Panchen, A. L. (1967) 'The nostrils of choanate fishes and early tetrapods'. *Biol. Rev.*, **42**, 374–420.

Romer, A. S. (1937) 'The braincase of the Carboniferous crossopterygian *Megalichthys nitidus*'. *Bull. Mus. comp. Zool. Harv.*, **82**, 1–73.

Romer, A. S. (1941) 'Notes on the crossopterygian hyomandibular and braincase'. *J. Morphol.*, **69**, 141–60.

Säve-Söderbergh, G. (1934) 'Some points of view concerning the evolution of the vertebrates and the classification of this group'. *Ark. Zool.*, **26A**, 1–20.

Säve-Söderbergh, G. (1936) 'On the morphology of Triassic stegocephalans from Spitsbergen, and the interpretation of the endocranium in the Labyrinthodontia'. *K. svenska VetenskAkad. Handl.*, (3) **16**, 1–181.

Schaeffer, B. (1941) 'A revision of *Coelacanthus newarki* and notes on the evolution of the girdles and basal plates of the median fins in the Coelacanthini'. *Amer. Mus. Nov.*, **1110**, 1–17.

Schaeffer, B. (1952) 'The Triassic coelacanth fish *Diplurus*, with observations on the evolution of the Coelacanthini'. *Bull. Am. Mus. nat. Hist.*, **99**, 25–78.

Schaeffer, B. (1962) 'A coelacanth fish from the Upper Devonian of Ohio'. *Scient. publs. Cleveland Mus. nat. Hist.*, N.S. **1**, 1–14.

Schaeffer, B. (1965) 'The rhipidistian-amphibian transition'. *Am. Zool.*, **5**, 267–76.

Schaeffer, B. (1967) 'Osteichthyan vertebrae'. *J. Linn. Soc. (Zool.)*, **47**, 185–95.

Schaeffer, B. and Gregory, J. T. (1961) 'Coelacanth fishes from the Continental Triassic of the Western United States'. *Amer. Mus. Nov.*, **2036**, 1–18.

Schultze, H. P. (1969) 'Die Faltenzähne der Rhipidistiiden Crossopterygier, der Tetrapoden und der Actinopterygier-gattung *Lepisosteus*'. *Palaeontogr. ital.*, O.S. **65**, N.S. **35**, 63–136.

Schultze, H. P. (1970) 'Folded teeth and the monophyletic origin of tetrapods'. *Amer. Mus. Nov.*, **2408**, 1–10.

Stensiö, E. A. (1921) *Triassic fishes from Spitsbergen* (I. Holtzhausen, Vienna).

Stensiö, E. A. (1932) 'Triassic fishes from East Greenland'. *Medd. Grønland*, **83**, 1–345. Atlas.

Stensiö, E. A. (1937) 'On the Devonian coelacanthids of Germany with special reference to the dermal skeleton'. *K. svenska VetenskAkad. Handl.*, (3) **16**, 1–56.

Stensiö, E. A. (1963) 'The brain and cranial nerves in fossil, lower craniate vertebrates'. *Skr. norske VidenskAkad. Oslo Mat-naturv. Kl.* (1963) 1–120.

Thomson, K. S. (1962) 'Rhipidistian classification in relation to the origin of the tetrapods'. *Breviora*, **117**, 1–12.

Thomson, K. S. (1964a) 'Revised generic diagnoses of the fossil fishes *Megalichthys* and *Ectosteorhachis* (family Osteolepidae)'. *Bull. Mus. comp. Zool. Harv.*, **131**, 283–311.

Thomson, K. S. (1964b) 'The comparative anatomy of the snout in rhipidistian fishes'. *Bull. Mus. Comp. Zool. Harv.*, **131**, 313–57.

Thomson, K. S. (1964c) '*Gyroptychius* (Rhipidistia, Osteolepidae) from the Middle Devonian of Scotland'. *Ann. Mag. nat. Hist.*, (13) **7**, 725–32.

Thomson, K. S. (1965) 'The endocranium and associated structures in the Middle Devonian rhipidistian fish *Osteolepis*'. *Proc. Linn. Soc. Lond.*, **176**, 181–95.

Thomson, K. S. (1966) '*Glyptolepis* from the Middle Devonian of Scotland'. *Postilla*, **99**, 1–10.

Thomson, K. S. (1967a) 'Mechanisms of intracranial kinetics in fossil rhipidistian fishes (Crossopterygii) and their relatives'. *J. Linn. Soc. (Zool.)*, **178**, 223–53.

Thomson, K. S. (1967b) 'Notes on the relationship of the rhipidistian fishes and the ancestry of the tetrapods'. *J. Paleont.* **41**, 660–74.

Thomson, K. S. (1968a) 'A new Devonian fish (Crossopterygii: Rhipidistia) considered in relation to the origin of the Amphibia'. *Postilla*, **124**, 1–13.

Thomson, K. S. (1968b) 'A critical review of certain aspects of the diphyletic theory of tetrapod relationships'. *Nobel Symposium*, **4**, 285–305.

Thomson, K. S. (1968c) 'Further note on the structure of rhipidistian fishes'. *J. Paleont.*, **42**, 243.

Thomson, K. S. (1969) 'The biology of the lobe-finned fishes'. *Biol. Rev.*, **44**, 91–154.

Thomson, K. S. and Hahn, K. V. (1968) 'Growth and form in fossil rhipidistian fishes (Crossopterygii). *J. Zool. Lond.*, **156**, 199–223.

Thomson, K. S. and Vaughn, P. P. (1968) 'A new pattern of vertebral structure in a fossil rhipidistian fish (Crossopterygii)'. *Postilla*, **127**, 1–19.

Vorobjeva, E. I. (1959) 'A new genus of a crossopterygian fish, *Platycephalichthys*, from the Upper Devonian of Lovat River'. *Paleont. Jour. Akad. Nauk. U.S.S.R.* (1959) 95–106. (In Russian.)

Vorobjeva, E. I. (1960), 'New facts about the genus *Panderichthys* from the Devonian of the U.S.S.R'. *Paleont. Journ. Akad. Nauk. U.S.S.R.*, (1960) 87–96. (In Russian.)

Vorobjeva, E. I. (1962) 'Rhizodont crossopterygian fishes from the Main Devonian area of the U.S.S.R'. *Trudy Paleont. Inst.*, **94**, 1–108. (In Russian.)

Watson, D. M. S. (1926) 'The evolution and origin of the Amphibia', *Phil. Trans. R. Soc.*, (B) **214**, 189–257.

Watson, D.M.S. and Day, H. (1916) 'Notes on some Palaeozoic fishes'. *Mem. Proc. Manchr. lit. phil. Soc.*, **60**, 1–52.

Westoll, T. S. (1936) 'On the structure of the dermal ethmoid shield of *Osteolepis*'. *Geol. Mag.*, **73**, 157–71.

Westoll, T. S. (1937) 'On a specimen of *Eusthenopteron* from the Old Red Sandstone of Scotland'. *Geol. Mag.*, **74**, 507–24.

Westoll, T. S. (1938) 'Ancestry of the tetrapods'. *Nature, Lond.*, **141**, 127–28.

Westoll, T. S. (1939) 'On *Spermatodus pustulosus* Cope, a coelacanth from the "Permian" of Texas'. *Amer. Mus. Nov.*, **1017**, 1–23.

Westoll, T. S. (1940) 'New Scottish material of *Eusthenopteron*'. *Geol. Mag.*, **77**, 65–73.

Westoll, T. S. (1941) 'Latero-sensory canals and dermal bones'. *Nature, Lond.*, **148**, 168.

Westoll, T. S. (1943*a*) 'The origin of the tetrapods'. *Biol. Rev.*, **18**, 78–98.

Westoll, T. S. (1943*b*) 'The origin of the primitive tetrapod limb'. *Proc. R. Soc. Lond.*, B **131**, 373–93.

Westoll, T. S. (1943*c*) 'The hyomandibular of *Eusthenopteron* and the tetrapod middle ear'. *Proc. R. Soc. Lond.*, B **131**, 393–414.

CHAPTER SEVEN

Subclass Osteichthyes. Infraclass Dipnoi

7.1. CLASSIFICATION

Order 1, Dipterida
  e.g. *Chirodipterus*, U. Dev; *Dipnorhynchus*, L. Dev; *Dipterus, Pentlandia*, M. Dev; *Rhinodipterus*, U. Dev; *Uranolophus*, L. Dev; ?*Melanognathus*, L. Dev.
Order 2, Holodipterida
  e.g. *Devonosteus, Holodipterus*, U. Dev.
Order 3, Rhynchodipterida
  e.g. *Griphognathus, Rhynchodipterus*, U. Dev; *Soederberghia*, U. Dev. or L. Carb.
Order 4, Phaneropleurida
  e.g. *Fleurantia*, U. Dev; *Jarvikia, Oervigia*, U. Dev or L. Carb; *Phaneropleuron, Scaumenacia*, U. Dev.
Order 5, Uronemida
  e.g. *Uronemus*, L. Carb; ?*Conchopoma*, U. Carb—L. Perm.
Order 6, Ctenodontida
  e.g. *Ctenodus, Sagenodus*, L.–U. Carb; *Straitonia, Tranodis*, L. Carb.
Order 7, Ceratodontida
  e.g. *Ceratodus*, L. Trias—U. Cret; *Neoceratodus*, Extant.
Order 8, Lepidosirenida
  e.g. *Lepidosiren, Protopterus*, Extant; ?*Gnathorhiza*, U. Carb—L. Perm.

L., Lower; M., Middle; U., Upper, Dev, Devonian, Carb, Carboniferous; Perm, Permian; Trias, Triassic; Cret, Cretaceous.

7.2. DIPNOAN CHARACTERISTICS

The dipnoans or lung-fishes are an extremely long-lived group of moderately-sized fishes appearing in the Lower Devonian and continuing to the present day. During this time a steady evolution has been taking place within the group, which can be reconstructed with a long series of 'normal' forms (Dollo, 1895; Westoll, 1949). This evolution is particularly interesting since as in most other groups of fishes which have existed for a long time there is a steady loss of ossification, and in dipnoans it is accompanied by a degeneration of other characters, particularly the return to continuous median fins, which may be interpreted as a return in many respects to the larval condition. So great have the changes within the group been that the Lower Devonian *Uranolophus* (Denison, 1968*a*, *b*) is only distinguishable from primitive osteolepidids by its cranial morphology, which although primitive is already typically dipnoan (Fig. 7.1). On the other hand, the living *Lepidosiren* has hardly any obvious features which would connect it with the primitive members of any osteichthyan group. Since it was the modern lung-fishes whose anatomy was first described in detail, it is hardly surprising to find that workers originally separated the dipnoans from other bony-fishes. The debate about the relationships of the group has continued to this day (see Relationships of teleostomes; §6).

The main results of the reduction in ossification and the return to the larva-like condition of the median fins become clear if we contrast a living lung-fish with a primitive Devonian form. *Neoceratodus* is the most primitive living genus; it has a few large bones in the skull, they are thin, deeply

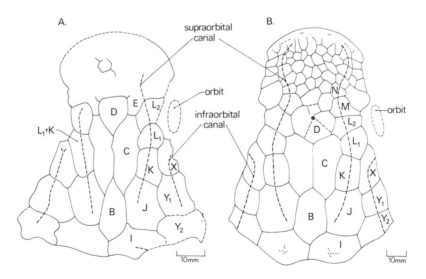

Fig. 7.1. Plans of the skull-roofs of two Lower Devonian dipnoans. (After Denison.); A. *Uranolophus wyomingensis*; B. *Dipnorhynchus sussmilchi.*

142

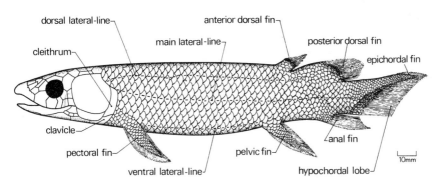

Fig. 7.2. *Dipterus valenciennesi*. Restoration in lateral view. (After Forster-Cooper.)

seated and separated from the lateral-line canals, and there are no gular plates; the dentition comprises a pair of upper vomerine and pterygo-palatine tooth-plates and a lower mandibular tooth-plate; the scales are thin and embedded in the skin; the tail is diphycercal and continuous with the dorsal and anal fins, and the fin-rays are horny camptotrichia. In a primitive Devonian genus such as *Uranolophus*, the dermal bones and scales are thick and include a cosmine layer, they have a superficial position and enclose the lateral-line canals; there are many small bones in the skull and large gular plates; there are no tooth-plates; the tail is heterocercal (see *Dipterus*, Fig. 7.2) and there are separate anterior dorsal, posterior dorsal and anal fins; and the fin webs are stiffened with bony lepidotrichia.

The profound changes that have taken place in the history of lung-fishes make it difficult to formulate a satisfactory definition for the group as a whole. However, throughout dipnoan history it appears that the palato-quadrate has been fused to the neurocranium (autostyly) (Säve-Söderbergh, 1952; Schaeffer, 1968), and the hyomandibula, no longer functional as a suspensory element, has been reduced. There are never marginal tooth-bearing bones, or marginal teeth comparable with those of other osteich-thyans. The external nasal openings are ventral, with the anterior opening on the edge and the posterior opening on the roof of the mouth (Fig. 7.3). The posterior opening was long mistaken for a choana, comparable with that of rhipidistians or tetrapods, but recent work has confirmed that it is the homologue of the actinopterygian posterior opening, secondarily dis-placed into the buccal cavity (Jarvik, 1942; Thomson, 1965*b*; Bertmar, 1965, 1966; Panchen, 1967). All dipnoans have lobate fins, which are usually covered with scales (Jarvik, 1959). The internal skeleton of the fins was primitively concentrated, but that of the paired fins probably had a more elongated axis than in those rhipidistians where fin supports are

143

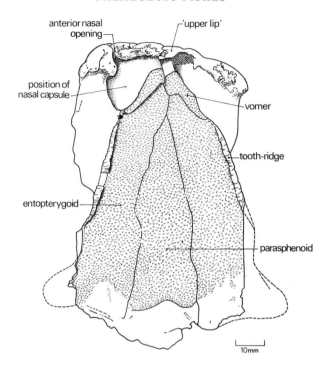

Fig. 7.3. *Uranolophus wyomingensis*. Palate and 'upper lip'. (After Denison.)

known, being more like that of the modern *Neoceratodus*, which is a biserial 'archipterygium' (see xenacanths, Chapter 9 §7).

7.3. STRUCTURE AND DIVERSITY

Dipnoans reached the zenith of their evolution in late Devonian and Carboniferous times, when they were adapted for a considerable range of habitats and diets. The dipterids include the most primitive forms from the Lower Devonian, as well as 'normal' Middle and Upper Devonian genera. An account of the basic structure of Palaeozoic lung-fishes may be based on this group.

7.3.1. Structure

In *Dipterus* (Fig. 7.2) there are two lobed dorsal, an anal, and acutely lobed, long pectoral and pelvic fins (Forster-Cooper, 1937). The tail is heterocercal with a small epichordal and a large hypochordal lobe. The body scales are cycloid, overlapping and rather thin, but both the scales and the dermal bones are covered with a smooth layer of cosmine, as in osteolepidids. These elements have a thick base of lamellar bone. The scales of *Uranolophus* are significantly different from those of *Dipterus* and other lung-fishes, and show striking similarities to those of primitive crossopterygians (Denison, 1968*a*). The exposed part of the scale is rhombic, and the overlapped zone is narrow. The flank scales have a dorsal peg, recalling that of *Porolepis*, which fits into a depression on the inner surface of the scale above.

What is known of the limb girdles seems to indicate that they do not differ significantly from those of other osteichthyans (Jarvik, 1944*b*). In *Uranolophus* the shoulder-girdle includes a large cleithrum and clavicle, and possibly a small rhipidistian-like interclavicle. The anocleithrum and supracleithrum have only been reported in later forms, although both are probably present in *Dipterus*. The scapulocoracoid is perichondrally ossified in *Uranolophus* and *Chirodipterus*. It is· a small structure attached to the cleithrum, and is similar to that of *Eusthenopteron*. The notochord is persistent in primitive lung-fishes and the vertebrae comprise separate dorsal and ventral arches. Most Palaeozoic lung-fishes have long, well-ossified pleural ribs.

The course of the sensory canals (Fig. 7.4) of the head has the same general plan as in other osteichthyans, but the dermal bones are more numerous and may in many ways be considered to be more primitive. The cheek canals show the characteristic rhipidistian arrangement, particularly in the course of the preopercular line (Stensiö, 1947; Lehmann and Westoll, 1952). In *Dipnorhynchus* and *Uranolophus* (Westoll, 1949; Lehmann and Westoll, 1952; Denison, 1968*a*, *b*) the supraorbital canal extends far back on the skull-roof, to include a section which corresponds to the anterior pit-line of later forms (see Jarvik, 1968*a*); it has no connection with the infraorbital line. This connection develops later, as in *Dipterus*, much as it develops in later actinopterygians (holosteans). There are no premaxillaries or maxillaries. The absence of these bones is connected with the peculiar dentition. There is no ethmoid commissure, probably as a result of the migration of the posterior nasal opening into the roof of the mouth. There may be a rostral commissure, as in *Dipterus* (White, 1962, 1965), and an occipital cross-commissure.

The dermal bones of the skull-roof and cheek appear at first sight (Fig. 7.4) to be entirely incomparable with those of other osteichthyans. Comparison becomes possible if those bones developed in connection with the sensory canals considered as series, as has been done for the other groups of osteichthyans. Two systems of nomenclature have been applied to the skull bones of lung-fishes. One is based on the standard actinopterygian terminology (e.g. Lehman, 1959), and the other is a series of letters and numbers (Forster-Cooper, 1937) that makes no assumptions about bone homologies. The alphabetical scheme used here (Figs. 7.1, 7.4) is based on the versions

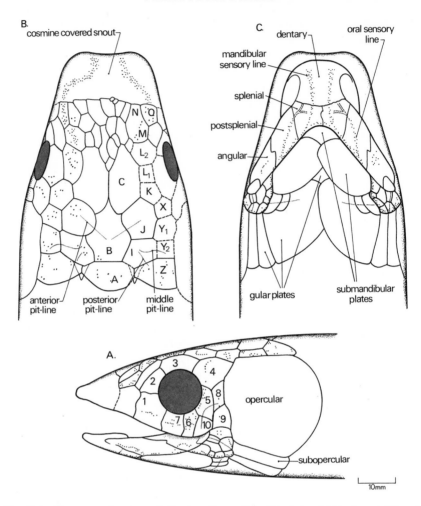

Fig. 7.4. *Dipterus valenciennesi*. Restorations of skull in lateral (A), dorsal (B) and ventral (C) views. Courses of the lateral-lines indicated only by their external pores. (After Westoll.)

applied by Westoll (1949) and Denison (1968a). In *Dipterus* three bones are found on the occipital commissure, Z, A, Z, which may be regarded as extra-scapulars, and three on the otic-postotic section of the main canal, X, Y_1, Y_2, which are comparable with the supratemporal series of actinopterygians and the intertemporal, supratemporal and tabular of rhipidistians. Six bones are found on the infraorbital line, 4,5,6,7,1A,1B; bone 4 being comparable with the postorbital of rhipidistians; and a varying number, K to N, on the supraorbital canal, the naso-parietal series. Bone 8 on the preopercular line can be regarded as a squamosal, and bone 9 as a preopercular. The postrostral and parietal regions are occupied by a very variable number of bones lying between the main and supraorbital canal series. The medium bone B and the paired bones C are the most important of these. In front of them, in *Dipnorhynchus*, bone D is related to a pineal foramen. Other small bones in the skull are shown in Fig. 7.4. The opercular is very large relative to the subopercular, and there is a series of large gulars, perhaps including homologues of the rhipidistian submandibular series (Jarvik, 1967). In most dipnoans the snout has no exoskeleton. However, it is sometimes present in *Dipterus* and other dipterids, being formed of cosmine and loosely cancellar bone tissue. Probably it appeared only at a late stage of growth in *Dipterus* (White, 1965). In *Dipnorhynchus* and *Uranolophus* (Fig. 7.1) the snout is more heavily ossified, and consists of a mosaic of small bones (Campbell, 1965; Denison, 1968a). This is a primitive feature also seen in rhynchodipterids. The anterior external nostrils form notches on the ventral edge of the snout.

The dermal bones of the lower jaw present the same problems of homologization and terminology as those of the skull-roof (Jarvik, 1967; Schultze, 1969). We shall apply the most widely used bone names. Thus in *Dipterus* and *Uranolophus* there is a lateral series with the splenial, postsplenial and angular developed in relation to the mandibular and oral lateral-lines. The front of the jaw is formed by the dentary, which reaches back on the inner face of the jaw to suture with the prearticular. There is a small adductor fossa and the meckelian cartilage is ossified, forming at its posterior end a stout articular.

The neurocranium (Fig. 7.5) has been described for *Chirodipterus* and *Dipterus* (Säve-Söderbergh, 1952; Gross, 1964; White, 1965), in which it is ossified in a single piece and can be compared very closely with that of the living *Neoceratodus*, particularly to young stages of development. The main difference lies in the greater degree of ossification in the fossil genera. Clearly the fusion of the palatoquadrate with the neurocranium and the development of the typical dipnoan jaw mechanism, in which the adductor muscles extend their area of origin up on to the roof of the neurocranium, took place at an early stage of evolution. This has limited the capacity for evolutionary change in the head, other than in the dermal skeleton and in the proportions of the snout. The endocast of *Chirodipterus* indicates that the brain was also developed much as in *Neoceratodus*. In *Uranolophus*, and to a lesser extent in *Dipnorhynchus*, the prepineal region of the skull is shorter than in later genera and the eyes are more anteriorly situated. This indicates smaller nasal capsules, a longer otic region and longer jaws.

147

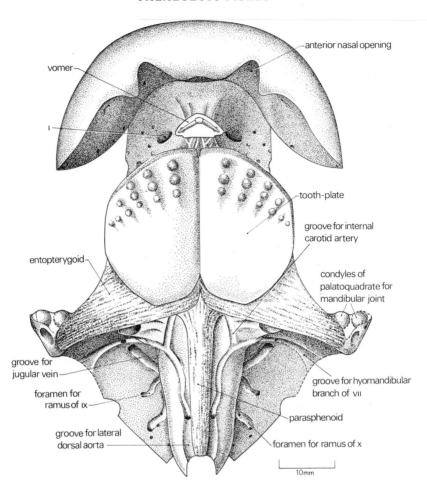

Fig. 7.5. *Chirodipterus wildungensis*. Restoration of palate. (After Säve-Söderbergh.)

The palate includes a parasphenoid, which in *Dipterus* and all well-known lung-fishes stretches back to the hind margin of the neurocranium. This bone is flanked by large entopterygoids and anteriorly there are small vomers. It has been suggested that *Dipnorhynchus* and *Uranolophus* had a posteriorly short parasphenoid and separate parotic plates, as in *Eusthenopteron*, but this is uncertain. The primitive condition of the dentition is well shown by *Uranolophus* (Fig. 7.3). Here the lower surface of the palate and the upper surface of the prearticulars are strewn with small denticles of dentine. On the margins of the mouth and on the dentary these denticles fuse into low tooth-

148

ridges, composed of a hypermineralized hard tissue similar to the tubular dentine of holocephalans (Chapter 10 §2). *Dipterus* and other Middle Devonian genera, however, already show the typical lung-fish dentition of a pair of large dentine-covered, triturating plates in the upper and lower jaw, borne by the entopterygoids and prearticulars respectively (Fig. 7.6). It is nevertheless evident that there was some experimentation in the dentition in early lung-fishes. In *Dipnorhynchus sussmilchi* areas of the palate and pre-articulars are thickened as bulbous crushing surfaces (White, 1966). The primitive marginal tooth-ridges sometimes persist in later dipnoans, and from time to time have been described as vestigial premaxillaries and maxillaries.

The gill-skeleton is ossified in some Devonian genera, but has yet to be described in detail. The hyomandibula is a non-suspensory element, sup-porting the gill-cover. In some genera it closely anticipates the hyoman-dibula of *Neoceratodus*. The ceratohyals are large and joined to the basi-branchial by small hypohyals. The basibranchial frequently bears thin tooth-plates, and may have an anterior projection very similar to the sublingual rod of *Eusthenopteron*.

7.3.2. Diversity

The basic structure and principal modifications found in the dipterids have now been given. Two genera are of additional interest. *Rhinodipterus* (Gross, 1956; Ørvig, 1961; White, 1962) has an elongated snout, a modification also found in other orders, and one apparently evolved independently several times in the Upper Devonian. In the lower jaw the symphysial region is elongated (Fig. 7.6). The Middle Devonian *Pentlandia* (Watson and Day, 1916; Westoll, 1949) is very similar to *Dipterus* but shows some signs of advance towards the condition of later forms. The posterior dorsal fin is larger, longer based and not lobed, from which it may be inferred that the internal skeleton of the fin is not concentrated.

The holodipterids are poorly known (Jaekel, 1927; Gorizdro-Kulczycka, 1950). They have a dentition of swollen crushing areas, forming ill-defined tooth-plates, somewhat as in *Dipnorhynchus sussmilchi*. Whether this means that they are related to this Lower Devonian species or not cannot be decided.

The rhynchodipterids are basically an Upper Devonian group with an interesting mixture of primitive and specialized characters (Säve-Söder-bergh, 1937; Lehman, 1959; Schultze, 1969). The primitive features include the completely ossified snout and large number of bones in the head, the *Uranolophus*-like dentition with the teeth not fused into tooth-plates, and the *Dipterus*-like scale structure and body form (Fig. 7.7). The specialized

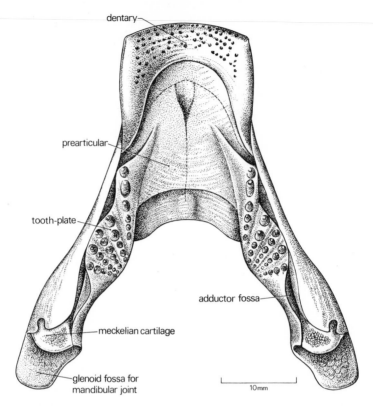

dentary

prearticular

tooth-plate

adductor fossa

meckelian cartilage

glenoid fossa for
mandibular joint

10mm

Fig. 7.6. *Rhinodipterus ulrichi*. Restoration of lower jaw in dorsal view. (After Jarvik.)

features include the elongated snout; the lower jaw, which in contrast to *Rhinodipterus* has the ramus elongated and a posterior retroarticular process; and the vertebral column which includes well-developed ring-like centra with separate neural and haemal arches (Jarvik, 1952; Schultze,

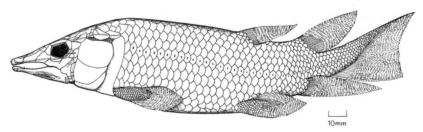

10mm

Fig. 7.7. *Griphognathus sculpta*. Restoration in lateral view. (After Schultze.)

150

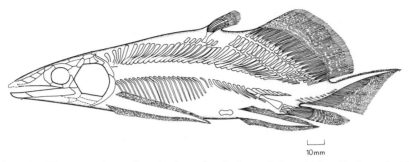

Fig. 7.8. *Fleurantia denticulata*. Restoration in lateral view. (After Graham-Smith and Westoll.)

1969). *Griphognathus* has a well-ossified neurocranium which retains a lateral occipital fissure of actinopterygian type.

The phaneropleurids (Figs. 7.8, 7.9) are another basically Upper Devonian group in which the skull tends to be elongated, as in *Fleurantia*, *Jarvikia* and *Oervigia* (Graham-Smith and Westoll, 1937; Lehman, 1959). The lower jaw is known in *Fleurantia* and has the ramus elongated as in rhynchodipterids. The group shows an advance on the condition in dipterids and rhynchodipterids. *Scaumenacia* (Jarvik, 1959) has an even longer based posterior dorsal fin than *Pentlandia*, and the anterior dorsal fin is longer based and not lobed. The epichordal lobe of the tail is larger and the tail less heterocercal. In *Phaneropleuron* (Fig. 7.9) the two dorsal fins and the epichordal lobe of the caudal fin are confluent, the tail being diphycercal. Accompanying these changes in the structure of the fins in the phaneropleurids is a loss of any ossification in the snout, the loss of the cosmine layer on the scales and dermal bones, and a reduction in the number and thickness of the latter. *Fleurantia* (Fig. 7.8) stands a little apart from *Scaumenacia* and *Phaneropleuron*, and it probably represents a side branch of the order with some primitive features. The anterior dorsal fin is small, lobate and separate from the posterior, and the

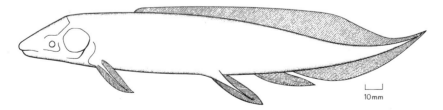

Fig. 7.9. *Phaneropleuron andersoni*. Restoration in lateral view. (After Dollo.)

151

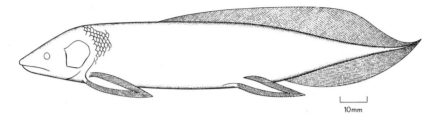

Fig. 7.10. *Uronemus lobatus.* Restoration in lateral view. (After Dollo.)

dentition includes small granular teeth as well as poorly-developed tooth-plates.

In the ctenodontids (e.g. the Carboniferous *Ctenodus* and *Sagenodus*) and the uronemids (e.g. the Carboniferous *Uronemus* Fig. 7.10), the dorsal and anal fins are both continuous with the diphycercal tail, and the dermal bones of the head are further reduced in number (Watson and Gill, 1923; Westoll, 1949). In addition to these changes in the dermal bones the neurocranium becomes progressively less well-ossified, until finally, as in modern forms, only one pair of cartilage bones is left, the exoccipitals. Among the cteno-dontids, genera such as *Tranodis* and *Sagenodus* tend to have sectorial tooth-plates with a reduced number of ridges and denticles, whereas in *Ctenodus* the tooth-plates have become specialized for crushing, with an increased number of ridges and denticles (Thomson, 1965*a*, 1969). The uronemids appear to have the tooth-plates reduced to granular teeth, although they may in fact exhibit a primitive condition. In *Conchopoma* (Weitzel, 1926; Denison, 1969) the dentition is made up of scattered teeth on the palate, which are opposed by a large basibranchial tooth-plate, and small teeth on the margins of the jaws. Although *Conchopoma* (Fig. 7.11) is usually classified with *Uronemus*, which it closely resembles in body form, this relationship is not well-established. It is now clear that continuous median fins and a diphycer-cal tail have been acquired independently several times in Carboniferous and Permian lung-fishes. At least one species of *Conchopoma* is known to have

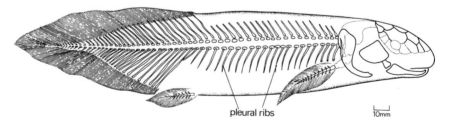

pleural ribs

Fig. 7.11. *Conchopoma gadiforme.* Restoration in lateral view. (After Weitzel.)

152

had very long paired fins, comparable to those of the living *Protopterus*.

It remains to mention the Carboniferous and Permian genus *Gnathorhiza* (Romer and Smith, 1934; Olson, 1951; Berman, 1968). This remarkable form has its tooth-plates reduced to a few deep shearing blades, which show some resemblance to those of living genera; and burrows have been found which show that like *Lepidosiren* and *Protopterus*, it had the ability to aestivate. It has been suggested that *Gnathorhiza* was an ancestral lepidosirenid. An alternative explanation is that the lepidosirenids diverged from the ceratodontids in the Mesozoic (Stromer, 1938), and that the similarities to *Gnathorhiza* in structure and behaviour are due to parallel evolution.

7.4. EVOLUTION AND MODE OF LIFE

The classification of dipnoans employed here is a rather arbitrary attempt to separate the most distinct assemblages of genera as orders. So far it has not proved possible to group dipnoans in a satisfactory phyletic arrangement. Our arrangement differs little from a frankly horizontal classification (Lehman 1959, 1966), which recognizes levels of organization based on the evolution of the median fins. The main tendencies in dipnoan evolution are well known and have been described above. They involve changes in the configuration of the median fins, the loss of ossification in both the endoskeleton and exoskeleton, and the shortening of the cheek and otic region in the skull. Westoll (1949) has shown that the rate of evolution for dipnoans was very high in Devonian times, when there was a rapid 'modernization' of their complex of characters, and thereafter it fell away markedly, so that since Palaeozoic times they have been characterized by a very slow rate. A similar pattern of evolution can be seen in coelacanths (Schaeffer, 1952).

There have been only few prominent side branches of the main line of lung-fish evolution, notably the rhynchodipterids among the better known forms. The widest adaptive radiation of the infraclass occurred in the Devonian, when there was some experimentation in the length and proportions of the head, the structure of the vertebral column, and the dentition. It is interesting to note that some of the forms which became specialized in the head, but retained a primitive arrangement of the fins and cosmoid scales (e.g. rhynchodipterids), were contemporaries of 'normal' dipnoans that had become 'advanced' in fin and scale structure. Experimentation in the dentition persisted into post-Devonian times, and even in groups which have well-defined tooth-plates, there are various specializations for shearing and crushing. The eventual adoption of a triturating dentition may have been correlated with a progressively more sluggish locomotion (Westoll, 1949).

It has often been supposed that the characteristic autostyly of dipnoans was developed to support crushing tooth-plates. But we now know that this

153

was not the case, as even the most primitive species with a granular dentition over large areas of the palate and lower jaw had fully autostylic jaws (see holocephalans, Chapter 10 §10).

As far as one can judge, the overall biology of lung-fishes was much the same in the Palaeozoic as it is today, although many early species were marine and must have had some special adaptations (Thomson, 1969). There has been little fundamental change in body form if we exclude the median fins, and throughout its history the group seems to have been adapted primarily for life on the bottom, in shallow waters. *Fleurantia* and *Scaumenacia* are notable as dipnoans with a deep, compressed body, and were probably fast swimming predators. A stenophagous diet may have been the rule in dipnoans, with emphasis on a particular part of the diet as the dentition became specialized. The well-formed opercular apparatus indicates that gill breathing was much more important in the Palaeozoic than in subsequent times. However, the discovery of lung-fish burrows in Devonian, Carboniferous and Permian rocks (Romer and Olson, 1954; Vaughn, 1964; Carroll, 1965; Thomson, 1969) shows that the faculty of air breathing was acquired early, and probably it was widely distributed in the group.

7.5. GROWTH OF COSMOID SCALES AND BONES

Primitive dipnoans and rhipidistians have the exposed surface of the scales and dermal bones coated with a smooth layer of cosmine (Chapter 6 §2). This layer may extend without interruption over the suture lines between adjacent bones on the head. However, in dipnoans the outer surface is often scored by narrow *Westoll-lines*, which divide the cosmine layer into separate sheets bearing no relation to the underlying bone pattern. Cosmine has an enameloid superficial layer, and individual sheets of cosmine, once formed, are incapable of growth or of fusion with neighbouring sheets. Growth of cosmoid scales and plates, therefore, involves first the resorption of the cosmine layer, then the increase in size of the isopedin in both thickness and area, so that it comes to bear concentric markings, and finally the redeposition of the cosmine layer. Probably this cycle took place seasonally, resorption taking place all over the body at about the same time (Westoll, 1936; Forster-Cooper, 1937).

Whilst the existence of the cosmine growth cycle is well-established, the details of the process are poorly understood, and they may not have been the same on the head as on the scales of the body (Jarvik, 1950a; Gross, 1956; Ørvig, 1969). It has been shown in a Devonian dipnoan (Ørvig, 1969), that the formation of cosmine on the lower surface of the trunk involved successive waves of deposition gradually spreading out laterally from a primordial cosmine patch. On each scale cosmine formation took place centrifugally, successive zones of growth of cosmine being separated by *Westoll-lines*. However, the marginal growth of the isopedin layer was not synchronized with the deposition of zones of cosmine.

A somewhat different mechanism is found in the Lower Devonian dipnoan *Uranolophus* and the primitive holoptychiid *Porolepis* (Gross, 1966; Denison, 1968a; Ørvig, 1969). In these genera it appears that resorption did not play a significant part in the growth of the scales. Instead the scales were initially covered with a layer of free-standing odontodes, which then became covered by further layers of odontodes each separated by a thin sheet of bone, as the scales grew in thickness and area. Eventually the superimposed layers of odontodes became covered by zones of growth of cosmine, deposited centrifugally so that no one cosmine layer came to overlie another. Once cosmine formation was completed, the growth of the scales must have terminated, although it is interesting to note that the growth of the head-shield in *Uranolophus* involved a cosmine resorption-redeposition cycle, much as in later forms.

The mode of growth of the scales in *Porolepis* and *Uranolophus*, with the superposition of successive superficial layers, is significantly closer in principal to the mechanism found in actinopterygians than is the resorption-redeposition mechanism found in later crossopterygians and dipnoans.

7.6. RELATIONSHIPS OF TELEOSTOMES

In this book we have divided the gnathostomatous fishes into two major, collateral groups, the teleostomes and elasmobranchiomorphs. It is reasonably clear that the elasmobranchiomorphs are a natural group (Chapter 10 §11), but there is some doubt about the interrelations of the forms grouped as teleostomes. Accordingly it is necessary to examine the relationships of dipnoans to other osteichthyans, and the relationships of acanthodians to osteichthyans. The interesting subject of the origin of tetrapods falls outside the scope of this book, and has frequently been reviewed (Westoll, 1943a; Jarvik, 1955, 1962, 1965a; Szarski, 1962; Parsons and Williams, 1963; Thomson, 1962, 1969; Andrews and Westoll, 1970).

Although Jarvik (1967; 1968a, b) in particular has stressed some chondrichthyan features of dipnoans, particularly in the degenerate living species, there are no strong reasons for excluding them from the osteichthyans (Schaeffer, 1968). Within the osteichthyans, however, the dipnoans are variously held to be most closely related to crossopterygians, to actinopterygians, or to have diverged at an early stage from the common stock of these two groups.

The evidence from Palaeozoic materials apparently favours a close relationship between dipnoans and crossopterygians (Westoll, 1949; Lehmann and Westoll, 1952; Denison, 1968*b*; Schultze, 1969). The primitive members of these two groups have a well-developed cosmine layer in the dermal bones and scales; a heterocercal tail with an epichordal lobe; two dorsal fins; the paired, dorsal and anal fins with a well-developed fleshly lobe and a concentrated internal skeleton; and a similar course for the preopercular sensory line on the cheek. In addition, *Uranolophus* has rhombic scales closely similar to those of primitive rhipidistians such as *Porolepis*, and vertebrae which may be similar to the rhipidistian type with distinct inter- or pleurocentra. The mode of growth, involving the resorption and redeposition of the cosmine layer, is a further similarity between dipnoans and rhipidistians, although as previously noted, the growth of the scales did not involve resorption in the earliest members of each group.

Unfortunately the value of much of this evidence is open to question. Thus in the structure and disposition of the fins, dipnoans and crossopterygians possibly resemble each other in primitive osteichthyan characters, and these are also found to some extent in elasmobranchs. Again, with respect to cosmine, a pore-canal system associated with the dentinal layer is found in some osteostracans, and its presence may not be phylogenetically significant. However, there is a much closer agreement between dipnoans and crossopterygians in the arrangement of the pore-canal system than between either of these groups and osteostracans (Schultze, 1969).

The suggestion that dipnoans are most closely related to actinopterygians comes mainly from embryological work on Recent species (Bertmar, 1966, 1968*b*) that is difficult to evaluate (Jarvik, 1968*a*). Palaeozoic species provide no additional evidence in favour of this view. However, if the specializations of the skull associated with autostyly are taken into account, the structure of the skull shows that this suggestion merits consideration (Schaeffer, 1968). Although the 'choanae' of dipnoans have been shown to be the posterior external nasal openings, this merely brings these fishes into line with the primitive osteichthyan condition, with separate anterior and posterior nostrils, and does not specifically associate them with actinopterygians.

The third view, that the dipnoans diverged from the primitive common stock of actinopterygians and crossopterygians, is the most challenging, because it demands a close examination of the significance of the dermal bone pattern. This hypothesis supposes that the mosaic of small dermal bones in the skull of dipnoans is a primitive feature, and that these plates cannot be homologized with the bones of other osteichthyans (White, 1965). Remnants of the primitive mosaic may also be seen in the snout of rhipidistians. However, it is probable that the parasphenoid, opercular series and bones of the dermal shoulder-girdle are homologous in all osteichthyans, and it must be assumed that these bones, at least, had formed in the dermal mosaic before the three groups diverged. The alternative explanation of the bone pattern in the dipnoan skull is that it originated from the pattern seen in crossopterygians and actinopterygians, by the loss of the tooth-bearing marginal bones (the maxillary and premaxillary) and the subdivision of the skull-roof into a mosaic. Such changes might well have taken place in connection with the evolution of autostyly and an increase in the breadth of the otic and orbital regions. The strongest argument against this interpretation is that it would involve a radical alteration in the direction of evolutionary change. The greatest number of bones is found in the oldest dipnoans, and they are rapidly reduced in number in the Devonian, leading in some cases (*Soederberghia*) to a pattern which is strikingly similar to that of other osteichthyan groups (Schaeffer, 1968).

The relationship between dipnoans and other osteichthyans must still be regarded as an unsolved problem. For this reason the dipnoans are ranked here as an independent infraclass, and not grouped with crossopterygians in the 'Sarcopterygii'.

Acanthodians have frequently been regarded as an offshoot of the elasmobranch stock, and the name 'spiny-sharks' has been applied to the group. However, many of the characters that have been used to link acanthodians with sharks are either primitive gnathostome features or superficial similarities without significance. In the first category fall such features as body form and the unconstricted notochord, and in the second, the presence of spines, deeply-seated fin-rays ('ceratotrichia'), sensory lines running between the scales, large scapulocoracoid, and possibly the posterior orientation of the pharyngobranchials. Most of these characters have already been discussed in Chapter 4, but it must be stressed that spines have evolved independently several times in the history of fishes (Jarvik, 1959), and that acanthodians differ strongly from elasmobranchs in having spines in front of the paired as well as the median fins. As far as the pharyngobranchials are concerned, they show no elasmobranch characters apart from their supposed posterior orientation.

The alternative hypothesis that acanthodians are related to osteichthyans is supported by detailed morphological evidence. It is unfortunate, however, that much of this evidence is derived from *Acanthodes*, one of the last and most specialized members of the group. The evidence for osteichthyan affinities (Miles, 1965, 1968) includes the presence of a long series of mobile branchiostegal rays in the main gill-cover; the large, compact otoliths in the ear; the palatobasal articulation between the palatoquadrate and the neurocranium; the spiracular groove on the neurocranium and its relationships to structures in the basisphenoid region; and the presence of a lateral occipital fissure separating the narrow occipital region of the neurocranium from the broad otic region. In addition the skull has a narrow base (tropybasy) with a thin interorbital wall; small, closely situated nasal capsules;

and a short occipital region. This is quite different from the condition of the skull in fossil and living sharks (Chapter 9), which is broad based (platybasy), with widely separated nasal capsules and a long occipital region. The neurocranium of *Acanthodes* also lacks such typical elasmobranch features as the basal angle, broad suborbital shelf, rostrum and precerebral cavity. The hypochordal radials of the tail in acanthodians resemble those of osteichthyans, particularly crossopterygians, in their short, unjointed condition. They are distinct from those of elasmobranchs, which became modified in another way, first becoming jointed and then shortened.

The neurocranium of *Acanthodes* is very suggestive of that of palaeoniscoids in its general architecture; and the tail of acanthodians resembles that of actinopterygians in the lack of an epichordal lobe. It is unlikely, however, that acanthodians and actinopterygians are particularly closely related. All osteichthyan groups have in common a dermal shoulder-girdle of characteristic structure, and dermal bones on the palate and (but cf. dipnoans) margins of the jaws. Characters such as these suggest that osteichthyans separated into actinopterygian, crossopterygian and dipnoan lines after their forebears diverged from the acanthodians. Therefore the acanthodians and osteichthyans probably represent two divergent lines of evolution within the teleostomes.

Although acanthodians are specialized in the presence of fin-spines, they are more primitive than osteichthyans in the lack of dermal bones on the palate and jaw margins, large bones covering the skull-roof and cheek, and a lateral dermal shoulder-girdle series of bones; also in the undifferentiated condition of the branchiostegal series and dermal fin-rays. The type of neurocranium seen in *Acanthodes* and palaeoniscoids may well be close to the primitive teleostome kind, the neurocranium of crossopterygians and dipnoans having been strongly modified in connection with the intracranial joint in the first group and autostyly in the second.

REFERENCES

References given in Chapters 5 and 6 are not repeated.

Berman, D. S. (1968) 'Lungfish from the Lueders Formation (Lower Permian, Texas) and *Gnathorhiza*-lepidosirenid acestry questioned'. *J. Paleont.*, **42**, 827–35.

Bertmar, G. (1965) 'The olfactory organ and upper lips in Dipnoi, an embryological study'. *Acta zool. Stockh.*, **47**, 43–59.

Bertmar, G. (1966) 'The development of skeleton, blood-vessels and nerves in the dipnoan snout, with a discussion on the homology of the dipnoan posterior nostrils'. *Acta. zool. Stockh.*, **47**, 81–150.

Bertmar, G. (1968a) 'Phylogeny and evolution in lungfishes'. *Acta zool. Stockh.*, **49**, 189–201.

Bertmar, G. (1968b) 'Lungfish phylogeny'. *Nobel Symposium*, **4**, 259–83.

Campbell, K. S. W. (1965) 'An almost complete skull roof and palate of the dipnoan *Dipnorhynchus sussmilchi* (Etheridge)'. *Palaeont.* **8**, 634–37.

Carroll, R. L. (1965) 'Lungfish burrows from the Michigan coal basin'. *Science, N.Y.*, **148**, 963–64.

Denison, R. H. (1968a) 'Early Devonian lungfishes from Wyoming, Utah, and Idaho'. *Fieldiana, Geol.*, **17**, 353–413.

Denison, R. H. (1968b) 'The evolutionary significance of the earliest known lungfish, *Uranolophus*'. *Nobel Symposium*, **4**, 247–57.

Denison, R. H. (1969) 'New Pennsylvanian lungfishes from Illinois'. *Fieldiana, Geol.*, **12**, 193–211.

Dollo, L. (1895) 'Sur la phylogénie des Dipneustes'. *Bull. Soc. belge. Géol. Paléont. Hydrol.*, **9**, 79–128.

Forster-Cooper, C. (1937) 'The Middle Devonian fish fauna of Achanarras'. *Trans. R. Soc. Edinb.*, **59**, 223–39.

Gorizdro-Kulczycka, Z. (1950) 'Les Dipneustes Dévoniens du Massif de S-te Croix'. *Acta geol. pol.*, **1**, 53–105.

Gross, W. (1964) 'Über die Randzähne des Mundes, die Ethmoidal-region des Schädels und die Unterkiefersymphyse von *Dipterus oervigi* n. sp.'. *Paläont. Z.*, **38**, 7–25.

Gross, W. (1965) 'Über den Vorderschädel von *Ganorhynchus spledens* Gross (Dipnoi, Mitteldevon)'. *Paläont. Z.*, **39**, 113–33.

Graham-Smith, W. and Westoll, T. S. (1937) 'On a new long-headed dipnoan fish from the Upper Devonian of Scaumenac Bay, P.Q., Canada'. *Trans. R. Soc. Edinb.*, **59**, 241–66.

Jaekel, O. (1927) 'Der Kopf der Wirbelthiere'. *Ergebn. Anat. EntwGesch.*, **27**, 815–974.

Jarvik, E. (1967) 'On the structure of the lower jaw in dipnoans: with a description of an early Devonian dipnoan from Canada. *Melanognathus canadensis* gen. et sp. nov.' *J. Linn. Soc. (Zool.)*, **47**, 155–83.

Lehman, J. P. (1959) 'Les Dipneustes du Dévonien du Groenland'. *Medd. Grønland*, **160**, 1–58.

Lehmann, W. and Westoll, T. S. (1952) 'A primitive dipnoan fish from the Lower Devonian of Germany'. *Proc. R. Soc. Lond.*, (B) **140**, 403–21.

Miles, R. S. (1965) 'Some features in the cranial morphology of acanthodians and the relationships of the Acanthodii'. *Acta zool. Stockh.*, **46**, 233–55.

Miles, R. S. (1968) 'Jaw articulation and suspension in *Acanthodes* and their significance'. *Nobel Symposium*, **4**, 109–27.

Olson, E. C. (1951) 'Fauna of Upper Vale and Choza. 3. Lung fish of the Vale 4. The skull of *Gnathorhiza dikeloda* Olson'. *Fieldiana, Geol.*, **10**, 104–24.

Parsons, T. S. and Williams, E. E. (1963) 'The relationships of the modern Amphibia'. *Q. Rev. Biol.*, **38**, 26–53.

Romer, A. S. and Olson, E. C. (1954) 'Aestivation in a Permian lungfish'. *Breviora*, **30**, 1–8.

Romer, A. S. and Smith, H. J. (1934) 'American Carboniferous dipnoans'. *J. Geol.*, **42**, 700–19.

Säve-Söderbergh, G. (1937) 'On *Rhynchodipterus elginensis*, n.g., n.sp., representing a new group of dipnoan-like Choanata from the Upper Devonian of East Greenland and Scotland'. *Ark. Zool.*, **29**B, 1–8.

Säve-Söderbergh, G. (1952) 'On the skull of *Chirodipterus wildungensis* Gross, an Upper Devonian dipnoan from Wildungen'. *K. svenska VetenskAkad. Handl.*, (3) **4**, 1–28.

Schaeffer, B. (1952) 'Rates of evolution in the coelacanth and dipnoan fishes'. *Evolution*, (1952) 101–11.

Schultze, H. P. (1969) '*Griphognathus* Gross, ein langschnauziger Dipnoer aus dem Oberdevon von Bergisch-Gladbach (Rheinisches Schiefergebirge) und von Lettland'. *Geol., Palaeont., Marburg*, **3**, 21–79.

Schultze, H. P. (1970) 'Die Histologie der Wirbelkörper der Dipnoer'. *N. Jb. Geol. Paläont. Abh.*, **135**, 311–36.

Stromer, E. (1938) 'Der Wüstenfisch *Ceratodus* Ag. 1838 und seine meso-und känozoischen Verwandten'. *N. Jb. Min. Geol. Paläont.*, **80**B, 248–63.

Szarski, H. (1962) 'The origin of the Amphibia'. *Q. Rev. Biol.*, **37**, 189–241.

Thomson, K. S. (1964) 'The ancestry of the tetrapods'. *Sci. Progr.*, **52**, 451–59.

Thomson, K. S. (1965*a*) 'On the relationships of certain Carboniferous Dipnoi; with descriptions of four new forms'. *Proc. R. Soc. Edinb.*, **69**B, 221–45.

Thomson, K. S. (1965*b*) 'The nasal apparatus in Dipnoi, with special reference to *Protopterus*'. *Proc. zool. Soc. Lond.*, **145**, 207–238.

Thomson, K. S. (1967) 'A new genus and species of marine dipnoan fish from the Upper Devonian of Canada'. *Postilla*, **106**, 1–6.

Vaughn, P. P. (1964) 'Evidence of aestivating lungfish from the Sangre de Cristo Formation, Lower Permian of northern New Mexico'. *Sci. Contrib. Los Ang. Co. Mus.*, **80**, 1–8.

Watson, D. M. S. and Gill, E. S. (1923) 'The structure of certain Palaeozoic Dipnoi'. *J. Linn. Soc. (Zool.)*, **25**, 163–216.

Weitzel, K. (1926) '*Conchopoma gadiforme* Kner, ein Lungenfisch aus dem Rotliegenden'. *Abh. Senck. Naturf. Ges.*, **40**, 159–78.

White, E. I. (1962) 'A dipnoan from the Assise de Mazy of Hingeon'. *Bull. Inst. roy. Sci. nat. Belgique.*, **38**, 1–8.

White, E. I. (1966) 'A little on lung-fishes'. *Proc. Linn. Soc. Lond.*, **177**, 1–10.

CHAPTER EIGHT

Subclass Placodermi.

8.1. CLASSIFICATION

Order 1, Arthrodira
  Suborder 1, Dolichothoraci
    e.g. *Actinolepis*, L.–M. Dev; *Arctolepis*, L. Dev; *Groenlandaspis*, U.
    e.g. Dev; *Coccosteus*, M. Dev; *Dunkleosteus*, U. Dev; *Euleptaspis*,
    L. Dev.
  Suborder 2, Brachythoraci
    e.g. *Belosteus, Brachydeirus, Brachyosteus*, U. Dev; *Buchanosteus*, L.
    Dev; *Coccosteus*, M. Dev; *Dunkleosteus*, U. Dev; *Euleptaspis*,
    L.–M. Dev; *Gemuendenaspis*, L. Dev; *Gorgonichthys, Hadrosteus,
    Heintzichthys*, U. Dev; *Heterostius*, M. Dev; *Holonema*, M.–U.
    Dev; *Homostius*, M. Dev; *Leiosteus, Leptosteus*, U. Dev; *Mylos-
    toma, Oxyosteus, Pachyosteus, Pholidosteus*, U. Dev; *Rhachiosteus*,
    M. or U. Dev; *Rhinosteus, Synauchenia, Tapinosteus, Titanichthys,
    Trematosteus*, U. Dev.
Order 2, Ptyctodontida
    e.g. *Ctenurella*, U. Dev; *Palaeomylus, Ptyctodus*, M.–U. Dev; *Rham-
    phodopsis*, M. Dev; *Rhynchodus*, M.–U. Dev.
Order 3, Phyllolepidida
    e.g. *Phyllolepis*, U. Dev; ?'*Wuttagoonaspis*', M. Dev.
Order 4, Petalichthyida
    e.g. *Lunaspis*, L. Dev; *Macropetalichthys*, M. Dev.
Order 5, Rhenanida
  Suborder 1, Palaeacanthaspidoidei
    e.g. *Holopetalichthys* (= *Radotina*), *Kosoraspis, Palaeacanthaspis*, L.
    Dev.
  Suborder 2, Gemuendinoidei
    e.g. *Asterosteus*, M. Dev; *Gemuendina*, L. Dev; *Jagorina*, U. Dev.
Order 6, Antiarchi
    e.g. *Asterolepis*, M. Dev; *Bothriolepis*, U. Dev; *Byssacanthus*, M.–U.
    Dev; *Gerdalepis, Grossaspis, Pterichthyodes*, M. Dev; *Remigolepis*,
    U. Dev or L. Carb.

Incertae sedis Stensioellidae

e.g. *Nessariostoma, Paraplesiobatis, Pseudopetalichthys, Stensioella,*
L. Dev.

L., Lower; M., Middle; U., Upper; Dev, Devonian; Carb, Carboniferous.

8.2. PLACODERM CHARACTERISTICS

Among Recent fishes it is clear that the elasmobranchs and holocephalans are closely related groups, and are correctly classified together as chondrichthyans. Chondrichthyans are typified chiefly by their internal skeleton of cartilage, which never ossifies although it may become encrusted with prismatic calcifications, and their outer skeleton of placoid denticles, which becomes modified into teeth on the margins of the jaws. Although placoderms do not share these characteristics, they seem nevertheless to be more closely related to chondrichthyans than to any other group. Consequently the category Elasmobranchiomorphi has been erected to bring these fishes together in the system. Some of the evidence for this relationship is discussed in Chapter 10 §11.

Placoderms are a much diversified group of *bony fishes*. They flourished in the Devonian and are almost entirely restricted to this period. A few fragmentary remains have been described from the Upper Silurian and Lower Carboniferous (Miles, 1967c; Mark-Kurik, 1969). Typically, placoderms are dorsoventrally compressed, although there are rare exceptions. They always have a head-shield movably articulated with a trunk-shield covering the anterior part of the body (Fig. 8.1.), both of which are formed of a number of bony plates containing bone cells. Posterior to the trunk-shield the body tapers, and in most species the tail is heterocercal. The posterior region of the body is usually found without any dermal covering, but in some placoderms a few thick, contiguous scales have been described (Traquair, 1894;

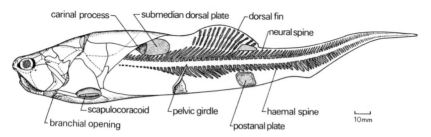

Fig. 8.1. *Coccosteus cuspidatus*. Restoration in lateral view. (After Miles and Westoll.)

Forster-Cooper, 1934; Gross, 1961; Miles, 1969), and in others a vestigial squamation of small rhomboidal scales is preserved (Miles and Westoll, 1968).

The plate armour is normally constructed in three layers (Fig. 8.2); a basal layer of laminar bone; a middle layer of trabecular bone; a superficial layer of laminar bone, with in more primitive forms a dentinal tissue with enclosed cell spaces (semidentine) (Heintz, 1932b; Gross, 1935, 1957; Bystrow, 1957; Ørvig, 1967). The superficial layer may bear an ornament of tubercles or ridges, and it carries the laterosensory lines in grooves. The armour was formed early in the life of the individuals. The growth processes of the armour included the marginal addition of bone to the middle and basal layers, and the successive apposition of new superficial layers.

Because of the diversity that exists within the subclass, the individual orders can most conveniently be described separately. The arthrodires are the largest order, containing more than 60% of all known placoderm genera, including some of the earliest and most primitive members.

8.3. ORDER 1, ARTHRODIRA

The arthrodires (Stensiö, 1959, 1963a, 1969a, b; Denison, 1958; Miles and Westoll, 1968; Miles 1969) are characterized by having a full complement of dermal bones in the head and primitively in the trunk-shield as well. They

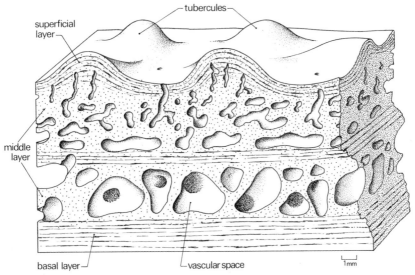

Fig. 8.2. *Bothriolepis canadensis*. Diagram to show structure of exoskeleton. (After Goodrich.)

163

are first found in the early Lower Devonian and continue to the Upper Devonian or Lower Carboniferous. They vary in total length from less than 100 mm to over two metres.

8.3.1. Structure

The head-shield is composed of a number of dermal bones in a constant pattern (Fig. 8.3). Dorsally there is a median nuchal posteriorly, with paired paranuchals lateral to it, and anteriorly paired median centrals with paired marginals, postorbitals, and preorbitals laterally to them. The latter may meet in front of the centrals, but are commonly separated for all or most of their length by the median pineal and rostral plates. Paired postmarginals lie at the lateral angles of the skull-roof. The cheek unit is formed beneath the orbit from a large suborbital and behind this a postsuborbital and submarginal. The head-shield is completed on the anterior face of the snout by a pair of postnasals associated with the incurrent nostrils, and ventrally there is sometimes a median internasal between the excurrent nostrils (Fig. 8.4). A parasphenoid lies behind the internasal on the floor of the neurocranium, and may be perforated by a pair of buccohypophysial foramina. In some families small extrascapular plates lie in the dorsal nuchal gap between the head- and trunk-shield (Fig. 8.3).

The orbits, surrounded by a ring of four dermal sclerotic plates, are laterally placed and far forward. The nostrils are small and close to the middle line. The neurocranium (Stensiö, 1963a, b, 1969a; White, 1952; Westoll and Miles, 1963) may be lined by perichondral bone, which forms a continuous sheet from the occipital to the ethmoid region in primitive forms such as the Lower Devonian 'Kujdanowiaspis'; but in others like the Upper Devonian Pholidosteus, Tapinosteus and Leiosteus, is divided into several ossifications separated by cartilage.

The cavities and canals of the neurocranium are almost completely lined with perichondral bone in 'Kujdanowiaspis' and are known in great detail from Stensiö's work with serial grindings (1963a, b; Fig. 8.5). The neurocranium is platybasic and comprises a very long, robust postethmo-occipital bone with thick lateral walls. The ethmoid region was very short, with the nasal capsules separate and situated over an anterior subnasal shelf. The orbits are floored by long suborbital shelves, and bounded posteriorly by short anterior postorbital processes. The orbits are divided into ocular and postocular divisions by the supraorbital processes. Further back there are large posterior postorbital processes and supravagal processes, which support the hind part of the skull-roof, and posterior glenoid processes which articulate with the anterior face of the vertebral column to form the cranio-

164

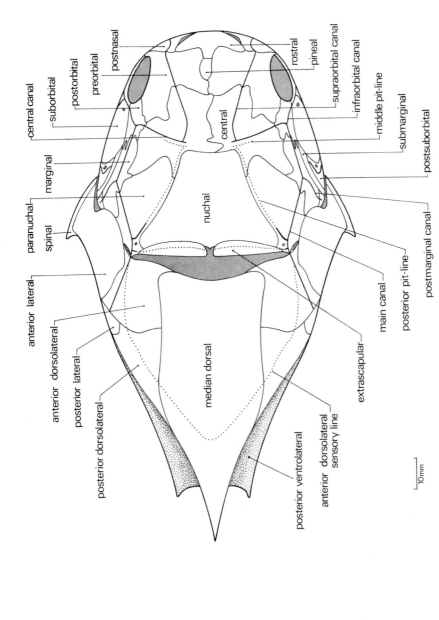

Fig. 8.3. *Coccosteus cuspidatus*. Restoration of head and trunk shields in dorsal view. (After Miles and Westoll.)

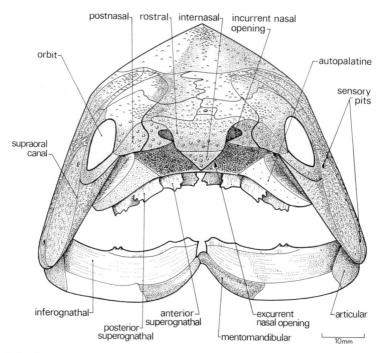

Fig. 8.4. *Coccosteus cuspidatus*. Restoration of skull in anterior view. (After Miles and Westoll.)

vertebral neck joint. The notochord persisted in the floor of the neuro-cranium, but ended well short of the hypophysial region.

The brain and cranial nerves have been interpreted by comparison with elasmobranchs. The hypophysis was situated in an anterior position, as it is in the embryos of living fishes, and opened on to the roof of the mouth through the buccohypophysial foramen. The pineal organ was double, probably representing the parapineal and pineal organs of lampreys. The proportions of the different brain regions are clear from the endocast. Notably there was a long medulla oblongata, which was probably only slightly differentiated from the spinal cord. The cranial nerves had the typical gnathostome disposition, with the hyomandibular branch of the facial nerve (VII) passing out through the anterior postorbital process. Several spino-occipital nerves pierced the lateral wall of the occipital region, posterior to the vagus (X) canal. Posterior and anterior eye muscle canals have been described in the orbit, but their function is in doubt. The eye may have been supported on an eyestalk. There are three semicircular canals, each with an ampullary swelling. The external semicircular canal loops dorsally to the posterior semicircular canal, and with the anterior canal they open directly into the utriculus. Thus, as in elasmobranchs, there is no crus commune (sinus utriculi superior) connecting the two vertical canals. No statoliths have been found, but there is evidence of elasmobranch-like statoconia in the sacculus. The endolymphatic duct passes upwards from the sacculus to open to the outside on the paranuchal plate.

The palatoquadrate is usually surrounded by two perichondral ossifications, an anterior autopalatine articulating with the neurocranium, and a posterior quadrate fused with the inner surface of the postsuborbital (Figs.

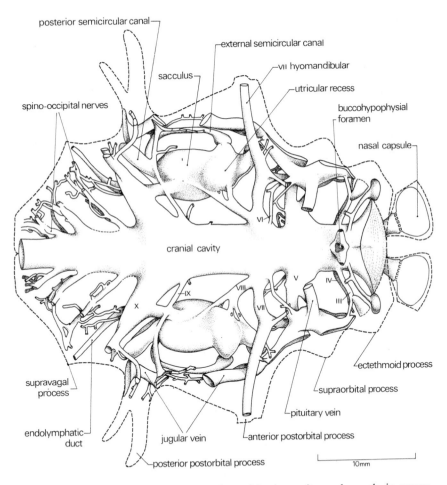

Fig. 8.5. *Kujdanowiaspis* sp. Restoration of brain cavity and canals in neurocranium, in ventral view. Canals labelled according to the structure they housed without further explanation. (After Stensiö.)

167

8.4, 8.9B). The quadrate bears a condyle for the articulation of the lower jaw. There are two pairs of upper tooth-plates, the anterior and posterior superognathals. The former are supported by the ventral surface of the neurocranium, just behind the nasal capsules, and the latter by the auto-palatines. The left and right autopalatines are separate anteriorly, there being no palatoquadrate symphysis.

The lower jaw includes a large tooth-plate, the inferognathal, closely associated with the meckelian cartilage, which also ossifies in two regions, an anterior mentomandibular and a posterior articular (Fig. 8.4). The infero-gnathal bites inside the superognathals, unless the gnathals are modified for crushing, in which case they oppose each other with broad faces. The gnathals are comparable in histology with the dermal bones of the armour, and their 'teeth' are simply cusps on the bone surface which become worn away during life. Teeth comparable with those of chondrichthyans or tele-ostomes are not found in placoderms.

The fusion of the quadrate with the dermal skeleton of the cheek means that the jaw suspension was autostylic (Miles, 1969; Stensiö, 1969a). The hyomandibula is not satisfactorily known, but it did not have the same suspensory functions as in advanced elasmobranchs and actinopterygians. The gill skeleton is also largely unknown (Stensiö, 1963a, 1969a), but was situated in an extensive gill-chamber under the back of the neurocranium, covered by the posterior plates of the cheek. A single, low branchial opening was present between the head- and trunk-shield at each side.

The trunk-shield is formed from a definite number of bones which, how-ever, may be reduced in number in some families. Normally (Fig. 8.3) there are a median dorsal, paired anterior and posterior dorsolaterals, paired anterior and posterior laterals, paired spinals; and ventrally (Fig. 8.6) there are paired interolaterals, paired anterior and posterior ventrolaterals, and an anterior and posterior median ventral. Paired anteroventrals are also found in some early forms (Denison, 1958). The anterior lateral and intero-lateral plates have strongly ornamented internal laminae which combine to form the hind wall of the gill-chamber. The median dorsal has a median ventral keel in advanced forms (Figs. 8.1, 8.7, 8.8B), which may be enlarged in to a posterior carinal process.

A fenestra behind the spinal is for the articulation of the pectoral fin with the scapulocoracoid, which lies within the shield. The scapulocoracoid may be perichondrally ossified (Stensiö, 1944, 1959; White, 1952). It has a mesial coracoid process and a lateral process filling the cavity of the spinal plate (Fig. 8.6). The scapulocoracoid is a low structure without a scapular blade. There is a lateral, horizontal crest for the articulation of the fin skeleton, and muscle attachment areas for the dorsal and ventral fin muscles. The scapulo-coracoid is also pierced by perichondrally lined canals for the pectoral

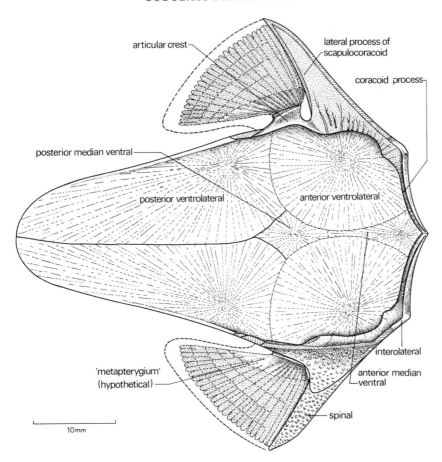

Fig. 8.6. *Pholidosteus* sp. Restoration of ventral plates of trunk-shield in dorsal view, with endoskeletal shoulder-girdle and pectoral fin skeleton. (After Stensiö.)

nerves and blood vessels. Basically the fin seems to have been innervated by diazonal, spinal nerves, each accompanied by a segmental artery and vein. However, the formation of nerve and vessel plexuses tended to obscure this simple arrangement. A series of short skeletal elements in the fin have been interpreted as basals, and there is a tendency for the posterior elements to fuse into a basipterygium. However, it is possible that the articular crest of the scapulocoracoid is homologous with the basal series of primitive elasmobranchs, situated within the body wall (Chapter 9 §4). If this is so, the 'basals' of arthrodires should be reinterpreted as radials (Miles and Westoll, 1968).

Directly behind the trunk-shield there is a pelvic fin, supported by a few radials and a girdle (Fig. 8.1) in two separate pieces, which touch ventrally. Each half of the girdle has a lateral articular crest and is pierced by diazonal nerve foramina. There is a dorsal fin supported by two rows of skeletal elements, the most posterior members of the basal row fusing into a triangular plate. A large ventral plate is present in the anal region, though there is no evidence that it supported an anal fin, and a similar plate articulated with the keel of the median dorsal plate. The notochord is unconstricted and extends to the tip of the heterocercal tail. The vertebrae comprise separate neural and haemal arches with long spines. Anteriorly, within the trunk-shield, these elements from several segments are contiguous around the notochord to form a synarcual element, which articulated with the glenoid processes of the neurocranium. There are no ribs.

The lateral-line sensory canal system consists of open grooves, which are of two kinds, large and small grooves, corresponding to the canals and pit-lines.

The main canal of the body passes over the posterior and anterior dorso-laterals on to the paranuchals, the marginals, and the postorbitals and thence as the infraorbital canal beneath the eye on to the suborbital, where it gives off a posterior supraoral branch (Fig. 8.3). From the main canal in the paranuchal an occipital commissure passes mesially across the extra-scapulars or nuchal, and more anteriorly the posterior pit-line passes mesially on to the centrals, where it ends behind the middle pit-line. A branch from the post-orbital, the central line, may or may not meet the supraorbital canal in the centrals. The supraorbital canal joins the infra-orbital in front of the eye. A ventrally directed branch in the marginals is the postmarginal (or preopercular) canal; and a branch in the postsuborbital is the postsuborbital canal. On the venter a ventral canal crosses in the anterior ventrolaterals and anterior median ventral, and there may be a second line in the interolaterals. Pits and depressions, which housed cutaneous sense organs similar to the ampullae of elasmobranchs, are sometimes found associated with the sensory line on the interolaterals, and on the cheek plates and margins of the skull-roof (Ørvig, 1960; Miles, 1965, 1966a).

8.3.2. Diversity and tendencies in evolution

It is usual to divide arthrodires into two large subdivisions, the primitive dolichothoracids and the advanced brachythoracids. These two groups grade into each other in many respects, so that the differences between them are not clear-cut. There is some doubt, therefore, as to whether this is a natural classification of arthrodires (Denison, 1958; Westoll, 1958; Miles, 1969). Generally speaking, dolichothoracids have a long trunk-shield with long spinal plates and small pectoral fenestrae; a head-shield with small, anterior orbits, small preorbital plates, the extrascapular plates not differentiated from the nuchal; and small inferognathals restricted to the anterior part of the lower jaw rami. Brachythoracids have a reduced trunkshield with enlarged pectoral fenestrae; the preorbitals are enlarged so that they come to form the anterodorsal margins of the orbital openings, the extrascapulars exist as separate elements or are completely reduced, and the nuchal plate is enlarged posteriorly; the inferognathals are enlarged and each differentiated into an anterior biting division and a posterior blade which occupies the posterior part of the jaw and gave insertion to the adductor mandibulae muscles.

The significance of these differences becomes apparent if arthrodires are described in four successive levels of organization (Fig. 8.7), each of which can be defined by characters relating to broad adaptations in the locomotor and feeding mechanisms. The lowest two levels embrace the dolichothoracids, the highest two the brachythoracids. It is necessary to describe arthrodire evolution in this way because the individual lines of descent are largely unknown.

Trends of change in the trunk-shield include the enlargement of the pectoral fenestra, scapulocoracoid and base of the pectoral fin, the reduction of the posterior extent of the armour on the flank, and the reduction in length of the spinal plate. These changes signify an increased efficiency in swimming and control in the water, as progressively more of the body

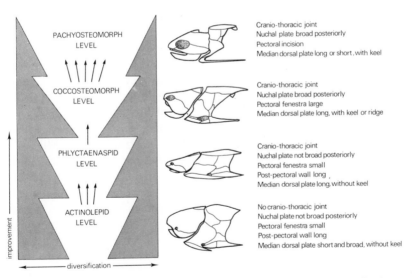

Fig. 8.7. Successive levels of organization in arthrodires. (After Miles.)

171

muscles became free for use in swimming and large flexibly-mobile pectoral fins were developed as gliding planes and props. Trends of change in the skull-roof include the enlargement of the nuchal gap and the development of powerful muscles to raise and lower the head, with an extensive insertion on the posterodorsal face of the neurocranium and posterior margin of the skull-roof. Correlated with these changes there is often an increase in the size of the keel and carinal process of the median dorsal plate. These changes are associated with the widening of the gape, and the development of specialized tooth-plates for varied diets. They are closely concerned with the development of the neck-joints.

In the most primitive arthrodires, at the actinolepid level, the anterior dorsolateral bears a flange over which the hind margin of the paranuchal could slide as the head was raised and lowered. Such movements of the head were very limited. At more advanced levels this simple sliding mechanism is modified into the cranio-thoracic hinge joint. The cranio-thoracic neck joint is co-axial with the endoskeletal cranio-vertebral joint, and these joints progressively allow more up-and-down movement of the head as the fishes pass up through the phlyctaenaspid, coccosteomorph and pachyosteomorph levels. The neck joints are important in feeding because they enable the head to be tilted back as the mandibles are dropped, so that the mouth can be widely opened (Miles, 1967b, 1969). Clearly this would be impossible if the plate armour was a continuous unit. The up-and-down movement of the head may have had subsidiary functions in pumping water through the gill chambers, and in the control of pitching (Westoll, 1945; White, 1952).

Arthrodires show little differentiation at the lower levels of organization, but as different lines of brachythoracids passed through the coccosteomorph and attained the pachyosteomorph level in the late Middle and early Upper Devonian, the group underwent a considerable secondary adaptive radiation. Brachythoracids are classified in at least seventeen distinct families (e.g. Obruchev, 1967; Miles, 1969, Stensiö, 1969b), and it is only possible to mention some of the more interesting forms here.

Primitive, Lower Devonian brachythoracids such as *Euleptaspis* and *Gemuendenaspis* have a long, dolichothoracid-like trunk-shield (Miles, 1962, 1969), and others like *Buchanosteus* and *Holonema* retain prominent dolichothoracid features in the neurocranium and skull-roof (White, 1952; Stensiö, 1963a, 1969a, b). The coccosteids (*Coccosteus*) and pholidosteids (*Pholidosteus*, *Tapinosteus*) are relatively unspecialized Middle and early Upper Devonian arthrodires, and can be regarded as the central members of the order (Stensiö, 1963a; Miles and Westoll, 1963, 1968).

At the pachyosteomorph level the reduction of the flank plates from behind has continued until the pectoral fenestra had been modified into a posteriorly open pectoral incision. *Rhachiosteus* is one of the least modified genera, although it has lost the posterior series of plates in the trunk-shield (Miles, 1966*a*). The homosteids and heterosteids are large, depressed Middle Devonian forms. In *Homostius* (Heintz, 1934; Mark, 1963) the head-shield has an exceptionally long occipital region, and the postorbital and preorbital plates characteristically meet under the orbit (Fig. 8.8A). The lower jaw is unusual, with the inferognathal having a smooth, toothless upper surface. The trunk-shield has its ventral part far forward and apparently lacks a posterior median ventral and posterior ventrolaterals, and has greatly reduced spinals. *Heterostius* (Fig. 8.8B) has an even more reduced trunk-shield, with a single large median plate on the venter, but its skull-roof is of more normal proportions (Heintz, 1930; Ørvig, 1969).

The early Upper Devonian fauna of Wildungen in Germany includes many highly specialized brachythoracids (Gross, 1932; Stensiö, 1959, 1963*a*; Miles, 1969). These forms usually have very large orbits and the cheek plates

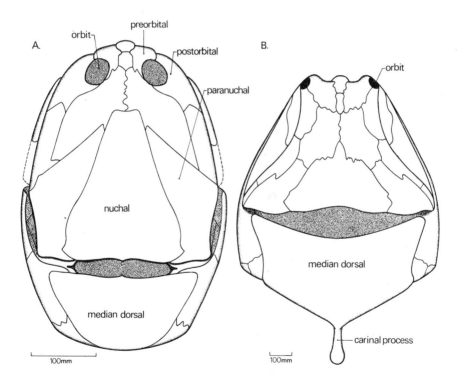

Fig. 8.8. Restorations of head and trunk shields in dorsal view. (After Miles.); A. *Homostius sulcatus*; B. *Heterostius ingens*.

173

tend to become firmly interlocked with the plates of the roof. The spinal has disappeared in almost all members. In the trematosteids (*Belosteus, Trematosteus, Brachyosteus*) and pachyosteids (*Leiosteus, Rhinosteus, Pachyosteus*), the biting division of the inferognathal and the posterior superognathal have greatly elongated shearing edges, and the back of the head-shield is markedly embayed to accommodate the powerful levator muscles that inserted on the back of the skull (Fig. 8.9A–C). The very large gape permitted the long gnathals to be used to major effect. The cheek was deepened in genera such as *Belosteus* and *Brachyosteus* (Fig. 8.9A, B), and the jaw articulation was dropped to a low position to accommodate long, powerful adductor mandibulae muscles. In *Brachyosteus* there is a further modifica-

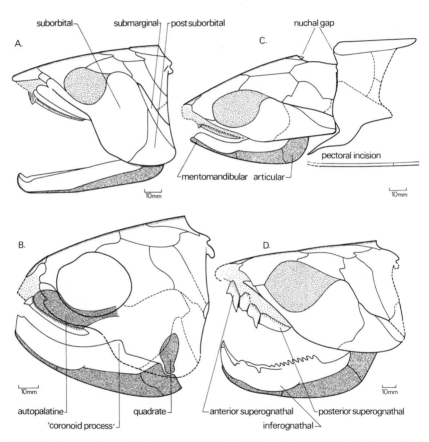

Fig. 8.9. Restorations of head-shields in lateral view. Trunk-shield also shown in C. (After Miles.); A. *Belosteus major*; B. *Brachyosteus dietrichi*; C. *Leiosteus inflatus*; D. *Hadrosteus rapax*.

174

tion, with the lower jaw transformed into a bent lever by the development of a 'coronoid process'. This parallels changes found in actinopterygians and coelacanths. Most of the trematosteids and pachyosteids were predators with a fast jaw action employing the elongated edges of the posterior supero- and inferognathals. *Pachyosteus* has an unusual 'dentition' of numerous small cusps on the gnathals, which presumably acted as friction pads to hold the prey before it was swallowed.

The hadrosteids include only *Hadrosteus* (Fig. 8.9D), a predator with an enormous gape and large anterior and posterior superognathals, each with a single pick-like cusp, and a long inferognathal with stout anteriorly curving cusps and a long shearing edge.

A different adaptive type is found in two unrelated Wildungen families, the leptosteids (Fig. 8.10A) and brachydeirids (Fig. 8.10B, C) (Gross, 1932, 1933; Stensiö, 1963a, 1969a, b), with the latter being the most highly modified forms. These are laterally compressed, deep-bodied, surface-water fishes, showing a reversal of the usual brachythoracid trends of change in the head (Miles, 1967b, 1969). In brachydeirids the nuchal gap becomes reduced, and there is a progressive reduction of the up-and-down movement of the head on the trunk, and simplification of the cranio-thoracic neck joint. With these changes are associated modifications in the gnathals and feeding mechanism. In *Brachydeirus* and *Oxyosteus* the nuchal gap is already small, and the gnathals are short, anteriorly situated crushing plates. As a consequence of the forward position of the gnathals the snout tends to be long, and in *Oxyosteus rostratus* (Fig. 8.10B) it is drawn out into a long rostrum. The most specialized brachydeirid is *Synauchenia* (Fig. 8.10C). In this genus the head- and trunk-shield have fused into a single rigid carapace. This is the only placoderm in which this change has taken place, and it is significant that it is found in a family showing special modifications of the feeding mechanism, and one adapted for a nektonic mode of life.

The last major radiation of pachyosteomorph arthrodires is found in the late Upper Devonian Cleveland shales of Ohio. The fauna (Fig. 8.11) includes giants such as *Dunkleosteus*, *Heintzichthys* and *Titanichthys*, which reached a length of over two metres (Heintz, 1932a; Dunkle and Bungart, 1942, 1943, 1946). *Heintzichthys* (Fig. 8.11B) is adaptively similar to some of the Widungen genera, with a long slender inferognathal, greatly elongated posterior superognathal and large nuchal gap. It has, however, the skull-roof and cheek plates as discrete units. *Dunkleosteus* (Fig. 8.11A) has small eyes and a contrasting jaw mechanism with short powerful gnathals. The anterior superognathal and inferognathal have large anterior picks. Probably *Dunkleosteus* had a slow, powerful bite, with great force concentrated on the picks (Miles, 1967b, 1969). *Dunkleosteus* is also of interest because it retains a small spinal plate (Heintz, 1932a, 1968), and shows many signs

175

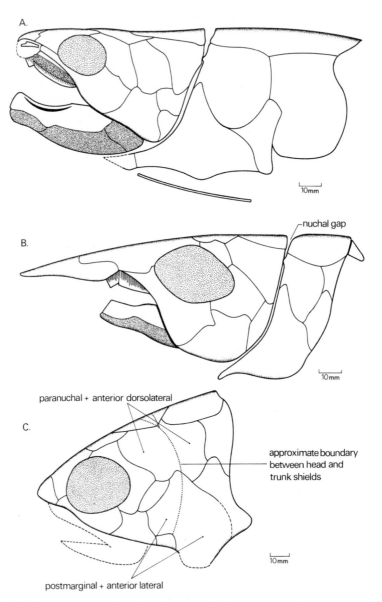

Fig. 8.10. Restorations of head and trunk shields in lateral view. (After Miles.);
A. *Leptosteus bickensis*; B. *Oxyosteus rostratus*; C. *Synauchenia coalescens*.

176

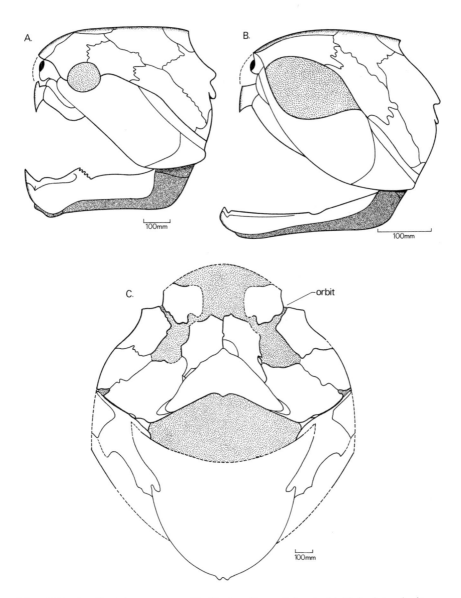

Fig. 8.11. A. *Dunkleosteus terrelli*. Restoration of head-shield in lateral view; B. *Heintzichthys gouldi*. Restoration of head-shield in lateral view; C. *Titanichthys termieri*. Restoration of head and trunk shields in dorsal view. (After Miles.)

177

of close relationship with the Middle Devonian coccosteids. *Gorgonichthys* has a similar inferognathal to *Dunkleosteus* but with a larger pick, and it reaches 0.5 m in length. *Mylostoma* has a crushing dentition with the upper gnathals modified into broad plates and the inferognathal is downwardly arched forwards to accommodate lengthened adductor muscles (Dunkle and Bungart, 1943; Miles, 1969). Mention may also be made of *Titanichthys* (Fig. 8.11C), which was a strongly depressed genus with a broad armour, anterior eyes and a subterminal mouth. The inferognathal is a long, slender bone with a blunt biting region showing no signs of wear. Probably *Titanichthys* had no superognathals, and as the anterior region of the head-shield is unossified feeding may have involved the use of large fleshy lips (Dunkle and Bungart, 1942; Lehman, 1956, 1962).

8.4. ORDER 2, PTYCTODONTIDA

Ptyctodontids (Watson, 1938; Ørvig, 1960, 1962; Westoll, 1962; Miles, 1967*a*; Stensiö, 1969*a*) are a peculiar group of placoderms in which the dermal armour of both the head- and trunk-shield is greatly reduced (Figs. 8.12, 8.13). They are mainly found in the Middle and early Upper Devonian, although detached tooth-plates of Carboniferous age have been reported (Miles 1967*c*). Ptyctodontids are small fishes and probably only rarely exceeded 200 mm in length. They show some remarkable resemblances to living holocephalans (see Relationships of elasmobranchiomorphs, Chapter 10; §11).

Rhamphodopsis and *Ctenurella*, from the Middle and Upper Devonian respectively, are the best known genera. The number of plates in the head-shield is reduced, with the cheek unit represented only by a large opercular (submarginal) plate, and the snout is unarmoured. The orbital openings are large. The nuchal is not always present. The sensory lines are enclosed in

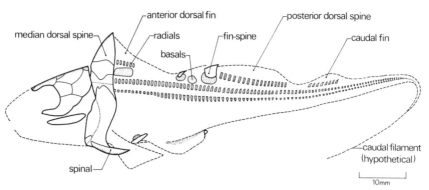

Fig. 8.12. *Rhamphodopsis threiplandi*. Restoration in lateral view. (After Miles.)

178

canals deep in the plates, which open to the outside through widely-spaced pores. A characteristic feature is the X-anastomosis of the pair of continuous supraorbital-posterior 'pit-line' canals on the median postpineal plate between the centrals. This shows some similarity to the arrangement in petalichthyids. A cranio-thoracic joint is present, but it is not as well differentiated as in arthrodires, and appears to be variable in its structure (Miles, 1967a).

The palatoquadrate is short, high and forwardly situated (Fig. 8.13), as in holocephalans. It is perichondrally ossified in separate autopalatine, metapterygoid and quadrate regions, and was firmly attached to the neurocranium under the orbit, at three areas on the inner face of the autopalatine. Thus there appears to be clear evidence in the skull that the hyomandibula was not suspensory, as in holocephalans (Chapter 10 §2). Rostral and labial cartilages, which have been compared with those of holocephalans (Ørvig, 1962), supported the fleshy snout and lips. The gill-chamber, situated under

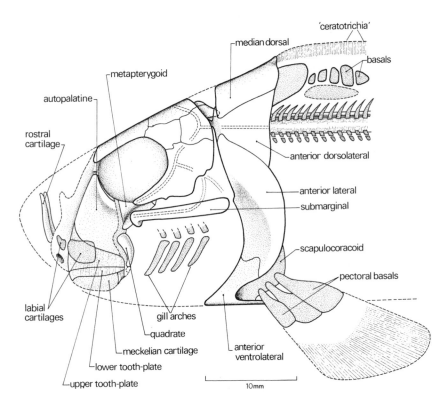

Fig. 8.13. *Ctenurella gladbachensis*. Restoration of head in lateral view. (After Ørvig.)

179

the back of the skull, is short and deep, and enclosed by a flexible gill-cover (Miles, 1967a).

The palatoquadrates carry a single pair of large upper tooth-plates, which were opposed by a smaller pair in the lower jaw. The tooth-plates are variously modified (Eastman, 1898; Hussakof and Bryant, 1918). They have a shearing edge in *Rhamphodopsis* and *Ctenurella*, a large central tritural area in *Ptyctodus* and separate tritural cusps in *Palaeomylus*. The tooth-plates of ptyctodontids are strengthened by an inwardly growing, hypermineralized columnar tissue ('secondary dentine', Gross, 1957, Ørvig, 1957, 1967), which is similar to that found in holocephalans and dipnoans. As the outer layer of bone or dentinal tissue on the surface of the tooth-plate becomes worn away, the hard columnar tissue is exposed, forming the tritural areas in *Ptyctodus* and *Palaeomylus*.

The trunk-shield is short, and in *Rhamphodopsis* (Fig. 8.12) has a stout dorsal spine and long spinals, all absent in *Ctenurella* (Fig. 8.13). The internal laminae of the anterior lateral and anterior ventrolateral plates, which form the hind wall of the gill chamber, are very large and strongly ornamented. There are no posterior lateral or posterior ventral plates, and therefore no armour on the flank behind the pectoral fin.

The vertebral column resembles that of arthrodires, with an unconstricted notochord and separate neural and haemal arches with long spines. A short, high synarcual is present under the median dorsal plate. There are two dorsal fins with an internal skeleton of basals and radials, and a small dorsal lobe in the caudal fin. The tail is long and tapering. The second dorsal fin has a small fin-spine. The pectoral fins are large and mobile, with a narrow base. They have three stout basals which articulated against a small scapulocoracoid (Stensiö, 1959).

The large pelvic fins are remarkable for their sexual dimorphism associated with internal fertilization, as in chondrichthyans (Chapter 9 §2). In males (Fig. 8.14B), claspers bearing a laterally-toothed dermal plate project ventrally from the root of the fin. These claspers worked against a spiny plate on the ventral surface of the fin. In front of the pelvic fins are holocephalan-like prepelvic claspers (tenacula), which bear spines in *Ctenurella*. In females (Fig. 8.14A) the fins are supported by large, immobile endoskeletal plates, and in *Rhamphodopsis* are clothed by numerous, overlapping scales. The prepelvic claspers of males are represented by flat plates in the skin in females.

8.5. ORDER 3, PHYLLOLEPIDIDA

Phyllolepis (Stensiö, 1934a, 1936, 1939) is a very specialized Upper Devonian placoderm, with a characteristic ornamentation of concentric and transverse

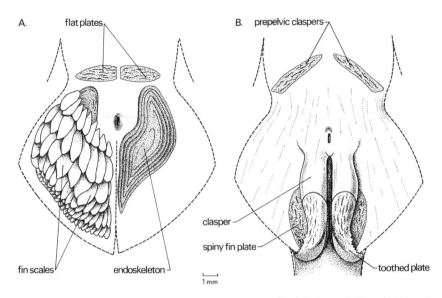

A. flat plates

B. prepelvic claspers

clasper

spiny fin plate

fin scales endoskeleton

toothed plate

1 mm

Fig. 8.14. *Rhamphodopsis threiplandi*. Restorations of pelvic fins of a female (A) and a male (B) in ventral view. (After Miles.)

ridges. It is very much dorsoventrally flattened (Fig. 8.15). The plates of the trunk-shield are greatly reduced in number; there is a large median dorsal, but only a single dorsolateral plate and no median ventral. The spinals are broad, well-developed and denticulated along their outer edge. The pectoral fins were situated behind the flank plates. In the head a median plate, probably the nuchal, has become enormously enlarged at the expense of the other dermal bones which are all rather small. The pattern of plates is not easy to compare with that of arthrodires. Shallow grooves which converge on the centre of the large median plate, mark the course of the sensory lines. The most anterior part of the skull appears to have been unossified.

'*Wuttagoonaspis*' (Ritchie, 1969) from the Middle Devonian of Australia may prove to be a primitive phyllolepid when better known, and to connect this group with early arthrodires.

8.6. ORDER 4, PETALICHTHYIDA

The petalichthyids (Stensiö, 1925, 1963*b*, 1969*a*; White, 1952; Ørvig, 1957; Gross, 1961) are an order of placoderms ranging from the Lower to the Upper Devonian which in many ways resemble the arthrodires. They seldom exceed 0.5 m in length, are dorsoventrally flattened, and have a head- and a trunk-shield, the latter with long spinal plates (Fig. 8.16). The orbits,

181

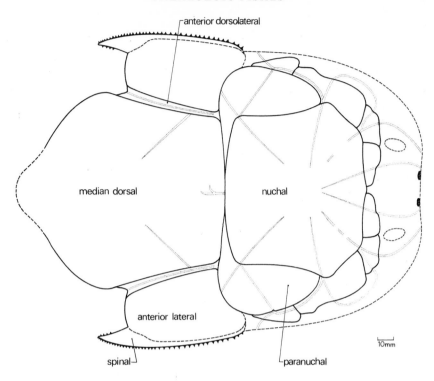

Fig. 8.15. *Phyllolepis* sp. Restoration of head and trunk shields in dorsal view. (After Stensiö.)

however, have a dorsal position and the cranio-thoracic joint is of peculiar structure. Further, the occipital region is greatly elongated, and this has had a marked effect on the dermal plate pattern and the structure of the neurocranium. There is a characteristic arrangement of the dermal plates, in which the sensory canals are deeply sunk. The body is only known in the Lower Devonian *Lunaspis* (Fig. 8.16). It was covered behind the trunk-shield with contiguous bony scales and tapered away posteriorly to a point, the tail apparently being diphycercal. Three large ridge scales, similar to those found in early arthrodires, stand in place of a dorsal fin.

The bones of the head-shield always consist on the dorsal surface of a long unpaired nuchal, and smaller median pineal and rostral plates, which may be combined into a single rostropineal. Laterally to these median plates are paired anterior and posterior paranuchals, centrals and preorbitals. Laterally to the centrals lies paired marginals. Beneath the orbit there is a postorbital, immediately behind which lies a large plate, probably the submarginal, which almost certainly served as an operculum covering the gill-chamber.

182

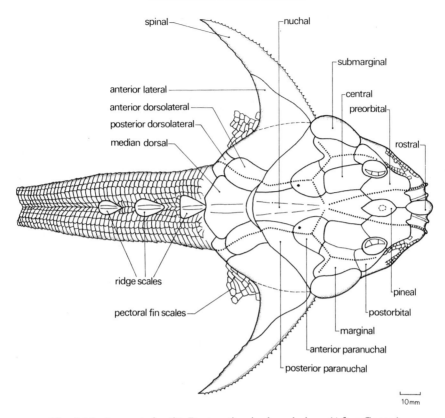

Fig. 8.16. *Lunaspis broilii*. Restoration in dorsal view. (After Gross.)

The rest of the cheek is represented in *Lunaspis* by a mosaic of scales around the front of the head-shield.

The neurocranium (Fig. 8.17), which is well known in the Middle Devonian *Macropetalichthys* (Stensiö, 1925, 1963*b*, 1969*a*), is platybasic with a characteristically long, narrow occipital region. The entire structure is ossified as a single piece, although it does not include the nasal capsules. As in early arthrodires, the lateral walls are very thick. The eyes are situated in the posterior part of the orbital cavity, just in front of the labyrinth cavity. At the anterior end of the neurocranium is a prominent ectethmoid process for the orbital articulation of the palatoquadrate. The anterior postorbital process is short and continuous with the posterior process. Behind these processes there is a very large supravagal process, and at the hind end of the brain-case there is a pair of dorsal craniospinal processes to support the skull-roof. On the floor of the neurocranium, the hypophysial fenestra is completely closed.

183

The trunk-shield is similar to that of arthrodires, both dorsally and ventrally, although in *Lunaspis* a small pair of additional plates may be present behind the posterior ventrolaterals. There are, however, no plates on the flank behind the base of the pectoral fin.

The main lateral-line canal of the body passes on to the trunk-shield across the posterior and anterior dorsolaterals as in arthrodires, whence it is continued into the posterior paranuchal plate of the head-shield to the anterior paranuchal, and is continued through the marginal into the post-orbital as the infraorbital canal (Fig. 8.16). From the anterior paranuchal a median branch, representing the posterior pit-line, meets one from the other side on the nuchal plate, to form a transverse commissure. A posterior branch from the marginal forms the postmarginal (or preopercular) canal. The two supraorbital canals which pass back over the preorbital plate on to the nuchal may as in *Marcropetalichthys* meet at a point on the transverse commissure or be separate as in *Lunaspis*, stopping short of the transverse commissure. The former condition is similar to that found in ptyctodontids.

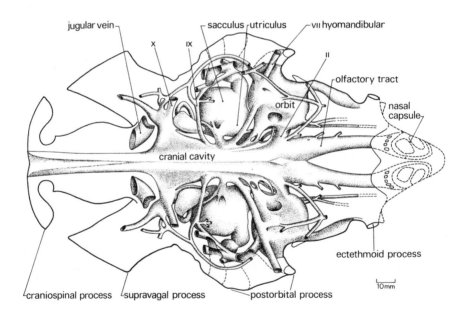

Fig. 8.17. *Macropetalichthys rapheidolabis*. Restoration of brain cavity and canals in neurocranium, in ventral view. Canals labelled according to the structures they housed without further explanation. (After Stensiö.)

184

8.7. ORDER 5, RHENANIDA

Included in the rhenanids are a few Devonian fishes, the majority of which are still poorly known. They are armoured with a head- and trunk-shield basically of placoderm type, although they differ from other groups in having·a mosaic of small bones between the outer surfaces of the large plates on the head-shield. They are small fishes, rarely exceeding 0.3 m in length, and show special adaptations for a benthic mode of life in the dorsal position of the nasal openings and subterminal mouth. Two suborders, the Palaea-canthaspidoidei and Gemuendinoidei, can be distinguished. The former are primitive forms, adaptively similar to early arthrodires, but they are still poorly known and there is not general agreement about their affinities. The latter are strongly depressed forms, which have a *superficial* resemblance to modern rays. This resemblance is so great that some writers have considered them to be closely related to elasmobranchs (Holmgren, 1942; Jarvik, 1964, 1968). Nevertheless, there are very good reasons for not doing so (see Relationships of elasmobranchiomorphs, Chapter 10 §11).

8.7.1. Suborder 1, Palaeacanthaspidoidei

These are mostly Lower Devonian placoderms (Stensiö, 1944, 1969*a*; Gross, 1958, 1959), with a more extensive trunk-shield than in gemuendinoids. The variable structure of the head-shield is of particular interest.

In *Holopetalichthys* the skull-roof can apparently occur in two main condi-tions in the same species (Fig. 8.18). Thus the major plates may appear to be separated by an extensive mosaic of scale-like plates, or they may be joined into a continuous shield, with the mosaic strongly reduced or absent. The arrangement of the major plates has been compared with that in petalich-thyids (Westoll, 1967). The orbits have a lateral position, outside the post-nasal, preorbital and postorbital plates. The nuchal is short, and may be preceded by a median postpineal plate on which the supraorbital sensory lines converge, as in ptyctodontids. The dorsal position of the nasal openings is associated with major changes in the snout, so that the rostral and pineal plates are interorbital in position, and in front of them is a large plate with no obvious counterpart in arthrodires, but possibly comparable with the premedian of antiarchs. On the cheek there is a large opercular-like sub-marginal.

Gross (1959) regarded the mosaic of scale-like plates as a hold-over from a primitive stage in the evolution of placoderms, before the plate-armour was established. Stensiö (1963*a*) believed it to be a secondary state resulting from the disintegration of the major plates. Westoll (1967) has attempted a more rigorous examination of the different conditions found in any one

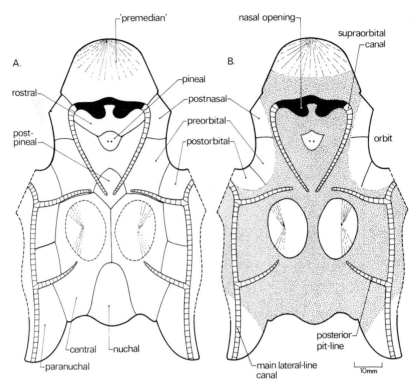

Fig. 8.18. *Holopetalichthys kosorensis*. Restorations of head-shield in dorsal view, with fully developed plates (A) and maximum area covered by mosaic of small scale-like plates (B). Areas of scale-like plates stippled. (After Westoll.)

species. He suggests that several successive processes of dermal skeleto-genesis may be inferred, including:

(1) 'the development of the large dermal bones';
(2) 'the development of separate thin tesserae, which may apparently be-come attached to underlying flanges of dermal bones';
(3) 'development of new generations of tubercles';
(4) 'probably a late development of the superficial layer, tending to obli-terate all sutures, at least in some individuals'.

There is no good evidence to show whether the mosaic of small plates is a primitive or secondary feature, but the trend of change in gemuendinoids supports the second interpretation. The secondary appearance of the mosaic over flanges of the main plates, if confirmed, is a striking parallel with changes in psammosteid heterostracans (Chapter 3 §3.2). The final stage of the skeletogenetic processes can only be compared with the changes observed

186

in amphiaspid heterostracans. Finally, as in agnathans, there is clear evidence here of a degree of morphogenetic independence between the superficial and deeper layer of the exoskeleton.

The neurocranium is preserved in *Kosoraspis* and *Holopetalichthys*, but as this structure is much better known in gemuendinoids, it will only be described in that group.

The trunk-shield is short and high with a reduced number of ventral plates (Fig. 8.19). In *Palaeacanthaspis* (Stensiö, 1944) the anterior and posterior median ventrals and the posterior ventrolaterals are absent. The

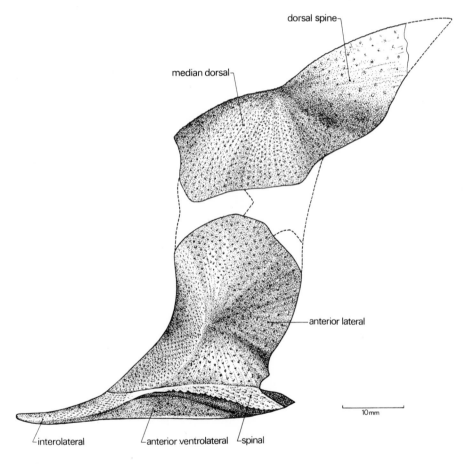

Fig. 8.19. *Palaeacanthaspis vasta*. Restoration of trunk-shield in lateral view. (After Stensiö.)

187

spinal is large, but has no long spine, and the median dorsal is drawn out into a large dorsal spine.

There is no sign of the cranio-thoracic joint, but the anterior region of the vertebral column is modified into a synarcual, which articulated with the glenoid processes of the neurocranium in a cranio-vertebral joint. The scapulocoracoid is perichondrally ossified, with a posteriorly facing articular area for a narrow-based pectoral fin, much as in primitive arthrodires. There is, however, no armour behind the fin, and therefore no pectoral fenestra.

The sensory canals lie in deep grooves in the surface of the plates, and have an arrangement closely resembling that of arthrodires. They are, however, less constant in their relationships to the dermal plates than in other placoderm groups.

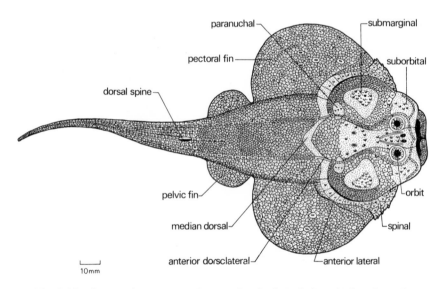

Fig. 8.20. *Gemuendina stuertzi*. Restoration in dorsal view. (After Gross.)

8.7.2. Suborder 2, Gemuendinoidei

The gemuendinoids include three well-known genera (Stensiö, 1950, 1959, 1963*b*; Gross, 1963; Westoll, 1967), the Lower Devonian *Gemuendina*, the Middle Devonian *Asterosteus*, and the Upper Devonian *Jagorina*.

Gemuendina (Fig. 8.20) is a small fish not exceeding 300 mm in length. It is dorsoventrally flattened with greatly enlarged pectoral fins, being thus superficially very like a ray. The head is armoured with a few large dermal

188

plates, a median unpaired plate covering the neurocranium with three paired plates lying on either side of it. The median plate probably includes equivalents of the nuchal, centrals and marginals of arthrodires. The lateral plates do not articulate closely with one another but lie loosely in the skin, which is studded with a mosaic of small plates. There seems every reason to suppose that the middle of the three plates is the submarginal, and that it lay in the skin that formed the operculum covering the gill-chamber. The posterior plate carries the main lateral-line canal from the trunk-shield and is clearly the paranuchal, whilst the anterior plate lies outside the orbit and is the suborbital. The mosaic of small plates becomes more extensive in *Asterosteus* and *Jagorina*, at the expense of the large plates. The eyes are rather small and surrounded by ten or more sclerotic plates. The external nasal openings are small, lying dorsally and close together, only a very short way in front of the orbits. The lateral-line system is superficial in position, running between pairs of tubercles on the plates. The main line runs forwards till it loops laterally around the eye as the infraorbital line, where on the suborbital it gives off a supraoral branch. The infraorbital lines join in a transverse commissure in front of the nasal openings. Short supraorbital lines run back between the orbits.

The internal skeleton of the head is only well known in *Jagorina* (Stensiö, 1950, 1969a), although *Gemuendina* and *Asterosteus* appear to be practically identical in structure. The neurocranium (Fig. 8.21) is a single ossification of both perichondral and endochondral bone, and is fused to the basal surface of the dermal skeleton. It is long and narrow, with small supraorbital and anterior postorbital processes, well-developed supravagal processes, and stout posterior glenoid processes which articulated with the synarcual. A separate antorbital ossification articulates with the anterolateral corner of the ethmoid region. This process is strongly reminiscent of the dermal suborbital plate of *Gemuendina* (Westoll, 1967). The nasal openings lie on the dorsal surface in front of the pineal opening. The eye is supported by an eyestalk. The sclera is ossified and with the thick sclerotic plates makes up a compact bony eye capsule. The occipital region of the neurocranium is pierced by four or five spino-occipital nerves.

Jagorina has a long palatoquadrate which ossified in one piece (Stensiö, 1969a), and was connected to its fellow anteriorly and by a ligament to the orbital region of the neurocranium (Fig. 8.21). Rhenanids are the only placoderms known to have had an elasmobranch-like symphysial connection between the palatoquadrates. The meckelian cartilage is a simple rod of bone. There are no tooth-plates of the usual placoderm sort, but the outer face of the palatoquadrate is armed with stellate tubercles. The whole arrangement of the jaws makes up a highly mobile apparatus, with a subterminal mouth that could be protruded, as in the Recent elasmobranch

189

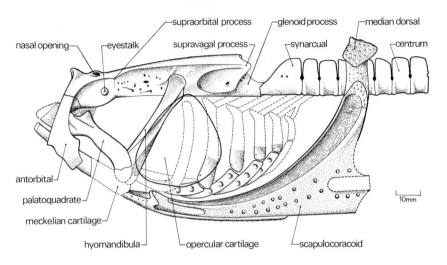

Fig. 8.21. *Jagorina pandora*. Restoration of skeleton of head and shoulder region in lateral view. (After Stensiö.)

Squatina. An important element in this mechanism is the long, stout hyomandibula. Dorsally the hyomandibula articulates against the neurocranium just behind the postorbital process, but in front of the foramen for the hyomandibular nerve. Ventrally it appears to have been in contact with both the palatoquadrate and meckelian cartilage, but to have been widely separated from the ceratohyal. This arrangement is similar to that found in Recent rays. An endoskeletal opercular cartilage is attached to the basal surface of the submarginal. Ossified ceratobranchials of four gillarches are known.

The trunk-armour is of very short rostro-caudal extent (Figs. 8.20, 8.21). It consists only of median dorsal, anterior dorsolateral, anterior lateral, spinal and large anterior ventrolateral plates. The anterior laterals and spinals are covered by a mosaic of small plates in *Gemuendina*, and the anterior lateral has a large internal lamina forming the hind wall of the gill chamber. The pectoral fins are very large and are formed of a single basal element having a narrow articulation with the scapulocoracoid, and long, jointed radials which extend right out to the fin margin. The pelvic fins are semicircular flaps, associated with a small pelvic girdle. The two halves of the girdle are separate, and each has a short iliac process. A single dorsal fin is represented by a small spine. There is no anal fin. The tail is long, tapering and diphycercal. The fins and body are covered with small denticle-like scales, which become enlarged into several irregular rows of ridge scales on the pectoral fins, and into more regular rows on the posterior part of the body. There are well-formed, ring-like centra in the vertebral column, the most anterior of which are fused together to form the synarcual.

8.8. ORDER 6, ANTIARCHI

The antiarchs (Traquair, 1894; Gross, 1931, 1941*a*, *b*; Stensiö, 1931, 1948; Westoll, 1945; Watson, 1961; Karatajute-Talimaa, 1960, 1963; Miles, 1968) are a group of highly specialized, widely distributed placoderms which first occur in the Lower Devonian and only become extinct at the very close of the Upper Devonian or in the early Carboniferous. They are mostly relatively small fishes not exceeding 30 mm in length.

As in arthrodires the head and front part of the body are covered with bony shields formed of overlapping plates made of bone with contained bone cells. The plates are arranged in a constant and characteristic manner. The posterior part of the body in the Middle Devonian *Pterichthyodes* (Traquair, 1894) is covered with overlapping cycloid bony scales, but in the Upper Devonian *Bothriolepis* the squamation is vestigial and the body almost naked (Fig. 8.22). There is either one dorsal fin as in *Pterichthyodes* or two as in *Bothriolepis* (Stensiö, 1948). The tail is heterocercal with a small hypochordal lobe and there is never an anal fin. Endoskeletal supports are found in the caudal fin of *Bothriolepis* (Jarvik, 1959), but the vertebral column is unknown.

The head-shield is smaller than the trunk-shield, which has a spine-like pectoral appendage movably articulated with it. The appendage is homologous with the pectoral fin of other placoderms, and is jointed about halfway down its length in all forms except *Remigolepis* (Fig. 8.23) (Stensiö, 1931). It is covered with a definite number of small bony plates, the most proximal of which clasp the helmet-shaped articular process of the trunk-

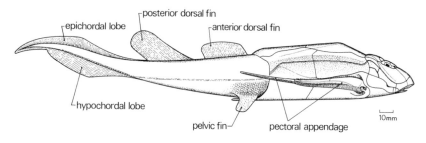

Fig. 8.22. *Bothriolepis canadensis*. Restoration in lateral view. (After Stensiö.)

shield (Figs. 8.24, 8.25). This joint permitted the appendage to make a closely defined series of movements in the horizontal and vertical planes, and some rotational movement about its long axis when it was folded back against the body (Watson, 1961). The endoskeleton of the appendage articulated with the scapulocoracoid, which protruded through the articular process of the shield. The muscles that moved the appendage were situated entirely within its bony plates, and inserted on the articular process. A foramen behind the articular process gave passage to the nerves and blood-vessels of the appendage. Pelvic fins have only been described in *Bothriolepis*, where they consist of folds of the skin directly behind the trunk-shield.

The trunk-shield (Figs. 8.22, 8.23) forms a large, box-like structure with a flattened base and consists of a number of bones easily comparable with those of the primitive arthrodire but differing most obviously in the presence of an anterior as well as a posterior median dorsal plate, and in the absence of anterior lateral, spinal and interolateral plates. The posterior lateral and posterior dorsolateral plates are represented by a single mixilateral in most forms, but are separate in *Remigolepis* and *Byssacanthus*. There is no anterior

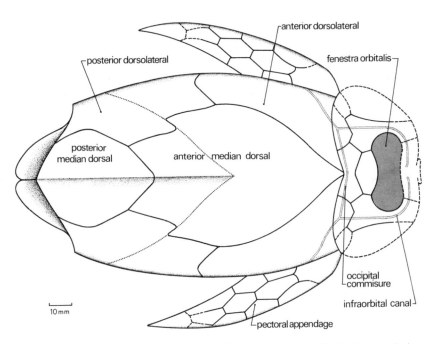

Fig. 8.23. *Remigolepis* sp. Restoration of head and trunk shields in dorsal view. (After Stensiö.)

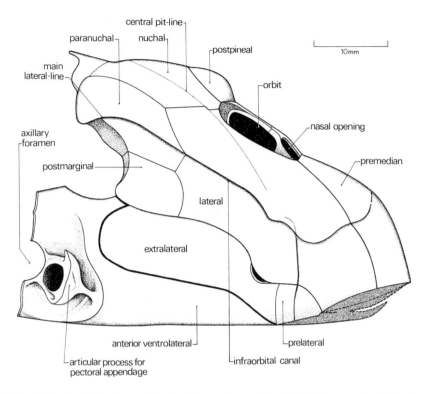

Fig. 8.24. *Bothriolepis canadensis*. Restoration of head-shield and part of anterior ventrolateral plate, in lateral view, (After Stensiö.)

median ventral, but there are usually one or two semilunar plates at the front of the ventral shield.

The head-shield bears condyles which articulate against fossae on the trunk-shield, the reverse of the arrangement in arthrodires. It is a continuous shield of overlapping plates, except in the region of the eyes which are dorsal and closely placed (Figs. 8.24, 8.25). Between the eyes, which were each surrounded by three sclerotic plates, lies a small loose plate, the pineal plate, with a foramen or depression for the pineal organ. Anteriorly to this plate lies another small loose plate, the rostral, notched anteriorly for the external nasal openings. The remainder of the skull-roof is formed dorsally of two median posterior plates, the nuchal and postpineal; an anterior median one, the premedian; and three pairs of lateral ones, the paranuchals, laterals and postmarginals. Laterally the gill-chamber is covered by one or two opercular plates, the prelateral (cf. arthrodiran postsuborbital) and extralateral (cf. arthrodiran submarginal). In *Bothrio-*

193

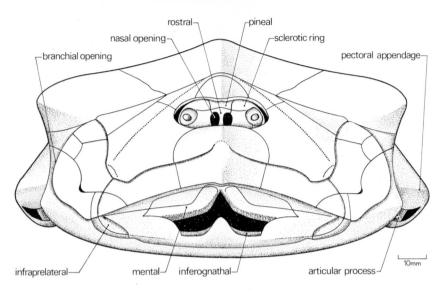

Fig. 8.25. *Bothriolepis canadensis.* Restoration of head and trunk shields in anterior view. (After Stensiö.)

lepis a further series of small plates is present on the undersurface of the head. One of these, the infraprelateral, carries a pit-line down on to the lower jaw (Stensio, 1947, 1948).

The neurocranium is unknown. The nasal capsules must have been small and lain close together. The mouth is anterior but ventral and is bounded dorsally by the mental plates (cf. arthrodiran suborbitals + posterior superognathals), and ventrally by the inferognathals, each of which has a denticulated biting edge.

As in arthrodires the lateral-line sensory canal system consists of open canals and pit-lines. The main canal of the body runs forward across the lateral plates of the pectoral shield on to the head, where in all cases it runs forwards under the eye as the infraorbital canal meeting its fellow in the middle line on the premedian plate. In some forms like *Pterichthyodes* there is an occipital commissure whereas in others this is apparently represented only by pit-lines. The position of the eyes makes the system rather difficult to compare with arthrodires (Stensiö, 1947), but in addition to the canals already mentioned the sclerotic ring has paired supraorbital lines, the central canal is represented by a pit-line running from the nuchal to the lateral plate, and another pit-line is continued from the lateral plate on to the mental plate with a ventral branch on to the lower jaw.

Antiarchs appear to have been fairly constant in general body form, and although one of the longest lived placoderms groups, they enjoyed little evolutionary change. The absence of the distal joint in the appendage of *Remigolepis* appears to be a secondary character (Gross, 1965a), although this is possibly a return to the primitive condition. One minor tendency in the group is for the median dorsals to be produced into a high ridge, as in *Bothriolepis cristata*, *Gerdalepis* and *Grossaspis*, or into a long spine as in *Byssacanthus* (Karatajute-Talimaa, 1960). In *Gerdalepis* (Gross, 1941b) a bony horizontal septum separates the top of the trunk-shield from the body cavity, forming a forwardly opening chamber, perhaps for the levator muscles of the head.

Denison (1941) has been able to restore some of the soft anatomy in favourably preserved specimens of *Bothriolepis canadensis*, by the study of the different sediments that fill the inside of the shields. He has shown that this was a mud swallowing species and that the intestine had an elasmobranch-like spiral valve. Another, much reiterated conclusion, that *Bothriolepis* had lungs, is probably incorrect (Myers, 1942; Stensiö, 1948).

8.9. INCERTAE SEDIS STENSIOLLIDAE

Five small, dorsoventrally flattened Lower Devonian fishes, none very well known, are classified together in this family (Gross, 1962a, 1965b). Although referred to four species in four separate genera, it is possible that they belong only to two monotypic genera. The specimens are too crushed for detailed examination and are not easy to interpret.

The skull-roof of *Pseudopetalichthys* is covered with dermal plates, and there are paired supraorbital lateral-line canals meeting posteriorly in the middle line as in petalichthyids. The main lateral-line canal branches on a plate which has been interpreted as the anterior paranuchal (Westoll, 1967) to give rise to the posterior pit-line. There are large orbits and a large submarginal (opercular) plate. The skeleton of the paired fins (Fig. 8.26) is

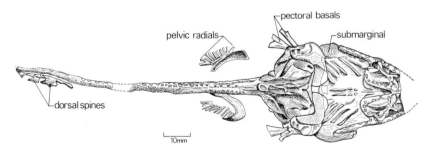

Fig. 8.26. *Pseudopetalichthys problematicus*. In ventral view. (After Gross.)

strikingly like that of a modern elasmobranch, but there is a dermal trunk-shield in which median dorsal, anterior lateral, spinal and anterior ventro-lateral plates have been recognized. The pectoral fin has two basal elements, the pro- and mesopterygium, articulated with the girdle. There is a long series of pelvic radials. There are centra in the vertebral column and traces of dermal spines or fulcral scales along the top of the body.

The jaw apparatus is particularly difficult to interpret, but both pala-toquadrate and meckelian cartilages appear to bear small round flattened plates. There are five branchial arches.

Paraplesiobatis is probably the same form as *Pseudopetalichthys* in a slightly different state of preservation.

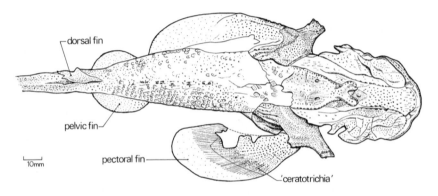

Fig. 8.27. *Stensioella heintzi*. In dorsal view. (After Gross.)

Stensioella (Fig. 8.27) and *Nessariostoma* are superficially very similar to *Pseudopetalichthys*. Both have the skull roofed with dermal plates, and scale-covered bodies. The eyes, however, are smaller and more laterally situated than in *Pseudopetalichthys*, the narrow-based pectoral fin is very large and stiffened with scales and 'ceratotrichia', and there is no indication of a spinal plate in the trunk-shield. The median spines along the back are also smaller than in *Pseudopetalichthys*, and there is a single, posteriorly situated dorsal fin. The dermal bones are not well known. The skull, however, has a long occipital region, and there is a well-defined neck joint between the back of the neurocranium and the synarcual. Traces of four gill-arches, the pala-toquadrate and meckelian cartilage are preserved. Again the jaw apparatus is difficult to interpret, but it appears to be different from that of *Pseudo-petalichthys*.

There is no good evidence that the stensioellids form a natural group, and no general agreement about their relationships. They are usually classified with the rhenanids (Gross, 1963) or petalichthyids (Westoll, 1967).

8.10. EVOLUTION AND MODE OF LIFE

The interrelations of the different placoderm orders are poorly understood and several major classifications have been proposed which bring them together in different ways (Westoll, 1945, 1967; White, 1952; Denison, 1958; Stensiö, 1959; 1963a; Obruchev, 1967; Miles, 1969). Many workers feel that the ptyctodontids and phyllolepids are closely related to arthrodires and should be included in the same order. This view has received some support with the discovery of '*Wuttagoonaspis*', a genus apparently sharing primitive arthrodiran and phyllolepid characters (Ritchie, 1969). More difficult problems are encountered in trying to relate arthrodires to antiarchs, petalichthyids and rhenanids. Stensiö (1959) has suggested that the non-antiarch placoderms divide naturally into those with a spinal plate and those without (the Spinothoracidi and Aspinothoracidi), but this classification widely separates families of arthrodires which on other evidence are closely related and there is good evidence that the spinal plate was lost independently several times in placoderms. Westoll (1967) has suggested that placoderms fall into two natural groups: those with a short occipital region and only one pair of paranuchal plates (arthrodires, phyllolepids, ptyctodontids and antiarchs), and those with a long occipital region and both anterior and posterior paranuchals (petalichthyids, rhenanids, stensioellids). This is a seminal suggestion, for it could give us some understanding of the basic diversification of placoderms. Unfortunately it cannot be readily accepted, for the skull-roof cannot be interpreted with a very high level of confidence in most members of the second group, and there are considerable differences to take into account between the neurocrania of petalichthyids and rhenaninds.

One way of looking at the evolution of placoderms in the absence of an established genealogy, is in terms of their relationship to the environment (Miles, 1969). Placoderms were almost entirely bottom-living fishes, and their adaptive radiation is concerned mainly with exploiting different ways of living on and just above the bottom. Thus the ptyctodontids resemble Recent chimaeroids in habit, and apparently adopted a chimaeroid-like mode of life on the bottom with a stenophagous diet (Miles, 1967a). The most advanced rhenanids are ray-like, and must have used their expanded pectoral fins to flip a concealing layer of sand and mud over the body, as they lay on the bottom in wait for prey. The antiarchs were narrowly adapted for propping themselves on the bottom with their stilt-like pectoral appendages, and like the rhenanids had dorsally situated eyes and nasal openings. They probably digested organic detritus out of the stream of mud which they ingested and passed through the intestine. The petalichthyids remained relatively unspecialized benthic fishes, adaptively similar to early arthrodires. If *Stensioella* is related to petalichthyids, it may be regarded as a more specialized benthic form, with large pectorals and a broad subterminal mouth.

Arthrodires underwent the widest adaptive radiation of all placoderm groups. The primitive forms of the Lower Devonian were moderately depressed, bottom-haunting scavengers and mud swallowers. Later the group radiated into strongly depressed, highly specialized benthic forms, such as the Middle Devonian *Homostius* and *Heterostius* and the Upper Devonian *Titanichthys*; lurking predators of ovate cross-section and mid-water predators such as the Upper Devonian dinichthyids, trematosteids and pachyosteids; and compressed surface-water types, the leptosteids and brachydeirids. The last two families, which comprise only four genera in all, were the only truly nektonic placoderms. The brachydeirids probably fed on small, hard-shelled invertebrates and have unique modifications in the jaw and neck joint mechanisms.

The secondary burst of adaptive radiation in arthrodires, as different lines passed through the advanced coccosteomorph to the pachosteomorph-level of organization in the late Middle Devonian and Upper Devonian, was attended by a sharp decline of the smaller placoderm groups. This was because the expanding adaptive zone of the competitively superior arthrodires came to overlap the adaptive zones of the other groups (Miles, 1969). The nonarthrodire placoderms were most successful in the early Middle Devonian, in the hiatus between the decline of the dolichothoracids and the rise of the brachythoracids.

Arthrodires and rhenanids are the only groups in which we have knowledge of any considerable evolutionary changes. The primitive members of each stock, dolichothoracids and palaeacanthaspidoids, were adaptively similar, but subsequently the groups became very different in both habit and mode of life. The other placoderm groups show little evolutionary change, and it is because of this that the interrelations of the placoderm orders are so poorly understood. The earliest members already show the typical characters of the group to which they belong, and in the absence of any marked trends of change it is not possible to extrapolate back to a hypothetical ancestor which may be compared with those of other groups. Thus it is not possible to say whether the trunk-shield ever extended posteriorly on the flank behind the pectoral fins in petalichthyids, ptyctodontids, phyllolepids and stensioellids, as it does in arthrodires and antiarchs, and we cannot say whether the long type of trunk-shield found in primitive arthrodires is primitive for all placoderm groups.

There was a long muscular body behind the trunk-shield in all placoderms.

This, together with the evidence of the unconstricted notochord in the vertebral column, indicates an eel-like mode of swimming. In advanced rhenanids the expanded pectorals were too stiffly armoured and had too narrow a base to have undulated in a ray-like way. The long muscular body shows that it is quite wrong to compare placoderms with modern trunk-fishes (Jarvik, 1964), in which the armour extends right back to the caudal fin. The first placoderms had small, poorly developed pectoral fins, and some of the functions of pectorals were apparently taken over in arthrodires by the enlarged spinal plates (Westoll, 1945, 1958). In the history of placoderms the evolution of the pectoral fins proceeded in two main directions, towards either the formation of muscular, mobile structure fulfilling the same functions in swimming as the pectorals of elasmobranchs, or towards the formation of stiff props. The second direction of change resulted in the most highly modified pectoral fins of all Palaeozoic fishes in the antiarchs, with their arthropod-like appendages.

The only good evidence of the reproductive system in placoderms is found in ptyctodontids (Miles, 1967a), in which the males have well-developed pelvic and prepelvic claspers. These structures indicate a chondrichthyan type of reproductive biology, although neither egg-cases nor evidence of viviparity have been found.

Apart from the rhenanids in which highly-specialized protrusible jaws were developed, and the arthrodire *Brachyosteus* in which a small "coronoid process' is found, the jaw mechanism of placoderms remained in a relatively unevolved state throughout the history of the group, with a simple mandibular lever. This is partly because the upper jaw tended to gain support either by fusing with the dermal armour as in arthrodires, or with the neurocranium as in ptyctodontids. This prohibited the formation of protrusible jaws, such as are found in advanced sharks and bony fishes, and restricted the possible side-to-side expansion of the oralobranchial chamber (Miles, 1967b). Another factor is the lack of true teeth in the group (Gross, 1967), of either the serially replaced 'selachian' type (Chapter 10 §2), or of the firmly attached, less-regularly replaced type of bony fishes. The dental apparatus apparently never evolved far from using slightly modified dermal bones as tooth-plates, which were gradually worn down during life and not replaced. However, the tooth-plates of ptyctodontids paralleled those of chimaeroids and lung-fishes in the development of a hypermineralized columnar tissue, as a response to a durophagous mode of life. The rapid replacement of placoderms by chondrichthyans at the close of the Devonian may have been partly due to the relatively primitive organization of the placoderm feeding mechanism.

REFERENCES

Bystrow, A. P. (1957) 'The microstructure of dermal bones in arthrodires'. *Acta zool., Stockh.*, **38**, 239–75.

Denison, R. H. (1941) 'The soft anatomy of *Bothriolepis*'. *J. Paleont.*, **15**, 553–61.

Denison, R. H. (1950) 'A new arthrodire from the New York State Devonian'. *Am. J. Sci.*, **248**, 565–80.

Denison, R. H. (1958) 'Early Devonian fishes from Utah. 3. Arthrodira'. *Fieldiana, Geol.*, **11**, 459–551.

Denison, R. H. (1960) 'Fishes of the Devonian Holland Quarry Shale of Ohio'. *Fieldiana, Geol.*, **11**, 555–613.

Denison, R. H. (1962) 'A reconstruction of the shield of the arthrodire *Bryantolepis brachycephalus* (Bryant)'. *Fieldiana, Geol.*, **14**, 99–104.

Dunkle, D. H. and Bungart, P. A. (1942) 'The infero-gnathal plates of *Titanichthys*'. *Scient. publs Cleveland Mus. nat. Hist.*, **8**, 49–59.

Dunkle, D. H. and Bungart, P. A. (1943) 'Comments on *Diplognathus mirabilis* Newberry'. *Scient. publs Cleveland Mus. nat. Hist.*, **8**, 73–84.

Dunkle, D. H. and Bungart, P. A. (1946) 'The antero-supragnathal of *Gorgonichthys*'. *Amer. Mus. Nov.*, **1316**, 1–10.

Eastman, C. R. (1898) 'Dentition of Devonian Ptyctodontidae'. *Amer. Naturalist*, **32**, 473–560.

Forster-Cooper, C. (1934) 'A note on the body scaling of *Pterichthyodes*'. *Palaeobiologica*, **6**, 25–30.

Gross, W. (1931) '*Asterolepis ornata* Eichw. und das Antiarch—Problem'. *Palaeontographica*, **75**, 1–62.

Gross, W. (1932) 'Die Arthrodira Wildungens'. *Geol. Palaont. Abh.*, **19**, 1–61.

Gross, W. (1933) 'Die Wirbeltiere des rheinishen Devons'. *Abh. Preuss. Geol. Landesanst.*, **154**, 1–83.

Gross, W. (1935) 'Histologische Studien aus Aussenskelett fossiler Agnathen und Fische'. *Palaeontographica*, **83A**, 1–60.

Gross, W. (1941*a*) 'Die *Bothriolepis*-arten der *Cellulosa*-Mergel Lettlands'. *K. Svenska VetenskAkad. Handl.*, (3) **19**, 1–79.

Gross, W. (1941*b*) 'Neue Beobachtungen an *Gerdalepis rhenana* (Beyr.)'. *Palaeontographica*, **93A**, 193–214.

Gross, W. (1957) 'Mundzähne und Hautzähne der Acanthodier und Arthrodiren'. *Palaeontographica*, **109A**, 1–40.

Gross, W. (1958) 'Über die älteste Arthrodiren—Gattung'. *Notizbl. Hess. Landesamt. Bodenforsch. Wiesbaden*, **86**, 7–30.

Gross, W. (1959) 'Arthrodiren aus dem Obersilur der Prager Mulde'. *Palaeontographica*, **113A**, 1–35.

Gross, W. (1960) '*Tityosteus* n.gen., ein Riesenarthrodire aus dem rheinischen Unterdevon'. *Paläont. Z.*, **34**, 263–74.

Gross, W. (1961) '*Lunaspis broilii* und *Lunaspis heroldi* aus dem Hunsrückschiefer (Unterdevon, Rheinland)'. *Notizbl. Hess. Landesamt. Bodenforsch. Wiesbaden*, **89**, 17–43.

Gross, W. (1962a) 'Neuuntersuchung der Stensiöellida (Arthrodira, Unterdevon)'. *Notizbl. Hess. Landesamt. Bedenforsch. Wiesbaden*, **90**, 48–86.

Gross, W. (1962b) 'Neuuntersuchung der Dolichothoraci aus dem Unterdevon von Overath bei Köln'. *Paläont. Z.*, *H. Schmidt-Festband*, 45–63.

Gross, W. (1963) '*Gemuendina stuertzi* Traquair, Neuuntersuchung'. *Notizbl. Hess. Landesamt. Bodenforsch. Wiesbaden*, **91**, 36–73.

Gross, W. (1965a) 'Über die Placodermen-Gattung *Asterolepis* und *Tiaraspis* aus dem Devon Belgiens und einen fraglichen *Tiaraspis*—Rest aus dem Devon Spitzbergens'. *Bull Inst. r. Sci. nat. Belg.*, **41**, 1–19.

Gross, W. (1965b) 'Über einer neuen Schadelrest von *Stensioella heintzi* und schuppen von *Machaeracanthus* sp. indet. aus dem Hunsrückschiefer'. *Notizbl. hess. Landesamt. Bodenforsch. Wiesbaden*, **93**, 7–18.

Gross, W. (1967) 'Über das Gebiss der Acanthodier und Placodermen'. *J. Linn. Soc. (Zool.)*, **47**, 121–30.

Heintz, A. (1929) 'Die downtonischen und devonischen Vertebraten von Spitzbergen. 2. Acanthaspida'. *Skr. Svalbard Ishavet*, **22**, 1–81.

Heintz, A. (1930) 'Eine neue Rekonstruction von *Heterostius* ASM'. *Protok. Obshch. Estest., Yur'ev*, **36**, 1–7.

Heintz, A. (1932a) 'The structure of *Dinichthys*. A contribution to our knowledge of the Arthrodira' *Am. Mus. nat. Hist.*, *Bashford Dean Mem. Vol.*, **4**, 115–224.

Heintz, A. (1932b) 'Untersuchungen über den Bau des Arthrodira'. *Acta zool., Stockh.*, **12**, 225–39.

Heintz, A. (1933) 'Some remarks about the structure of *Phlyctaenaspis acadica* Whiteaves'. *Norsk geol. Tidsskr.*, **14**, 127–44.

Heintz, A. (1934) 'Revision of the Estonian Arthrodira Pt.1. Family Homostiidae, Jaekel'. *Arch. Naturk. Eestis.*, **10**, 177–290.

Heintz, A. (1962) 'New investigation on the structure of *Arctolepis* from the Devonian of Spitsbergen'. *Norsk Polarinst Årb.*, (1961) 23–40.

Heintz, A. (1968) 'The spinal plate in *Homostius* and *Dunkleosteus*'. *Nobel Symposium*, **4**, 145–151.

Holmgren, N. (1942) 'Studies on the head of fishes. Pt. 3. The phylogeny of elasmobranch fishes'. *Acta zool. Stockh.*, **23**, 129–261.

Hussakof, L. and Bryant, W. L. (1918) 'Catalog of the fossil fishes in the museum of the Buffalo society of natural sciences'. *Bull. Buffalo Soc. nat. Sci.*, **12**, 1–198.

Jarvik, E. (1959) 'Dermal fin-rays and Holmgren's principle of delamination'. *K. svenska VetenskAkad. Handl.*, (4) **6**, 1–51.

Jarvik, E. (1964) 'Specializations in early vertebrates'. *Annls Soc. r. zool Belg.*, **94**, 11–95.

Jarvik, E. (1968) 'Aspects of vertebrate phylogeny'. *Nobel Symposium*, **4**, 497–527.

Karatajute-Talimaa, V. (1960) '*Byssacanthus dilatatus* (Eichw) from the Middle Devonian of the U.S.S.R.'. *Colnea Acta Geol. Lithuanica*, (1960) 293–305.

Karatajute-Talimaa, V. (1963) 'Genus *Asterolepis* from the Devonian of the Russian

Platform, in *The data of the geology of the Lithuania*, ed. Grigelis, A. and Karatajute-Talimaa, V. (In Russian with English summary.) p. 65.

Lehman, J. P. (1956) 'Les arthrodires du Dévonien Supérieur du Tafilalet (Sud marocain)'. *Notes Mém. Serv. Mines Carte Géol. Maroc.*, **129**, 1–70.

Lehman, J. P. (1962) 'A propos de la double articulation de la cuirasse des arthrodires'. *Colloques int. Cent. natn. Rech. Scient.*, **104**, 63–67.

Liu, T. S. and P'an, K. (1958) 'Devonian fishes from Wutung series near Nanking, China'. *Pal. Sinica*, **15** (n.s.C), 1–41. (In Chinese and English.)

Liu, T.-H. (1963) 'On the Antiarchi from Chutsing'. *Vertebr. Palasiat.*, **7**, 80–85. (In Chinese and English.)

Mark, E. J. (1953) 'Genus *Holonema* from the Middle Devonian of Estonian S.S.R.' *Loodusuurjate Seltsi Juubelekoguteos* (1853–1953), *Tallinn* (1953), 382–96. (In Russian.)

Mark, E. J. (1963) 'On the spinal plate of the Middle Devonian arthrodire *Homostius*'. *Geoloogia-Inst. Uurim.*, **13**, 189–99. (In Russian with English summary.)

Mark-Kurik, E. J. (1969) 'Distribution of vertebrates in the Silurian of Estonia'. *Lethaia*, **2**, 145–52.

Miles, R. S. (1962) '*Gemuendenaspis* n. gen., an arthrodiran fish from the Lower Devonian Hunsrückschiefer of Germany'. *Trans. R. Soc. Edinb.*, **65**, 59–77.

Miles, R. S. (1964) 'On some coccosteomorph arthrodires from the Devonian of Arizona'. *Ark. Zool.*, (2) **16**, 427–60.

Miles, R. S. (1964) 'A large arthrodire plate from Chautauqua County, New York'. *Ark. Zool.*, (2) **16**, 545–50.

Miles, R. S. (1965) 'Ventral thoracic neuromast lines of placoderm fishes. *Nature Lond.*, **206**, 524–25.

Miles, R. S. (1966*a*) 'The placoderm fish *Rhachiosteus pterygiatus* Gross and its relationships'. *Trans. R. Soc. Edinb.*, **66**, 377–92.

Miles, R. S. (1966*b*) '*Protitanichthys* and some other coccosteomorph arthrodires from the Devonian of North America'. *K. svenska VetenskAkad. Handl.*, (4) **10**, 1–49.

Miles, R. S. (1967*a*) 'Observations on the ptyctodont fish, *Rhamphodopsis* Watson'. *J. Linn. Soc. (Zool.)*, **47**, 99–120.

Miles, R. S. (1967*b*) 'The cervical joint and some aspects of the origin of the Placodermi'. *Colloques int. Cent. natn. Rech. scient.*, **163**, 49–71.

Miles, R. S. (1967*c*) 'Class Placodermi', in *The fossil record*, ed. Harland, W. B. *et al.* (Geol. Soc., London.) p. 640.

Miles, R. S. (1968) 'The Old Red Sandstone antiarchs of Scotland: Family Bothriolepididae'. *Palaeont. Soc. (Monogr.)*, (no. 552) **122**, 1–130.

Miles, R. S. (1969) 'Features of placoderm diversification and the evolution of the arthrodire feeding mechanism'. *Trans. R. Soc. Edinb.*, **68**, 123–70.

Miles, R. S. and Westoll, T. S. (1963) 'Two new genera of coccosteid Arthrodira from the Middle Old Red Sandstone of Scotland, and their stratigraphical distribution'. *Trans. R. Soc. Edinb.*, **65**, 179–210.

Miles, R. S. and Westoll, T. S. (1968) 'The placoderm fish *Coccosteus cuspidatus*

Miller ex Agassiz from the Middle Old Red Sandstone of Scotland. Pt. 1. Descriptive morphology'. *Trans. R. Soc. Edinb.*, **67**, 373–476.

Myers, G. S. (1942) 'The "lungs of *Bothriolepis*"'. *Stanford Ichthyol Bull.*, **2**, 134–36.

Obruchev, D. V. (1967) 'Class Placodermi', in *Fundamentals of Paleontology. 11. Agnatha, Pisces*, ed. Obruchev, D. V. (Israel program for scientific translations, Jerusalem) p. 168.

Obrucheva, O. P. (1962) *Armoured fishes of the Devonian of the U.S.S.R. (Coccosteidae and Dinichthyidae).* (Moscow, in Russian.)

Ørvig, T. (1957) 'Notes on some Palaeozoic vertebrates from Spitsbergen and North America'. *Norsk geol. Tidsskr.*, **37**, 285–352.

Ørvig, T. (1960) 'New finds of acanthodians, arthrodires, crossopterygians, ganoids and dipnoans in the Upper Middle Devonian Calcareous Flags (Oberer Plattenkalk) of the Bergisch Gladback-Paffrath Trough. Pt. 1.' *Palaont. Z.*, **34**, 295–335.

Ørvig, T. (1962) 'Y a-t-il une relation directe entre les arthrodires ptyctodontides et les holocephales?'. *Colloques int. Cent. natn. Rech. scient.*, **104**, 49–61.

Ørvig, T. (1967) 'Phylogeny of tooth tissues: evolution of some calcified tissues in early vertebrates', in *Structural and chemical organization of teeth*, ed. Miles, A. E. W. (Academic Press, New York and London).

Ørvig, T. (1969) 'A new brachythoracid arthrodire from the Devonian of Dickson Land, Vestspitsbergen'. *Lethaia*, **2**, 261–71.

Pageau, Y. (1969) 'Nouvelle faune ichthyologique du Devonién Moyen dans les Grès de Gaspé (Quebec). 2. Morphologie et systematique'. *Naturaliste can.*, **96**, 399–478, 805–89.

Ritchie, A. (1969) 'Ancient fish of Australia'. *Australian Nat. Hist.*, (September 1969) 218–23.

Robertson, G. M. (1970) 'The oral region of ostracoderms and placoderms: possible phylogenetic significance'. *Am. J. Sci*, **269**, 39–64.

Skeels, M. A. (1962) 'Two new fishes from the Middle Devonian Silica formation, Lucas County, Ohio'. *J. Paleont.*, **36**, 1039–46.

Stensiö, E. A. (1925) 'On the head of the macropetalichthyids with certain remarks on the head of the other arthrodires'. *Publs Field. Mus. nat. Hist. (Geol.)*, **4**, 87–197.

Stensiö, E. A. (1931) 'Upper Devonian vertebrates from East Greenland, collected by the Danish Greenland expedition in 1929 and 1930'. *Medd. Grønland*, **96**, 1–212.

Stensiö, E. A. (1934a) 'On the Placodermi of the Upper Devonian of East Greenland. I. Phyllolepida and Arthrodira'. *Medd. Grønland*, **97**, 1–58.

Stensiö, E. A. (1934b) 'On the heads of certain arthrodires. I. *Pholidosteus, Leiosteus* and acanthaspids'. *K. svenska VetenskAkad. Handl.*, (3) **13**, 1–79.

Stensiö, E. A. (1936) 'On the Placodermi of the Upper Devonian of East Greenland. Supplement to part 1'. *Medd. Grønland*, **97**, 1–52.

Stensiö, E. A. (1939) 'On the Placodermi of the Upper Devonian of East Greenland. 2nd Supplement to part 1'. *Medd. Grønland*, **97**, 1–33.

Stensiö, E. A. (1942) 'On the snout of arthrodires'. *K. svenska VetenskAkad. Handl.*,

(3) **20**, 1–32.

Stensiö, E. A. (1944) 'Contributions to the knowledge of the vertebrate fauna of the Silurian and Devonian of western Podolia. 2. Notes on two Arthrodires from the Dowtonian of Podolia'. *Ark. Zool.*, **35** A, 1–83.

Stensiö, E. A. (1945) 'On the heads of certain arthrodires. 2. On the cranium and cervical joint of the Dolichothoraci'. *K. svenska VetenskAkad. Handl.*, (3) **22**, 1–70.

Stensiö, E. A. (1947) 'The sensory lines and dermal bones of the cheek in fishes and amphibians'. *K. svenska VetenskAkad. Handl.*, (3) **24**, 1–195.

Stensiö, E. A. (1948) 'On the Placodermi of the Upper Devonian of East Greenland. 2. Antiarchi: subfamily Bothriolepinae. With an attempt at a revision of the previously described species of that family'. *Palaeozool. Groenland.* **2**, 1–622.

Stensiö, E. A. (1950) 'La cavité labyrinthique, l'ossification sclérotique et l'orbite de *Jagorina*'. *Colloques int. Cent. natn. Rech. scient.*, **21**, 9–41.

Stensiö, E. A. (1959) 'On the pectoral fin and shoulder girdle of the arthrodires'. *K. svenska VetenskAkad. Handl.*, (4) **8**, 1–229.

Stensiö, E. A. (1963a) 'Anatomical studies on the arthrodiran head. Pt. 1. Preface, geological and geographical distribution, the organization of the arthrodires, the anatomy of the head in the Dolichothoraci, Coccosteomorphi and Pachyosteomorphi'. *K. svenska VetenskAkad. Handl.*, (4) **9**, 1–419.

Stensiö, E. A. (1963b) 'The brain and cranial nerves in fossil, lower craniate vertebrates'. *Skr. norske VidenskAkad. Oslo, Mat.-naturv. Kl.* (1963) 1–120.

Stensiö, E. A. (1969a) 'Elasmobranchiomorphi Placodermata Arthrodires', in *Traité de Paléontologie*, 4:2, ed. Piveteau J. (Masson, Paris) p. 71.

Stensiö, E. A. (1969b) 'Anatomie des arthrodires dans leur cadre systématique'. *Annls Paléont.*, **55**, 151–92.

Stensiö, E. A. and Säve-Söderbergh, G. (1938) 'Middle Devonian vertebrates from Canning Land and Wegener Peninsula (East Greenland). Pt. 1. Placodermi, Ichthyodorulithes'. *Medd. Grønland*, **96**, 1–38.

Stevens, M. S. (=Skeels, M. A.) (1964) 'Thoracic armour of a new arthrodire (*Holonema*) from the Devonian of Presque Isle County, Michigan'. *Pap. Mich. Acad. Sci.*, **49**, 163–75.

Traquair, R. H. (1894–1914) 'A monograph of the fishes of the Old Red Sandstone of Britain. Pt. 2. The Asterolepidae'. *Palaeontogr. Soc. (Monogr.)*, 63–134.

Van Valen, L. (1963) 'The head shield of *Macropetalichthys* (Arthrodira)'. *J. Paleont.*, **37**, 257–63.

Watson, D. M. S. (1934) 'The interpretation of arthrodires', *Proc. zool. Soc. Lond.*, (1934) 437–64.

Watson, D. M. S. (1938) 'On *Rhamphodopsis*, a ptyctodont from the Middle Old Red Sandstone of Scotland'. *Trans. R. Soc. Edinb.*, **59**, 397–410.

Watson, D. M. S. (1961) 'Some additions to our knowledge of Antiarchi'. *Palaeontology*, **4**, 210–20.

Westoll, T. S. (1945) 'The paired fins of placoderms'. *Trans. R. Soc. Edinb.*, **61**, 381–98.

Westoll, T. S. (1958) 'The lateral fin-fold theory and the pectoral fins of ostracoderms and early fish', in *Studies of fossil vertebrates*, ed. Westoll, T. S. (The Athlone Press, London).

Westoll, T. S. (1962) 'Ptyctodont fishes and the ancestry of the Holocephali'. *Nature, Lond.*, **194**, 949–52.

Westoll, T. S. (1963) 'The hyomandibular problem in placoderm fishes'. *Contrd. pap. 16th Int. Congr. Zool.*, **1**, 176.

Westoll, T. S. (1967) '*Radotina* and other tesserate fishes'. *J. Linn. Soc. (Zool.)*, **47**, 83–98.

Westoll, T. S. and Miles, R. S. (1963) 'On an arctolepid fish from Gemünden'. *Trans. R. Soc. Edinb.*, **65**, 139–53.

White, E. I. (1952) 'Australian arthrodires'. *Bull. Br. Mus. nat. Hist., (Geol.)*, **1**, 249–304.

White, E. I. (1961) 'The Old Red Sandstone of Brown Clee Hill and the adjacent area. II. Palaeontology'. *Bull. Br. Mus. nat. Hist., (Geol.)*, **5**, 243–310.

White, E. I. (1968) 'Devonian fishes of the Mawson-Mutlock area, Victoria Land, Antartica'. *Scient. Rep. transantarct. Exped.*, **16**, 1–26.

White, E. I. (1969) 'The deepest vertebrate fossil and other arctolepid fishes'. *Biol. J. Linn. Soc.*, **1**, 293–310.

CHAPTER NINE

Subclass Chondrichthyes.
Infraclass Elasmobranchii

9.1. CLASSIFICATION

Order 1, Cladoselachida
    e.g. *Cladoselache*, U. Dev—U. Carb; ?*Coronodus*, ?*Diademodus*, U. Dev.

Order 2, Cladodontida
    e.g. '*Cladodus*', M. Dev—L. Perm; *Symmorium*, U. Carb; *Stethacanthus* U. Dev—U. Carb; *Denaea*, L.–U. Carb.

Incertae sedis *Cratoselache*, L. Carb; *Holmesella*, U. Carb; *Ohiolepis*, L. Dev; *Protacrodus*, U. Dev; *Tamiobatis*, L. or U. Carb.

Order 3, Selachii (=Euselachii)
    Suborder 1, Ctenacanthoidei
        e.g. *Bandringa*, U. Carb; *Ctenacanthus, Goodrichthys, Tristychius*, L. Carb.
    Suborder 2, Hybodontoidei
        e.g. *Arctacanthus*, U. Perm; ?'*Petrodus*', U. Carb; *Hybodus*, M. Trias—U. Cret.

Suborders of modern elasmobranchs not listed

Order 4, Xenacanthida (=Pleuracanthodii)
    e.g. *Dittodus*, M. Dev—U. Trias; *Xenacanthus*, U. Dev—M. Perm.

Incertae sedis Order 5, Helicoprionida
    e.g. *Campyloprion*, U. Carb; *Helicoprion*, U. Carb—M. Perm.

L., Lower; M, Middle; U., Upper; Dev, Devonian; Carb, Carboniferous; Perm, Permian; Trias, Triassic; Cret, Cretaceous.

9.2. CHONDRICHTHYAN CHARACTERISTICS

The chondrichthyans appear in the fossil record in the late Lower Devonian. They flourished during the Carboniferous and continue to the present day, where they are represented by the modern sharks, dogfishes, skates and rabbit-fishes. Their endoskeleton is entirely cartilaginous, and may be characteristically calcified into a superficial layer of prismatic granules. Their exoskeleton consists of small scales, sometimes enlarged (or fused?) into head-spines or fin-spines, and less frequently into armour plates. The web of the fin in most members is stiffened by horny fin-rays or ceratotrichia. The hyoidean gill-slit is always reduced to a spiracle or is absent, and typically the hyomandibula plays an important part in the suspension of the jaw apparatus. They have from five to seven gill-slits, which usually open directly to the outside, although in holocephalans there is an operculum. The olfactory capsules are relatively large, and the snout is produced into a rostrum which may be supported by internal rostral cartilages. As a result of this, the mouth is ventral. The nostrils are also more or less ventral, and may be confluent with the mouth; they are imperfectly divided by a flap into incurrent and excurrent openings. The teeth are typically not fused to the jaws and replace one another serially. Generally speaking, the branchial arches are >-shaped and not Σ-shaped as in osteich-thyans, although there are exceptions in both chondrichthyans and osteich-thyans (Nelson, 1968). The lateral-line canal runs between two rows of scales, and on the head is often closely associated with groups of ampullary sense organs. The labyrinth remains in open contact with the outside through the endolymphatic duct, and in elasmobranchs has statoconia in place of the compact statoliths of osteichthyans and acanthodians. Sexual dimorphism exists in the form of male claspers, i.e. a paired penis supported by the skeleton of the pelvic fins. This is an adaptation for internal fertilization, and typically the embryos develop in horny egg-cases.

The scales of Palaeozoic chondrichthyans show a wide range of form and structure, and differ in important respects from the placoid scales of later forms. They have been carefully studied in the Upper Carboniferous shark *Holmesella* and in some other chondrichthyans of the same age (*'Orodus'*, *Ornithoprion*; Zangerl, 1966, 1968; Ørvig, 1966). In these forms the scales are typically composite (Fig. 9.1) growing structures, that can be described in the terms of the lepidomorial theory (Chapter 3 §3.2), although very simple lepidomoria may also occur as discrete elements. In *'Orodus'* the shagreen shows marked regional differentiation. The ventral scales consist of a variable number of small, finger-like denticles (lepidomoria or odon-todes) fused at their bases. The individual denticles have thin walls of dentine around a large pulp cavity, and a base of bone. The lateral scales are similar, but have a group of large denticles at the anterior margin, with thick walls and a small pulp cavity, in addition to the finger-like denticles. The dorsal scales (Fig. 9.1) are the largest and most complex, having massive denticles and a thick, cushion-like base, which grew by the concentric addition of bone as denticles where added to the crown. Cellular bone has been reported

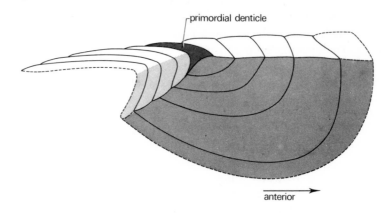

Fig. 9.1. Diagram to illustrate the mode of growth of a cyclomorial scale of the type found in '*Orodus*' sp. The first-appearing finger-like denticle is a simple lepido-morium. Additional finger-like elements develop posteriorly and massive denticles anteriorly. The latest additions to the scale are dotted. The fused base of the finger-like elements is lightly stippled; the fibrous cushion base of the massive denticles is more darkly stippled. (After Zangerl.)

in all of these scales, although the bony base of chondrichthyan scales usually lacks cell spaces. The placoid scales of later chondrichthyans are non-growing, synchronomorial structures. Their development from growing, cyclomorial scales can be explained as the result of heterochrony, i.e. changes in the relative times of appearance of structures during development. In placoid scales it is believed that the individual lepidomoria appear synchronously and fuse at the papillary stage before the dentinal crown is formed, so that there is a shortening of the total time of development of the scale. Depending on the exact degree of fusion of the lepidomoria, there may be a number of incompletely separated pulp cavities, or one large cavity (Stensiö, 1961). In a Permian edestid holocephalan, cyclomorial and synchronomorial scales occur in approximately equal numbers, and are presumably situated in different regions of the body.

Because the cartilaginous nature of the skeleton makes any fossil remains except teeth and spines exceedingly rare, the evolution of chondrichthyans is only understood in its broadest outlines (Moy-Thomas, 1939; Schaeffer, 1965, 1967). Many Palaeozoic genera are still known only by their teeth and other isolated fragments, and the affinities of some important groups are still uncertain. Two main lines of evolution can be distinguished in chondrichthyans, the elasmobranchs and holocephalans, and they are distinct from their first appearances in the record (Patterson, 1965; Stahl, 1967; Jarvik, 1968).

208

9.3. INFRACLASS ELASMOBRANCHII

Elasmobranchs can be distinguished from holocephalans most easily by the microscopic structure of the teeth (see also Chapter 10 §2) and the accompanying mode of jaw suspension, the palatoquadrate never being fused to the neurocranium but being either amphistylic or hyostylic. The teeth of typical elasmobranchs replace one another moderately quickly and have an outer layer of enamel-like substance, beneath which lies a layer of orthodentine containing numerous fine tubules, which surrounds a core of osteodentine (trabecular dentine). There is no operculum, the gill-slits always opening directly to the outside.

The elasmobranchs are an essentially predaceous group, relying on smell rather than sight for obtaining their food, consequently the eyes are usually rather small, and the olfactory capsules are relatively large. The detailed course of the lateral-line canals is unknown in Palaeozoic forms, but it may be assumed to have been similar to that of a primitive living shark such as *Chlamydoselachus* (Allis, 1923; Stensiö, 1947). The main canal of the body (Fig. 9.2) passes forward on to the head and bends down ventrally beneath the orbit as the infraorbital canal. The supraorbital canal connects dorsally with this canal both behind and in front of the eye. Dorsally there is a short median occipital branch of the main canal, which does not meet its fellow in the middle line. On the cheek arising from the infraorbital canal behind the

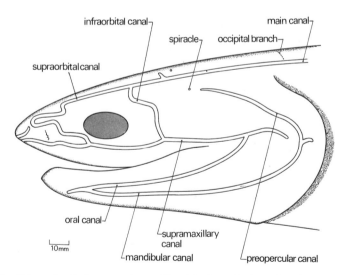

Fig. 9.2. *Chlamydoselachus anguineus*. Head in lateral view showing course of the sensory canals. (After Stensiö.)

209

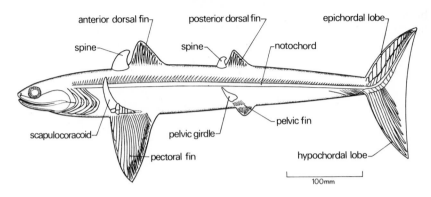

Fig. 9.3. *Cladoselache fyleri*. Restoration in lateral view. (After Schaeffer.)

eye there is a supramaxillary canal which is continued on to the lower jaw as the oral canal, and a preopercular canal arises near the spiracle and passes down on to the lower jaw as the mandibular canal.

9.4. ORDER 1, CLADOSELACHIDA

This order includes the well-known Upper Devonian fish *Cladoselache* (Dean, 1909; Harris, 1938), which has been thought to approach in structure a condition that would be expected in a hypothetical ancestral elasmobranch. However, in most respects it is now seen to represent a specialized side branch of the basal stock (Harris, 1950). The cladoselachids are characterized by the presence of two dorsal fins, paired fins which are little more than triangular flaps of the body wall, and the absence of an anal fin.

Cladoselache (Fig. 9.3) is the only really well-known member and is a fairly large fish, when fully grown about two metres long, with an elongated fusiform body. The trunk is almost naked, although composite, multicuspid scales are found on the free margins of the fins, in the mouth cavity, and around the eye where they are enlarged to form an orbital ring (Dean, 1909). The tail is almost symmetrical externally, but internally is strongly heterocercal. There are two dorsal fins, each provided with a short spine. These spines are superficial structures, probably consisting of osteodentine only; they do not have a basal part deeply inserted between the myotomes, and may not be homologous with the spines of other elasmobranchs. Although there is no anal fin, it has been suggested that it is represented by a pair of small, lateral keel-like flaps in the caudal region. This hypothesis is weak, particularly as similar streamlining structures are found in modern pelagic sharks with an externally symmetrical tail (Harris, 1950). The paired fins,

210

both pectoral and pelvic, are lateral triangular flaps similar to the embryonic fins of modern sharks. This was long taken to be the primitive condition in chondrichthyans, but these fins may be paedomorphic developments, by means of which the pelagic adult fish was provided with large hydrofoils. The cartilaginous supports of the fins are particularly characteristic. All the fins have an endoskeleton of unjointed branching cartilaginous radials and a row of basal cartilages in the paired fins (Fig. 9.6A). These fins are said to be plesodic (Stensiö, 1959; Jarvik, 1959), i.e. the radials extend throughout the web of the fin, ending at the fin margins. Small rays are intercalated between the pointed tips of the main rays in the paired fins. The limb girdles are little more than enlarged basals and do not fuse with their fellows in the middle line. The articular process of the scapulocoracoid is broad, with a long articulation for the pectoral fin. The vertebral column was without centra, the notochord being persistent. The dorsal vertebral arches are calcified and persist almost to the tip of the caudal fin. Beneath the notochord there is a segmented rod of cartilage at the base of the caudal fin, recalling the haemal arches of other forms. Ribs have not been observed. *Cladoselache* has no claspers, but claspers, are found in the coeval genus *Diademodus*, which may be closely related to *Cladoselache* despite an apparent lack of dorsal fin-spines.

The jaw suspension was amphistylic, the very long palatoquadrate having

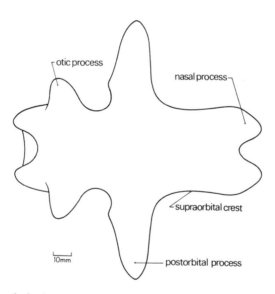

Fig. 9.4. *Cladoselache kepleri*. Outline restoration of neurocranium in dorsal view. (After Schaeffer.)

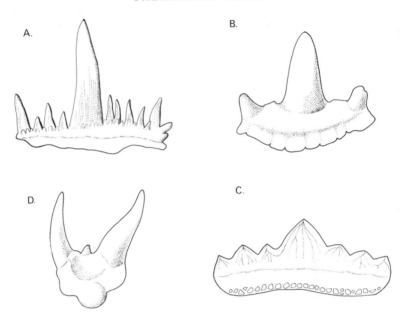

Fig. 9.5. Teeth of cladodont-level sharks. (After Schaeffer.); A. 'Cladodus' sp.;
B. 'Cladodus' sp.; C. *Protacrodus vetustus.*; D. *Xenacanthus* sp.

an otic and an orbital process for articulation with the neurocranium, and meeting its fellow in the middle line anteriorly. The mandibular joint was probably double as in other early sharks (Schaeffer, 1967), with both the palatoquadrate and meckelian cartilage having an articular process and fossa. There is a long hyomandibula and ceratohyal, and five branchial arches. The neurocranium (Fig. 9.4) is always crushed flat, but is similar in structure to those of other primitive elasmobranchs and the living *Chlamydoselachus* (Harris, 1938; Schaeffer, 1967). It has prominent postorbital processes. The ethmo-orbital region in front of the postorbital processes is about equal in length to the otico-occipital region behind. Anteriorly there are short nasal processes over the uncalcified nasal capsules, and posteriorly there are small otic processes. The orbits are floored by narrow subocular shelves and protected dorsally by the supraorbital crests. A large facet for the otic articulation of the palatoquadrate was probably present on the postero-dorsal surface of the postorbital process. Ventrally between the postorbital processes there is a median hypophysial fenestra, and paired foramina for the internal and external carotid arteries. The aortic canal is embedded in the floor of the neurocranium.

The teeth were 'cladodont' (see Fig. 9.5A, B), consisting of a large central cusp and a varying number of smaller lateral ones. Teeth of this type are

very common in the early elasmobranchs in the Devonian and Carboniferous, and it is on this evidence and on the variety of structure shown in the few
other known members, that this and the next order are presumed to have
been a very large complex of primitive sharks.

9.5. ORDER 2, CLADODONTIDA

Cladodontids in which the body structure is known are essentially similar to
Cladoselache in having the radials of the fins unsegmented and extending
almost to the edge of the fin, and in the absence of an anal fin. They differ,
however, in having only one dorsal fin, which is without a spine (Zangerl,
1969). Of these, the Lower Carboniferous *'Cladodus' neilsoni* (Traquair,

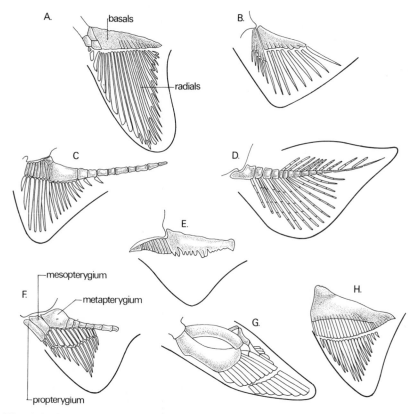

Fig. 9.6. Pectoral fin skeletons in various primitive sharks. (After Schaeffer.)
A. *Cladoselache* sp.; B. *Denaea fournieri*; C. *'Cladodus' neilsoni*; D. *Xenacanthus
sessilis*; E. *Symmorium reniforme*; F. *Ctenacanthus costellatus*; G. *Tristychius arcuatus;*
H. *'Ctenacanthus' clarki*

213

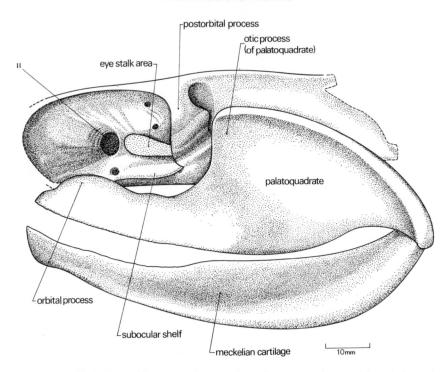

Fig. 9.7. '*Cladodus*' *wildungensis*. Restoration of neurocranium and jaws in lateral view. (After Gross and Schaeffer.)

1897) has a very long basal series in its pectoral fin, with a large meta-pterygium in the middle of the series and a chain of small cartilages extending back in the body wall (Fig. 9.6C). In *Denaea*, however, the basal series is apparently greatly reduced to two elements articulating with the shoulder-girdle, whereas *Symmorium* seems to exhibit an intermediate condition, with a long series of basals followed by a large metapterygium, but without the more posterior elements in the body wall (Fig. 9.6B, E). The scapulo-coracoid is better developed in cladodontids than in *Cladoselache*, but the right and left halves are still distinct from one another, and the articular process is narrow.

The name *Cladodus* has been given to a number of Devonian and Carbo-niferous species with 'cladodont' teeth, that are probably not closely related (see Fig. 9.5C). Uncrushed neurocrania are known for '*Cladodus*' from the Devonian of Germany (Fig. 9.7), and in other genera of uncertain position, e.g. *Tamiobatis* (Gross, 1937; Stensiö, 1937; Romer, 1964; Schaeffer, 1967). These specimens confirm what is known in *Cladoselache* and demonstrate that there is an anterior fontanelle and a short rostrum;

but they show considerable variation in the length of the otic region and in the corresponding length of the semicircular canals. The optic stalk and nerve foramina in the orbital region have a similar arrangement to that found in the living *Chlamydoselachus*; the postorbital process is pierced by the jugular vein; and the endolymphatic ducts open dorsally in a median depression. The jaws are long and the suspension of the palatoquadrate is amphistylic.

9.6. ORDER 3, SELACHII

The selachians, in our restricted sense of the word, range from the Carboniferous to the present day. They make up the central stock of the elasmobranchs, culminating in forms of modern aspect in the late Mesozoic, and they include all the living species. The majority of well-known Palaeozoic selachians are recognized as ctenacanthoids, a suborder which was particularly important in the Carboniferous. They are the most diversified of Palaeozoic elasmobranchs, and probably include primitive selachians which are closely related to the ancestors of all the later forms. The ctenacanthoids were subsequently replaced by the hybodontoids, which became the dominant selachians of the Triassic and Jurassic. Primitive hybodontoids are not sharply separated from ctenacanthoids in the Palaeozoic.

9.6.1. Suborder 1, Ctenacanthoidei

The ctenacanthoids (Figs. 9.8–9.10), which are contemporaries of *Cladoselache* in the Upper Devonian but more common in the Lower Carboniferous, differ from cladoselachids and cladodontids in several important respects. There are two dorsal ornamented fin-spines of osteodentine, with a considerable area inserted into the body between the myotomes; there is an anal fin; and the radials of the fins, both paired and unpaired, are jointed at least once and do not extend so near the fin margin. Although the basal series is still long in the best-known member, the Lower Carboniferous *Ctenacanthus costellatus* (Moy-Thomas, 1936), there are three elements enlarged to articulate with the well-formed pectoral girdle, the pro-, meso- and metapterygia (Figs. 9.6F, 9.8). It is particularly clear in this species that the large basal elements are the result of the fusion together of primitive, metamerically arranged cartilages (Jarvik, 1965). In ctenacanthoids, as in cladodontids, differing patterns of fusion have resulted in a variety of patterns in the basal skeleton. However, in the evolution of modern selachians, the tribasal pattern became fixed as the characteristic type (Schaeffer, 1967).

The ctenacanthoids were relatively very large fishes. *Ctenacanthus costel-*
215

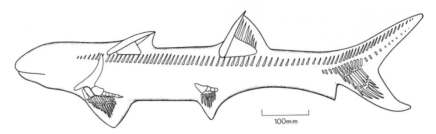

Fig. 9.8. *Ctenacanthus costellatus*. Restoration in lateral view. (After Moy-Thomas.)

latus measures from 0.5 to 1.5 m in length, but *Goodrichthys* was about 2.5 m long, and was therefore one of the larger Palaeozoic fishes. The teeth are of typical 'cladodont' type, and as in more primitive elasmobranchs the limb girdles are in two halves. The anal fin is situated posteriorly near the strongly heterocercal caudal fin. The dorsal fins are of particular interest in *Ctenacanthus* and *Goodrichthys* (Brough, 1935; Moy-Thomas, 1939). The anterior dorsal fin-spine makes an acute angle with the long axis of the body, and the fin is supported by a triangular basal plate and a single radial, whereas the posterior fin-spine is nearly vertical and the fin is supported by a basal plate and a number of radials. This is the condition found in the dorsal fin of hybodontoids. *Goodrichthys* has a cladodontid-like neurocranium with large postorbital and otic processes, and an elongated otic region. The jaws are long and the suspension is amphistylic.

    Tristychius arcuatus (Moy-Thomas, 1936) is a highly specialized ctena-canthoid species (Fig. 9.9). There are two smooth dorsal fin-spines, both sloping posteriorly at much the same angle, and the caudal fin has only elongated haemal spines and no radials to support its lower lobe, as is the case in modern sharks. The pectoral fins have single-jointed radials extending to the fin margin, but the fin has dibasal attachment to the shoulder-girdle (Fig. 9.6G). The notochord is persistent. The nature of the skull is not known, but the crushing teeth are tumid and without separate cusps. The body is almost naked, the scales being restricted to the margins of the pectoral fins

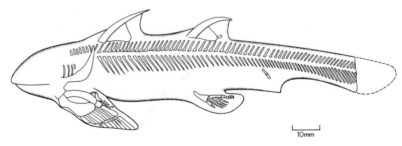

Fig. 9.9. *Tristychius arcuatus*. Restoration in lateral view. (After Moy-Thomas.)

216

and the head. *Bandringa rayi* is a differently specialized ctenacanthoid (Zangerl, 1969). This species is known from a single individual which is probably very immature (Fig. 9.10). It has a greatly elongated snout; the dorsal fin-spines are small with the anterior spine slightly more upright than the posterior; the anal fin is long; and the tail has a large epichordal and a small hypochordal lobe. The dentition comprises small 'cladodont' teeth, but the body seems to be devoid of scales.

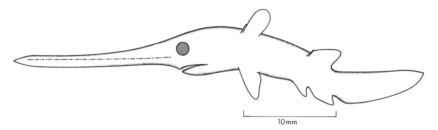

10 mm

Fig. 9.10. *Bandringa rayi*. Restoration in lateral view, probably of an immature individual. (After Zangerl.)

9.6.2. Suborder 2, Hybodontoidei

This suborder may occur as early as the Upper Carboniferous, being represented by forms like '*Petrodus*' (Moy-Thomas, 1935), but the earliest safely determined genus is *Arctacanthus* from the Permian of East Greenland (Nielsen, 1932; Patterson, 1967). Hybodontoids continue until the Cretaceous, but the Lower Jurassic *Hybodus hauffianus* is perhaps the best known. As noted above, the dorsal fin-spines are as in primitive ctenacanthoids, and since the earliest hybodontoids have 'cladodont' teeth, and the anal fins of both hybodontoids and ctenacanthoids are placed far back near the caudal, there can be little doubt that the two groups are closely related. In the paired fins hybodontoids differ from ctenacanthoids in much the same way as the latter differ from the cladoselachids. The radial cartilages of all the fins, both paired and median, have receded further from the fin margins and are frequently segmented throughout their length, the main web of the fin now being entirely supported by the more flexible ceratotrichia. The length of the basal series of cartilages in the pectoral fin is reduced, and the fin has become detached from the body wall at its posterior end. Three basal elements articulate with the shoulder-girdle, which seems primitively still to have its two halves distinct. The jaw suspension as in earlier forms is amphistylic, the notochord is persistent and ribs are present. In males one or two pairs of hooked spines above the eye probably functioned as cephalic claspers during copulation.

217

It is generally believed that the modern suborders of selachians are derived from hybodontoid-like fishes (Schaeffer, 1967). In modern species the notochord is constricted and the two halves of the limb girdles are fused with one another. The jaw suspension is only amphistylic in a few primitive species, the majority being hyostylic, in which the otic process is reduced and loses its connection with the neurocranium. This change in suspension can be correlated with the development of short, protrusible jaws. The row of basal elements in the pelvic fin becomes fused into a single piece, the basipterygium.

9.7. ORDER 4, XENACANTHIDA

The xenacanthids are a group of moderately-sized and easily distinguishable fresh-water fishes (Jaekel, 1906). They appear to be an early, highly-specialized side branch of the basal elasmobranch stock, and range from the Devonian to the Triassic. The distinctive features of the order, as seen in *Xenacanthus* (Fig. 9.11), are the biserially 'archipterygial' pectoral fins, the diphycercal tail, the elongated dorsal fins, the divided anal fin and the presence of a cephalic spine at the posterior end of the head.

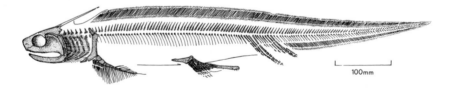

Fig. 9.11. *Xenacanthus sessilis*. Restoration in lateral view. (After Jaekel.)

The biserially 'archipterygial' pectoral fins (Fig. 9.6D) consist of a long segmented axis with both a row of preaxial and postaxial radials, which are jointed and stop some way short of the fin margin, the edge of the fin being stiffened by ceratotrichia. Possibly this type of fin was derived directly from the type of fin seen in cladoselachids and cladodontids (see particularly 'Cladodus' *neilsoni*) by a freeing of the fin at its posterior margin, the axis of the 'archipterygium' being formed by the basal series and a new row of radials being added postaxially. Alternatively, the axis may result from the extreme concentration of the basal series in the rostrocaudal direction, the segmentation of the axis being a secondary feature that does not correspond to the original segmentation of the basal cartilages (Jarvik, 1965). Whatever

218

the correct explanation, the pelvic fins are very similar to those of hybodon-toids and have well-formed pelvic claspers in males. The limb girdles are primitive in having the left and right halves unfused.

The dorsal fins are supported by at least two rows of radials proximally, and distally by ceratotrichia. The anal fins have their skeleton of radials concentrated. As in other early elasmobranchs the notochord is persistent, but small ribs are also present. There are no scales on the trunk.

The neurocranium of xenacanthids (Fig. 9.12) is essentially similar to that of other Palaeozoic elasmobranchs (Romer, 1966; Schaeffer, 1967). The occipital region is, however, rather prominently developed in connec-

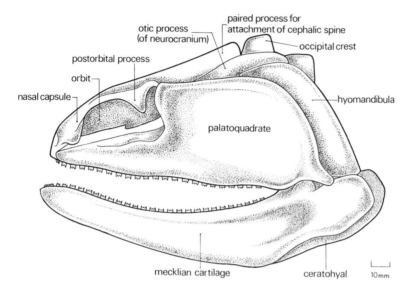

Fig. 9.12. *Xenacanthus* sp. Restoration of the neurocranium and jaws in lateral view. (After Romer and Schaeffer.)

tion with the articulation of the cephalic spine, and the otic processes are large. The jaw suspension is amphistylic (Hotton, 1952) and the dentition is peculiar to the group and apparently unvaried throughout it. The teeth are of the type known as '*Diplodus*' (Fig. 9.5D) and are clearly derived from the 'cladodont' type. They have two prominent lateral cusps and a single median smaller one, and a flat base with a button-like process which articulates with the succeeding tooth in the series. In some specimens dermal roofing plates have been described on the head. They appear to be composed of dentinal tissue, and have been unconvincingly compared with the bony plates of the skull-roof in an advanced arthrodire (Woodward, 1940).

219

9.8. INCERTAE SEDIS ORDER 5, HELICOPRIONIDA

This order, of which *Helicoprion* is the best known genus (Bendix-Almgreen, 1966), contains poorly known fishes in which enlarged mandibular symphysial teeth persist throughout life to form a remarkable whorl (Fig. 9.13). The whorl is supported between the jaw rami by a special symphysial crest. This crest encloses a ventrally open chamber, into which are displaced the oldest teeth in the inner coils of the whorl. The upper dentition is weak and supported by the palatoquadrate which is not fused with the neurocranium. The suspension of the jaws is thus either amphistylic or hyostylic. No other features of the head or postcranial skeleton are known.

The tooth-whorls of helicoprionids have a superficial similarity to the tooth-rows of edestid holocephalans (Chapter 10 §5), with which *Helicoprion* has often been classified. However, helicoprionids differ from edestids in the histology of the teeth, particularly in the presence of an outer enamel-

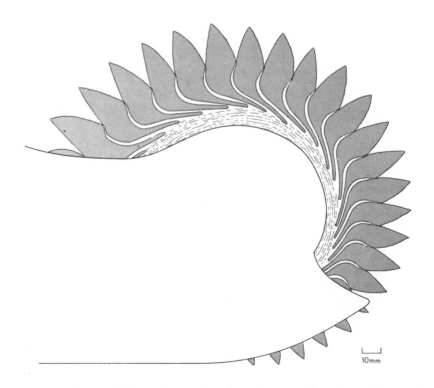

Fig. 9.13. *Helicoprion ferrieri*. Restoration of anterior part of lower jaw with exposed part of tooth-whorl, in lateral view. (After Bendix-Almgreen.)

220

like layer and in the absence of tubular dentine. The jaw suspension is another reason for separating these groups. Helicoprionids are probably elasmobranchs, but their origin and close affinities are quite unknown.

9.9. EVOLUTION

The ctenacanthoids and hybodontoids make up the main stock of Palaeozoic elasmobranchs, leading ultimately to the modern sharks and rays of the late Mesozoic and Tertiary. Presumably these primitive selachians originated from some cladodontid- or cladoselachid-like forms, although the actual ancestral type is unknown. *Cladoselache* was long thought to be an almost ideally primitive chondrichthyan, from which both later elasmobranchs and holocephalans could have been derived, but it is now believed to be a relatively advanced genus. *Cladoselache* is most obviously specialized in the tail skeleton, the externally symmetrical caudal fin, the presence of lateral keels at the side of the tail, and in the paucity of scales; and perhaps also in the absence of claspers, the presence of the ring of enlarged scales around the eye, and in the keel-like pectoral fins. *Diademodus* lacks most of these specializations and is provided with claspers in the males; nor have the peculiar dorsal fin-spines of *Cladoselache* been found in this genus (Harris, 1950). However, *Diademodus* is probably specialized in its polycuspid teeth.

Individual lines of descent have not yet been described in primitive elasmobranchs, and the hybodontoids in particular seem to be a horizontal grouping of species, possibly arising from distinct lines in the widely adapted ctenacanthoids. Because of the difficulties encountered in unravelling the phylogeny of the infraclass, it is convenient to consider its evolution in terms of levels of organization. Thus, more or less successive *cladodont* (cladoselachids, cladodontids and xenacanthids), *hybodont* (ctenacanthoids and hybodontoids) and *modern* levels have been recognized (Schaeffer, 1965, 1967), each typified by broad adaptations in the feeding (jaws and teeth) and locomotor (fin skeletons) mechanisms. Little progress has been made in tracing the ancestry of living forms down through the hybodontoid assemblage, although it is possible that the living hexanchid sharks are descended from some cladodontid (Patterson, 1967), and that the primitive living *Chlamydoselachus* is descended from some primitive amphistylic form without dorsal fin-spines (Glikman, 1967). Another possibility is that the modern odontaspids can be traced back to the ctenacanthoid *Bandringa* (Zangerl, 1969), although here in particular the evidence is slight. Lastly, *Heterodontus* has often been claimed as a living representative of the hybodontoids, although this view is now contested (Brough, 1935; Moy-Thomas, 1939).

The xenacanthids have a number of primitive characters which place them

221

at the cladodont level of organization (Schaeffer, 1967). But in other respects, such as in the pectoral fin skeleton, eel-like body, diphycercal tail, double anal fin and dorsal cephalic spine, they are highly specialized elasmobranchs. The other groups of elasmobranchs seem to be more closely related to each other than any one is to the xenacanthids, and should perhaps be classified together in opposition to the xenacanthids. This would reflect a basic dichotomy of the elasmobranch stock.

9.10. MODE OF LIFE

The earliest completely known elasmobranchs, *Cladoselache* and *Diademodus* in the Upper Devonian, are of normal shark-like habit. This is also true of other intact Palaeozoic elasmobranchs, and is strong evidence of a shark-like mode of life (Zangerl and Richardson, 1963). *Diademodus* may have been a relatively poorly-swimming carnivore, scavenging for food on the sea floor. As in typical modern sharks, the rostral region is well developed, indicating a strong sense of smell, and the eyes are small. *Cladoselache* is a less typical form, with large eyes and a short snout (Harris, 1950). Evidently it was highly modified for a carnivorous, pelagic mode of life, hunting its prey visually. The numerous species of *Cladoselache* show a wide adaptive radiation in the shape and proportions of the body and pectoral fins. Both *Cladoselache* and *Diademodus* have been found with gut contents of bony fish scales and shark teeth. Probably they seized their prey and swallowed it whole, or tore pieces from it, for the shearing and sawing adaptations of modern hyostylic sharks are not found in ancient amphistylic forms.

In the Mesozoic some hybodontoids developed a durophagous dentition of flat teeth. They probably adopted a varied diet, including shelled invertebrates. This adaptation is foreshadowed by several Palaeozoic forms with broad-crowned teeth, notably the ctenacanthoid *Tristychius*. As to the extremely depressed, durophagous adaptive type represented from the Upper Jurassic to the present day by the skates and rays, this is not found among the forms we have grouped as Palaeozoic elasmobranchs. This role is fulfilled by placoderms in the Devonian (Chapter 8 §10), and later by holocephalans, if we are correct in placing the petalodontids in this group (Chapter 10 §9). *Bandringa* is notable as a Carboniferous ctenacanthoid of similar adaptive type to the modern sand-sharks.

The form of the body and the presence of claspers show that swimming and internal fertilization were essentially the same in Palaeozoic elasmobranchs as in modern sharks. The long-based pectorals of primitive genera must, however, have acted only as rather stiff hydrofoils, in contrast to the flexible, narrow-based fins of modern species. In Recent elasmobranchs,

222

internal fertilization is correlated with the secretion of a horny egg case, in which the embryos develop. There is no evidence to show that egg cases were produced by Palaeozoic elasmobranchs, or alternatively that these fishes were viviparous.

REFERENCES

References given in Chapter 8 are not repeated

Allis, E. P. (1923) 'The cranial anatomy of *Chlamydoselachus anguineus*'. *Acta zool. Stockh.*, **4**, 123–221.

Bendex-Almgreen, S. E. (1966) 'New investigations on *Helicoprion* from the Phosphoria Formation of South-east Idaho, U.S.A.' *Biol. Skr. K. danske Videns-Akad.*, **14**, 1–54.

Blot, J. (1969) 'Holocéphales et élasmobranches. Systematique', in *Traité de Paléontologie*, 4:2, ed. Piveteau, J. (Masson, Paris) p. 702.

Brough, J. (1935) 'On the structure and relationships of the hybodont sharks'. *Mem. Proc. Manchr. lit. phil. Soc.*, **69**, 35–47.

Dean, B. (1909) 'Studies on fossil fishes (Sharks, chimaeroids and arthrodires)' *Mem. Am. Mus. nat. Hist.*, **9**, 211–87.

Fournier, G. & Pruvost, P. (1922) 'Découverte d'un poisson nouveau dans le marbre noir de Denée. *Bull. Acad. r. Belg. Cl. Sci.*, **8**, 210–18.

Glickman, L. S. (1967) 'Subclass Elasmobranchii (Sharks)', in *Fundamentals of Palaeontology, 11, Agantha, Pisces*, ed. Obruchev, D. V. (Israel program for scientific translations, Jerusalem) p. 292.

Gross, W. (1937) 'Das Kopfskelett von *Cladodus wildungensis*, 1. Endocranium und Palatoquadratum'. *Senckenbergiana*, **19**, 80–107.

Gross, W. (1938) 'Das Kopfskelett von *Cladodus wildungensis*, 2. Der Kieferbogen'. *Senckenbergiana*, **20**, 123–45.

Harris, J. E. (1938) '1. The dorsal spine of *Cladoselache*. 2. The neurocranium and jaws of *Cladoselache*'. *Scient. publs Cleveland Mus. nat. Hist.*, **8**, 1–12.

Harris, J. E. (1950) '*Diademodus hydei*, a new fossil shark from the Cleveland Shale'. *Proc. zool. Soc. Lond.*, **120**, 683–697.

Holmgren, N. (1941) 'Studies on the head in fishes. 2. Comparative anatomy of the adult selachian skull, with remarks on the dorsal fins in sharks'. *Acta zool., Stockh.*, **22**, 1–100.

Hotton, N. 3rd. (1952) 'Jaws and teeth of American xenacanth sharks'. *J. Paleont.*, **26**, 489–500.

Jaekel, O. (1906) 'Neue Rekonstructionen von *Pleuracanthus sessilis* und *Polyacrodus (Hybodus) hauffianus*'. *Sber. Ges. Naturf. Freunde Berl.* (1906) 155–59.

Jarvik, E. (1965) 'On the origin of girdles and paired fins'. *Israel J. Zool.*, **14**, 141–72.

Moy-Thomas, J. A. (1935) 'On the Carboniferous shark, *Petrodus patelliformis* M'Coy'. *Proc. Leeds phil. lit. Soc. (Sci. Sect.)*, **3**, 68–72.

Moy-Thomas, J. A. (1936) 'The structure and affinities of the fossil elasmobranch fishes from the Lower Carboniferous rocks of Glencartholm, Eskdale'. *Proc. zool. Soc. Lond.*, (1936) 761–88.

Moy-Thomas, J. A. (1939) 'The early evolution and relationships of the elasmobranchs'. *Biol. Rev.*, **14**, 1–26.

Moy-Thomas, J. A. and White, E. I. (1939) 'On the palatoquadrate and hyomandibula of *Pleuracanthus sessilis* Jordan'. *Geol. Mag.*, **76**, 459–63.

Nelson, G. J. (1968) 'Gill-arch structure in *Acanthodes*'. *Nobel Symposium,* **4**, 129–43.

Nelson, G. J. (1970) 'Pharyngeal denticles (placoid scales) of sharks, with notes on the dermal skeleton of vertebrates'. *Amer. Mus. Nov.*, **2415**, 1–26.

Nielsen, E. (1932) 'Permo Carboniferous fishes from East Greenland. *Medd. Grønland*, **86**, 1–63.

Ørvig, T. (1951) 'Histologic studies of placoderms and fossil elasmobranchs. 1. The endoskeleton with remarks on the hard tissues of lower vertebrates in general'. *Ark. Zool.*, (2) **2**, 321–454.

Ørvig, T. (1966) 'Histologic studies of ostracoderms, placoderms and fossil elasmobranchs. 2. On the dermal skeleton of two late Palaeozoic elasmobranchs'. *Ark. Zool.*, (2) **19**, 1–39.

Patterson, C. (1965) 'The phylogeny of the chimaeroids'. *Phil. Trans. R. Soc. (B)* **249**, 101–219.

Patterson, C. (1967) 'Elasmobranchii (Chondrichthys) in *The fossil record*, ed. Harland, W. B., *et al.* (Geol. Soc., London) p. 666.

Peyer, B. (1968) *Comparative Odontology.* Translated and edited by R. Zangerl (University of Chicago Press).

Pruvost, P. (1922) 'Description de *Denaea fournieri*, sélacien nouveau du Marbre noir de Denée'. *Bull. Acad. r. Belg. Cl. Sci.*, (1922) 213–18.

Romer, A. S. (1964) 'The braincase of the Palaeozoic elasmobranch *Tamiobatis*'. *Bull. Mus. comp. Zool. Harv.*, **131**, 89–105.

Romer, A. S. (1966) *Vertebrate paleontology.* 3rd. éd. (University of Chicago Press).

Schaeffer, B. (1965) 'The role of experimentation in the origin of higher levels of organization'. *Syst. Zool.*, **14**, 318–36.

Schaeffer, B. (1967) 'Comments on elasmobranch evolution', in *Sharks, skates and rays*, ed. Gilbert, P. W., Mathewson, R. F. and Rall, D. P. (John Hopkins Press, Baltimore) p. 3.

Stahl, B. S. (1967) 'Morphology and relations of the Holocephali with special reference to the venous system'. *Bull. Mus. comp. Zool. Harv.*, **13**, 141–213.

Stensiö, E. A. (1937) 'Notes on the endocranium of a Devonian *Cladodus*'. *Bull. geol. Inst. Upsala*, **27**, 128–44.

Stensiö, E. A. (1961) 'Permian vertebrates', in *Geology of the Arctic*, ed. Raasch, G. O. (University of Toronto Press) p. 231.

Traquair, R. H. (1897) 'On *Cladodus neilsoni. Trans. geol. Soc. Glasg.* **11**, 41.

Teichert, C. (1940) '*Helicoprion* in the Permian of Western Australia'. *J. Paleont.*, **14**, 140–49.

Woodward, A. S. (1924) 'Un nouvel Elasmobranche (*Cratosclache pruvosti* gen. et sp.

nov.) du calcaire carbonifere inférieur de Denée'. *Liège Soc. Géol. Belg. Livre jubilaire*, (1924) 59–62.

Woodward, A. S. (1940) 'The affinities of the Palaeozoic pleuracanth sharks'. *Ann. Mag. nat. Hist.* (11), **5**, 323–26.

Zangerl, R. (1966) 'A new shark of the family Edestidae, *Ornithoprion hertwigi* from the Pennsylvanian Mecca and Logan Quarry Shales of Indiana'. *Fieldiana, Geol.*, **16**, 1–43,

Zangerl, R. (1968) 'The morphology and the developmental history of the scales of the Palaeozoic sharks *Holmesella*? sp. and *Orodus*'. *Nobel Symposium*, **4**, 399–412.

Zangerl, R. (1969) '*Bandringa rayi*. A new ctenacanthoid shark from the Pennsylvanian Essex fauna of Illinois'. *Fieldiana, Geol.*, **12**, 157–69.

Zangerl, R. and Richardson, E. S. (1963) 'The paleoecological history of two Pennsylvanian black shales'. *Fieldiana; Geol. Mem.*, **4**, 1–352.

CHAPTER TEN

Subclass Chondrichthyes.
Infraclass Holocephali

10.1 CLASSIFICATION

Order 1, Chimaerida
  Suborder 1, Helodontoidei
    e.g. *Helodus*, L. Carb; *Psephodus*, L. Carb—M. Perm.
  Suborder 2, Chochliodontoidei.
    e.g. *Cochliodus*, L.–U. Carb.
  Suborder 3, Menaspoidei
    e.g. *Deltoptychius*, L. Carb; *Menaspis*, U. Perm.
  Suborder 4, Myriacanthoidei
    e.g. *Chimaeropsis*, U. Jur; *Metopacanthus*, L. Jur; *Myriacanthus*, L.–U. Jur.
  Suborder 5, Squalorajoidei.
    e.g. *Squaloraja*, L. Jur.
  Suborder 6, Chimaeroidei
    e.g. *Chimaera, Callorhynchus, Rhinochimaera*, Extant.
Order 2, Chondrenchelyida
    e.g. *Chondrenchelys, ?Eucentrurus*, L. Carb.
Order 3, Edestida
    e.g. *Agassizodus*, U. Carb; *Edestus*, L.–U. Carb; *Erikodus, Fadenia*, M. Perm; *Orodus*, L. Carb—L. Perm; *Sarcoprion*, M. Perm.
Incertae sedis *Ornithoprion*, U. Carb.
Order 4, Psammodontida
    e.g. *Psammodus*, L. Carb.
Order 5, Copodontida
    e.g. *Acmoniodus*, U. Dev; *Copodus, ?Mazodus*, L. Carb; *Solenodus*, U. Carb.
Incertae sedis Order 6, Petalodontida
    e.g. *Climaxodus, Ctenoptychius*, L.–U. Carb; *Janassa*, L. Carb—U. Perm; *Petalodus*, L. Carb—L. Perm; *Polyrhizodus*, L. Carb.

L., Lower; M., Middle; U., Upper; Dev, Devonian; Carb, Carboniferous; Perm, Permian; Trias, Triassic; Jur, Jurassic.

10.2 HOLOCEPHALAN CHARACTERISTICS

The holocephalans (Moy-Thomas, 1939; Patterson, 1965) represent the second major line of evolution in the chondrichthyans. They are represented by six genera of chimaeroids (rabbit-fishes) in the existing fauna, and can be traced back through the Mesozoic squalorajoids and myriacanthoids to the Palaeozoic menaspoids (Patterson, 1965). Although only the mandible and dentition are known in cochliodontoids, the forms classified here as the chimaerids probably share the following important characters. The neurocranium has a short, narrow preorbital region and widens suddenly into a long, broad orbitotemporal region. The eyes are large and both the otic and occipital regions are short. The jaws are short and broad, with holostylic suspension, i.e., the palatoquadrate is completely fused with the neurocranium and the hyoid arch is not modified with a hyomandibula. The mandibular joint is anteriorly placed, under the anterior part of the orbit, and the branchial arches are situated under the neurocranium, where they are covered by a single, large gill-cover. In the postcranial skeleton the notochord is persistent, and the first vertebral arches are fused into a synarcual which articulates with the back of the neurocranium. The pectoral fin is dibasal, with a large metapterygium and a stout first radial, and the shoulder-girdle has a high scapular blade. The pelvic fin has a long basipterygium and a long series of radials.

In living chimaeroids the spiracular gill-slit is closed, although the hyoid arch skeleton is unmodified and similar in shape to the gill-arches behind. As this appears to be the condition of the hyoid arch in fossil species as well, the unmodified condition is clearly an ancient character of the group. There is at present, however, no good evidence to show whether the complete state of the arch is a primitive or secondary character (de Beer and Moy-Thomas, 1935; Moy-Thomas, 1939; Patterson, 1965), although this is an important problem in considering the basic diversification of elasmobranchiomorphs (see Relationships of elasmobranchiomorphs § 11).

In addition to the chimaerids, there are other orders of Palaeozoic holocephalans, such as the edestids and chondrenchelyids, which are clearly divergently specialized side branches of the main stock; and further orders mostly known by their teeth, which are only doubtfully included in the infraclass.

Two sorts of dentition are found in holocephalans. In the 'selachian' type there are separate successional teeth as in elasmobranchs (Fig. 10.7), whilst in the 'dental plate' type, the teeth are fused into slowly replacing, crushing plates (Fig. 10.5B). The petalodontids, cochliodontoids, psammodontids and copodontids were originally brought together as 'bradyodonts', because of their slowly replacing teeth (Woodward, 1921), but the group was later expanded to include the edestids and chimaeroids (Nielsen, 1932; Moy-Thomas, 1939). 'Bradyodonts' typically have the crown of the tooth formed of numerous vertical parallel tubes of dentine (tubular dentine) (Fig. 10.1A), which gives the worn tooth a peculiar pitted appearance. The tubes of dentine, or dentions, are separated by a hard hypermineralized substance, and there is no outer layer of orthodentine or enamel. However, it has now been shown that tubular dentine is also found in some post-Palaeozoic elasmobranchs with a crushing dentition, and its value as a taxonomic criterion has thus been undermined (Radinsky, 1961; Bendix-Almgreen, 1968). Nevertheless 'bradyodonts' have not yet been found with an external layer of coronal orthodentine (pallial dentine) of the type found in durophagous elasmobranchs (Patterson, 1965, 1968); and in addition most Palaeozoic holocephalans have the base of the tooth closed by layers of thick, acellular tissue, which is not found in elasmobranchs (Fig. 10.1 B). This lamellar tissue is not found in petalodontids nor edestids, or later chimaeroids.

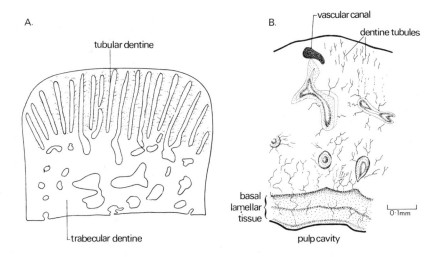

Fig. 10.1. A. Diagram of a 'bradyodont' tooth to show the structure of tubular dentine. (After Moy-Thomas.); B. *Menaspis armata*. Section through wall of frontal spine to show basal lamellar tissue similar to that closing the base of the tooth in many holocephalans. (After Patterson.)

Although all the major 'bradyodont' groups are considered in this chapter, and reasons can be found in the tooth structure for considering most of them to be closely related, it is questionable that the holocephalans are a natural group as classified above. In particular doubt attaches to the position of the petalodontids. Such reservations not withstanding, it is clear that the holocephalans were a much larger, more diverse group in the late Palaeozoic than in subsequent times, and that they were the dominant marine fishes of the Carboniferous.

10.3. ORDER 1, CHIMAERIDA

The chimaerids are typified by the characters listed above. The group is distinguished from the chondrenchelyids, which share many of these characters, by having fins of the ordinary chondrichthyan type, not a biserial 'archipterygium', and in not having the median fins continuous with a diphycercal tail. The three Palaeozoic suborders, the helodontoids, cochliodontoids and menaspoids can be considered separately. None of them exhibit the characteristic cranial specializations of living chimaeroids, such as the ethmoid canal, ventral position of the forebrain under the interorbital septum, large rostral cartilages and frontal clasper, which seem to be post-Palaeozoic acquisitions of the order (Patterson, 1965, 1968).

10.3.1. Suborder 1, Helodontoidei

The upper Carboniferous *Helodus simplex* (Moy-Thomas, 1936; Patterson, 1965) is one of the very few Palaeozoic chimaerids in which the structure of the head and body is known. *Psephodus magnus* is, however, known by an almost complete set of teeth (Traquair, 1884) similar to those of *Helodus*. These fishes are characterized by their numerous, simple, flattened teeth, which occur in about ten series on each jaw. Although some of the successional teeth fuse, the resulting tooth-plates are never large.

Helodus (Fig. 10.2) is a medium-sized fish about 300 mm in length, the body rather dorsoventrally flattened and covered with a shagreen of small synchronomorial scales. There is variation in the form of the scales, with both monocuspid and polycuspid types. The neurocranium (Fig. 10.3) is immovably fused with the palatoquadrates and is built on the same fundamental plan as in chimaeroids. It has some peculiar features, however, such as the paired upgrowths from the ethmoid region, which are of unknown function, and the fact that the cranioquadrate passages ventral to the orbits are not floored with cartilage. The pectoral fins (Fig. 10.2) are dibasal and have much-jointed radials which stopped well short of the fin margin. Of the two basal elements which articulate with the shoulder-girdle the

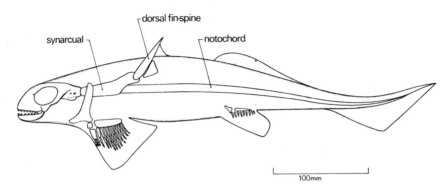

Fig. 10.2. *Helodus simplex*. Restoration in lateral view. (After Patterson.)

anterior is small and the posterior relatively large and long, almost exactly similar to those of living chimaeroids. Similarly as in chimaeroids, the two halves of the pectoral and pelvic girdles are not fused together, and the pelvic fin has an axis formed of a single basipterygium with which a few short radials articulate. Further resemblance to chimaeroids can be seen in the dorsal fins, only the anterior of which has a dorsal fin-spine and is small, whereas the posterior has no spine and is larger. The dorsal fin-spine is supported by the large synarcual. The notochord does not bear calcified

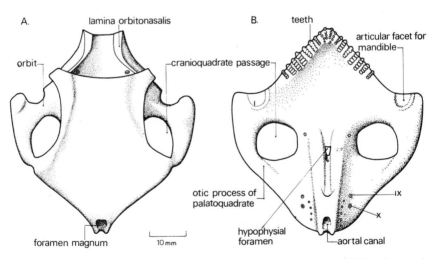

Fig. 10.3. *Helodus simplex*. Restorations of neurocranium in dorsal (A) and ventral (B) views. (After Patterson.)

rings, although the vertebral column is poorly preserved. The tail is hetero-cercal, but not strongly so.

10.3.2. Suborder 2, Cochliodontoidei

The members of this suborder are known by their teeth, and in the Lower Carboniferous *Cochliodus contortus*, by the upper and lower jaw cartilages and floor of the neurocranium (Patterson, 1968). Since the upper jaw cartilages were fused with the neurocranium, it is clear that cochliodontoids were holostylic. The dentition is made up of two or three large tooth-plates in each lower jaw ramus, and by a large tooth-plate preceded by smaller tooth-plates in each upper jaw ramus. The upper, small tooth-plates are composed of fused *Helodus*-like teeth.

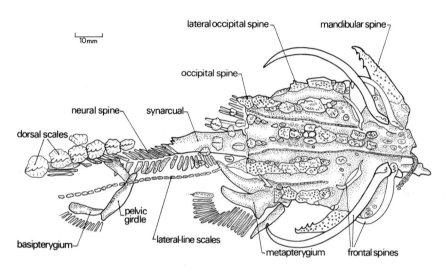

Fig. 10.4. *Menaspis armata*. In dorsal view. (After Patterson.)

10.3.3. Suborder 3, Menaspoidei

The menaspoids (Figs. 10.4, 10.5) are best represented by the Upper Permian *Menaspis* and the Lower Carboniferous *Deltoptychius* (Moy-Thomas, 1936; Patterson, 1965, 1968). They exhibit all the characteristic features of chimaerids listed above, in particular the peculiar proportions of the skull, the holostyly, the synarcual, and the dibasal pectoral fins. They also show characters which clearly separate them from helodontoids, some of which are important in connecting them with Mesozoic chimaerids.

231

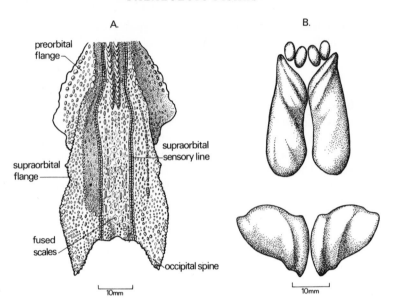

Fig. 10.5. *Deltoptychius armigerus*. (After Patterson.); A. Restoration of head-shield in dorsal view; B. Restoration of dentition as if seen from in front with the mouth wide open.

Menaspoids have a single large pair of tooth-plates in the lower jaw (Fig. 10.5B). These are opposed by an upper jaw dentition of one large posterior pair of tooth-plates and two small anterior pairs of *Helodus*-like teeth. The roof of the head is protected by a shield of dentinal tissue. The shield is less complete in *Menaspis* (Fig. 10.4) than in the earlier *Deltoptychius* (Fig. 10.5A), where it is a continuous unit of scale-like components. It bears a stout pair of dorsal occipital spines on its hind margin. In addition to these spines, in *Menaspis* there are also three pairs of long slender frontal spines. Both *Deltoptychius* and *Menaspis* have a paired mandibular spine on the posterior margin of the lower jaw, and a plate or lateral occipital spine above the gill-chamber. The importance of the armour in these genera, lies in the fact that comparable plates and spines are found in Mesozoic holocephalans, which menaspoids also resemble in their dentition. These features are not shared by helodontoids.

The trunk (Fig. 10.4) bears small polycuspid scales, and pairs of enlarged scales along the back. At least in *Deltoptychius* the scales were growing, i.e., cyclomorial structures, but of a complicated type in which synchronomorial units were added to the anterior and posterior margins of the primordial scale. The notochord was unconstricted and without calcification. Cartil-

232

aginous neural and haemal arches are preserved in the column of *Menaspis*, but the form of the body and median fins is unknown.

10.4. ORDER 2, CHONDRENCHELYIDA

The chondrenchelyids are known by a single Lower Carboniferous species, *Chondrenchelys problematica* (Fig. 10.6) (Moy-Thomas, 1935; Patterson, 1965), to which another poorly known Lower Carboniferous fossil *Eucentrurus* has doubtfully been related (Moy-Thomas, 1937). *Chondrenchelys* is a small, elongated fish, probably never more than 200 mm in length. All the median fins are continuous, the tail being diphycercal, and the pectoral fins biserial 'archipterygia' with a very short axis and the pelvics with long jointed axes and claspers. *Chondrenchelys* is the oldest holocephalan in which claspers are known, as they have not been found in helodontoids or menaspoids. Both the pectoral and pelvic girdles have their right and left halves unfused with one another, as in chimaerids. In all these respects *Chondrenchelys* resembles the xenacanth sharks. The vertebral column, skull and dentition, however, are entirely different. There are well-formed, calcified ring-like centra comparable with those of living chimaeroids, although the typical holocephalan synarcual is absent. The jaw suspension is holostylic and the proportions of the neurocranium are similar to those of chimaerids. The dentition consists of two large pairs of tooth-plates in each jaw and several smaller anterior plates. Simple, monocuspid scales occur on the body.

On account of the structure of the paired and median fins *Chondrenchelys* might be assumed to be closely related to the xenacanthid sharks, but the teeth and jaw suspension are so characteristically holocephalan that it must be assumed to have come to resemble the xenacanthids convergently, in connection with a similar mode of swimming.

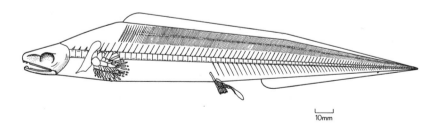

10mm

Fig. 10.6. *Chondrenchelys problematica*. Restoration in lateral view. (After Patterson.)

233

10.5. ORDER 3, EDESTIDA

This important group of holocephalans first appears in the Lower Carboniferous, and persists to the early Triassic. Typically in edestids the symphysial dentition in each jaw forms a curved row of rapidly replacing teeth. However, such teeth are absent in the primitive Lower Carboniferous genus *Orodus*, where the dentition comprises separate teeth (Fig. 10.7B) shaped like those of hybodontoid sharks and the lateral teeth of later edestids. *Orodus* teeth have typical 'bradyodont' tubular dentine in the crown, although lamellar tissue is not found in the base (Nielsen, 1932; Patterson, 1968). In later genera with a curved row of symphysial teeth, the crown of each tooth fits into the concave posterior edge of the tooth in front (Figs. 10.7A, 10.8). The teeth are more numerous and were more rapidly replaced than in other holocephalans with a 'selachian' dentition. The oldest members of the symphysial tooth rows dropped away at intervals as they became worn. In *Erikodus* and *Fadenia* (Nielsen, 1932, 1952) the symphysial teeth are enlarged and specialized for grinding with a low crown (Fig. 10.7A), whereas in *Edestus* and *Sarcoprion* they are laterally compressed so that the crowns form a series of narrow cutting blades (Fig. 10.8). In all edestids the lateral teeth are small and low crowned.

The head skeleton is partly preserved in the Permian genera *Sarcoprion*, *Fadenia* and *Erikodus* (Nielsen, 1952; Bendix-Almgreen, 1962, 1968). Our knowledge is very limited, but it appears that the general architecture of the neurocranium is broadly the same as in chimaerids. The orbits are large, the otic and occipital regions short and the mandibular joint is situated in an anterior position under the orbits. The palatoquadrate is completely fused with the neurocranium, so that the jaw suspension is holostylic, and the hyomandibula is not suspensory. The gill skeleton is mostly situated below the neurocranium. A specialized character of these genera seems to be

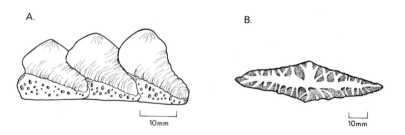

Fig. 10.7. A. *Fadenia crenulata*. Three adjacent teeth in lateral view. (After Nielsen.) B. *Orodus ramosus*. Tooth in coronal view. (After Moy-Thomas.)

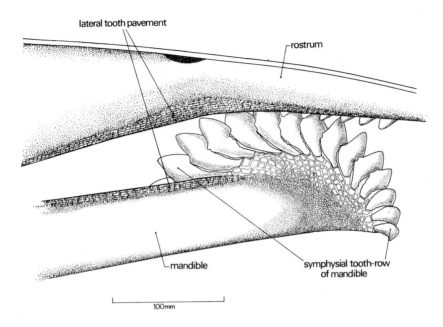

Fig. 10.8. *Sarcoprion edax*. Restoration of anterior region of skull with symphysial dentition, in lateral view. (After Nielsen.)

the elongated rostrum (Fig. 10.8), which may be correlated with the long symphysial tooth-rows. The lower jaw rami are fused at the symphysis to support the mandibular symphysial tooth-row. There is no head armour comparable with that of menaspoids, although enlarged scales which grade into the lateral tooth pavement are found in *Sarcoprion* and *Fadenia* (Nielsen, 1952).

The axial skeleton has an unconstricted notochord with separate neural and haemal arches. Anteriorly there is no synarcual element, but posteriorly the arches are fused into a plate supporting a caudal fin which resembles that of *Cladoselache*. The pectoral fin (Fig. 10.9) is also like that of *Cladoselache*, with a long series of unjointed, distally bifurcating radials, which extend to the edge of the fin web, and articulate proximally with a jointed basal series (Bendix-Almgreen, 1967). It is not clear whether the basal series was situated in the body wall, as in primitive elasmobranchs, or had already been freed by the formation of a metapterygial fissure. The first element of the basal series, or the metapterygium, articulates against a prominent crest on the scapulocoracoid. The two halves of the girdle are separate, as in chimaerids. The anterior dorsal fin is known in *Fadenia*, where it is supported by a triangular basal plate and a series of 12 radials. Fin spines

235

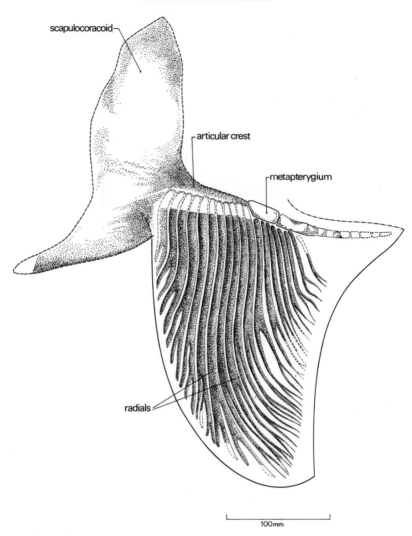

Fig. 10.9. *Fadenia crenulata*. Restoration of scapulocoracoid and pectoral fin skeleton in lateral view. (After Bendix-Almgreen.)

are unknown in edestids. In the Permian genera the squamation is made up of synchronomorial and cyclomorial scales in roughly equal numbers (see Chapter 9 § 2), but in the Carboniferous *Agassizodus* only cyclomorial scales and individual lepidomoria have been found (Zangerl, 1966).

236

10.6. INCERTAE SEDIS *Ornithoprion*

Ornithoprion hertwigi (Zangerl, 1966) is a small Upper Carboniferous chondrichthyan with a skull some 100 mm long. The neurocranium (Fig. 10.10) is very like that of edestids, to which group *Ornithoprion* has been referred. The eyes are large, the otic and occipital regions are short, the rostrum is elongated and there are rows of enlarged symphysial teeth in the upper and lower jaws. The symphysial region of the palatoquadrate is fused with the neurocranium to support the upper teeth, as in typical holocephalans, but the rest of the palatoquadrate is a separate chondrification which articulates against the neurocranium in front of the orbit and at the side of the otico-occipital region. Other unusual features of *Ornithoprion* include the posterior, elasmobranch-like position of the gill skeleton and the structure of the teeth, which have a crown of trabecular dentine covered with a thin layer of orthodentine. There is no tubular dentine. The meckelian cartilages articulate anteriorly with a median mandibular rostral cartilage, which projects far in front of the true rostrum and is tooth bearing. The scapulocoracoids are of the normal form and are not fused together ventrally. There is additionally a large sternal element. The notochord was persistent and there is no synarcual. The scales include simple lepidomoria and compound units. On the snout and mandibular rostrum the scales show a tendency to fuse by their bony bases to form bony plates.

Although the form of the skull and the symphysial tooth-rows seem to suggest that *Ornithoprion* is an edestid, this is not supported by the histology of the teeth, the free condition of most of the palatoquadrate, the posterior position of the gill skeleton, and the peculiar mandibular rostrum. These characters, particularly the tooth histology, suggest that *Ornithoprion* might be an elasmobranch that has parallelled edestides in some general features

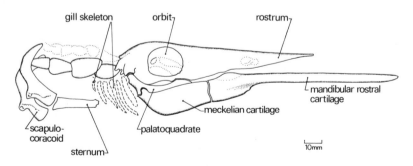

Fig. 10.10. *Ornithoprion hertwigi*. Restoration of skull and shoulder region in lateral view. (After Zangerl.)

237

of skull morphology (see *Helicoprion*, Chapter 9 §8). However, the evidence is inconclusive, and for this reason *Ornithoprion* is considered here after the group to which it has previously been referred.

10.7. ORDER 4, PSAMMODONTIDA

These fishes are known only by their teeth (Dean, 1909; Woodward, 1921; Radinsky, 1961; Patterson, 1968), which have the characteristic 'bradyodont' microscopic structure, including the thick basal lamellar layer. *Psammodus* (Fig. 10.11) is confined to the Carboniferous. The teeth are flat and quadrilateral and arranged in two longitudinal series. It has long been thought that the teeth of one side were wider than those of the other, this asymmetry being reversed in the upper and lower jaws. There is, however, no good evidence in favour of this view.

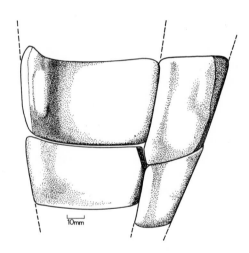

Fig. 10.11. *Psammodus rugosus.* Teeth in coronal view. (After Moy-Thomas.)

10.8. ORDER 5, COPODONTIDA

The copodontids are also known exclusively by their detached teeth (Moy-Thomas, 1939). The copodontid type of tooth (Fig. 10.12) is found in the Upper Devonian as *Acmoniodus* as well as in the Carboniferous as *Copodus* and *Solenodus*. It is a quadrilateral, slightly arched tooth, the dentition consisting of a single anterior tooth with possibly a second one behind, on the symphysis of the jaws. There is some doubt about the systematic position of these fishes, although the presence of tubular dentine in the crown of the

238

tooth, together with a thin basal lamellar layer suggests that their affinities lie with the Palaeozoic holocephalans. The Lower Carboniferous *Mazodus* may be allied to the copodontids. In this genus the dentition is made up of a large median tooth-plate surrounded by a number of small, asymmetrical teeth.

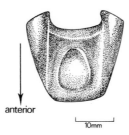

anterior

10mm

Fig. 10.12. *Copodus spatulatus*. Tooth in coronal view. (After Moy-Thomas.)

10.9. INCERTAE SEDIS ORDER 6, PETALODONTIDA

The petalodontids are a rather extensive group of chondrichthyans appearing in the Lower Carboniferous and continuing to the Permian. They are fairly small ray-like fishes. The teeth of typical petalodontids, such as the Lower Carboniferous *Climaxodus* (Woodward, 1919) and *Ctenoptychius* or the Permian *Janassa* (Hancock and Howse, 1870; Jaekel, 1899; Berman, 1967), are numerous, elongated and anteroposteriorly compressed, and arranged in close longitudinal and transverse rows (Fig. 10.13). The teeth are thus more shark-like than in helodontoids, for example, in that they are never fused into tooth-plates. They usually have a sharp cutting edge, which may be serrated, although in *Climaxodus* the teeth are bent in towards the mouth cavity so that the aboral face forms a grinding surface. The teeth are built up of circumpulpar dentine, with a thin layer of osteodentine on the outer surface of the crown (Radinsky, 1961; Berman, 1967). Convincing evidence that tubular dentine is present has not yet been produced.

Very little is known of the anatomy of petalodontids, but in *Ctenoptychius* and *Janassa* (Jaekel, 1899; Malzahn, 1968) the body was dorsoventrally compressed and ray-like with greatly enlarged pectoral fins. In *Janassa* (Fig. 10.13) there is a large rostral cartilage in the head, and some of the cartilages of the pectoral and pelvic fins are preserved. The pectoral fins have a segmented basal axis, and the pelvic girdle has an iliac process as in modern rays. The tail tapers to a point, but there is a large, semicircular epichordal

239

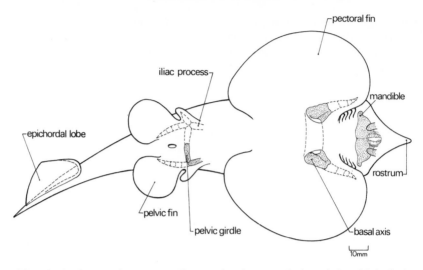

Fig. 10.13. *Janassa bituminosa*. Restoration in ventral view. (After Malzahn.)

lobe. The squamation comprises synchronomorial, mushroom-shaped scales (Ørvig, 1966). *Janassa* has no fin spines, although spines may be present in some Carboniferous genera.

The systematic position of petalodontids is questionable. Although Woodward (1921) regarded them as the typical 'bradyodonts', they have rapidly replaced teeth and show no convincing evidence of close affinity with any well-known Palaeozoic holocephalans, in either tooth histology or gross morphology. Moy-Thomas (1939) suggested that 'there is no evidence inconsistent with the view that Petalodonts were holostylic', but it must be admitted that the inclusion of this group in the holocephalans is at present a matter of convenience.

10.10. EVOLUTION AND MODE OF LIFE

The main stream of holocephalan evolution can be traced back from the living chimaeroids, through the Mesozoic myriacanthoids to the Palaeozoic menaspoids. As we have noted above, the dermal armour on the head is an important character connecting the last two groups. All of these forms are basically durophagous, with slowly replacing tooth-plates. They are specialized in their teeth in comparison with helodontoids, which retain a 'selachian' dentition of replacement teeth. Although helodontoids show some similarities to living chimaeroids in their cranial morphology, their dentition and lack of armour place them off the main line of ascent. The

240

relationships of the helodontoids to the menaspoid-myriacanthoid line is not clear, although probably they are not far removed from the main holocephalan stem. Again, while it is clear from the dentition that the cochliodontoids are closely related to helodontoids, the precise affinities of this poorly known group are obscure. Possibly they developed their 'dental plate' dentition independently of the menaspoids, as is also probable in the case of the chondrenchelyids, psammodontids and copodontids. The origin and relations of the last three groups are completely unknown. The edestids seemingly diverged from other holocephalans at an early stage in the history of the group, to develop their characteristic, specialized 'selachian' dentition.

It has been suggested that the fusion of the palatoquadrate with the neurocranium in holocephalans can be explained as a mechanism to give support to the powerful, grinding tooth-plates. However, the presence of a typical holostylic suspension in helodontoids, together with a primitive 'selachian' type of dentition, makes this doubtful. A similar problem is posed by the lung-fishes (Chapter 7:4).

Whilst the interrelations of the holocephalan taxa are badly understood, there can be no doubt about the ecological role of the group in the Palaeozoic. Holocephalans reached the peak of their evolutionary success in Carboniferous times, when, as mostly durophagous fishes, they occupied ecological niches that were previously filled by placoderms, and were to be occupied subsequently by elasmobranchs and actinoperygians. Holocephalans were almost entirely bottom living fishes. The body is dorsoventrally flattened in helodontoids and menaspoids, and this may well have been true of other groups such as the psammodontids and copodontids, at present known only by their teeth. The flattening of the body is carried farthest in the ray-like petalodontids, although there is some doubt about the inclusion of this group in the holocephalans. The edestids provide the main exceptions to the general durophagous mode of life of holocephalans. This order includes nektonic species with a shearing dentition, which suggests a predatory mode of life. Nevertheless even here there is a tendency to durophagy, and stomach contents of brachiopod shells have been found in *Fadenia*. The petalodontid *Janassa* was stenophagous, like the living chimaeroids, and its stomach contents include broken brachiopod shells, crinoids, foraminifera and fragments of large crabs. The mandibular rostrum of *Ornithoprion* has been explained as a device for stirring up the bottom organisms on which it fed.

Palaeozoic holocephalans show a wide range of swimming types, ranging from nektonic edestids such as *Fadenia*, with its *Cladoselache*-like pectoral and caudal fins, to the ray-like petalodontids. Although flattened forms clearly predominate, little is known of the body in most groups. *Chondrenchelys*

241

shows an interesting parallel to xenacanth sharks in body and fin form, and evidently swam in a similar eel-like way. However, the Recent chimaeroid adaptive type, in which the pectoral fins are enlarged to play an important part in locomotion, is not found in the Palaeozoic.

Male *Chondrenchelys* have pelvic claspers, providing the only evidence of typical chondrichthyan sexual dimorphism and its associated reproductive biology in early holocephalans.

10.11. RELATIONSHIPS OF ELASMOBRANCHIOMORPHS

It is generally accepted that placoderms are most closely related to elasmobranchs and holocephalans in the Recent fauna, although the exact nature of this relationship is much disputed. All three groups are quite distinct at their first appearance in the fossil record, and we can safely conclude that no one group known at present has given rise directly to any other.

A great amount of detailed morphological evidence has been put forward in support of the premise that placoderms are related to the cartilaginous fishes (Stensiö, 1963a; Miles, 1967a). Some of this evidence is inadmissible because it uses placoderm structures interpreted or restored specifically after an elasmobranch or holocephalan model (Westoll, 1960). Although the remaining points are not individually convincing, collectively they make up a strong case. Some of the best evidence comes from the snout (Stensiö, 1942), where arthrodires have been shown to have a strikingly elasmobranch-like arrangement of the incurrent and excurrent nasal openings. Again, in ptyctodontids the presence of pelvic claspers suggests that placoderms possessed the complicated reproductive biology that is otherwise found only in holocephalans and elasmobranchs, and that this is a part of the total elasmobranchiomorph heritage. The apparent absence of claspers in other placoderm groups is something of an obstacle to the full acceptance of this evidence, but perhaps the claspers were secondarily lost in forms with a long trunk-shield (Miles, 1967a).

The occipital joint, synarcual, large gill-cover and anteriorly placed gill-arches are placoderm characters also found in holocephalans. Consequently it has been suggested that placoderms and holocephalans are more closely related to each other than either group is to elasmobranchs (Patterson, 1965). In placoderms, however, it can be shown that these characters are a functionally interrelated complex, and they cannot be given much weight in phylogenetic discussions (Miles, 1967b). Stronger evidence for a particularly close relationship between placoderms and holocephalans has been found in the structure of ptyctodontid placoderms (Ørvig, 1960, 1962, 1967). In addition to the general placoderm characters listed above, ptyctodontids share with holocephalans the following features: a pair of rostral processes

242

to support the fleshy snout; large labial cartilages; a short, deep palato-quadrate firmly attached to the neurocranium in an anterior position under the large orbit; large tooth-plates adapted for durophagy, with a hyper-mineralized columnar hard tissue; prepelvic claspers in the males; and a long, 'rat-tail' body, with extensive dorsal fin development. This is an impressive list of similarities, but it is significant that they are characters shared by ptyctodontids and Recent holocephalans. If holocephalans are traced back through the geological record from the living chimaeroids to the Palaeozoic menaspoids and helodontoids, it can be seen that initially they were very different fishes from both the living forms and placoderms. Because of this, it seems likely that the similarities between ptyctodontids and living chimaeroids are the result of parallel evolution, due to the adoption of a similar benthic mode of life (Patterson, 1965).

The same explanation probably accounts for the similar habit of rhenanid placoderms and rays. Some authors (Holmgren, 1942; Jarvik, 1964, 1968) have suggested that these groups are particularly closely related, despite the fact that rays do not appear in the fossil record until the Jurassic. In this case, however, there is very strong morphological evidence that these fishes are phylogenetically widely separate. In rhenanids, for example, the nasal openings are dorsally situated, whereas they are ventral in rays; rhenanids are operculate fishes with dorsal branchial openings, whereas rays have a series of ventrally situated, separate gill-clefts; and rhenanids have narrow-based, unibasal pectoral fins, quite different internally from those of rays.

It must be concluded that a close relationship between placoderms and elasmobranchs or between placoderms and holocephalans has not been successfully demonstrated. There is, however, convincing evidence that together the elasmobranchs and holocephalans form a natural group. Some of this evidence has been given in the previous chapter (see Chondrichthyan characteristics, Chapter 9 §2). The most important points are that all of these fishes have a cartilaginous internal skeleton with prismatic calcification; an external skeleton of synchronomorial denticles that can be traced back in each group to one of similar cyclomorial scales; and in the primitive members of both groups a 'selachian' dentition of serially replaced teeth, which are little-modified scales, not fused to the jaws. None of these characters is found in placoderms, and they justify a classification of elasmobranchiomorphs in which elasmobranchs and holocephalans are grouped as chondrichthyans. The elasmobranch and holocephalan lineages apparently diverged after the basal elasmobranchiomorph stock separated into the placoderm and chondrichthyan lines of evolution.

It is not easy to say which of the two chondrichthyan groups is the most primitive. Both doubtlessly include mosaics of primitive, intermediate and

243

advanced characters. In holocephalans the holostylic jaw suspension can safely be regarded as a specialized feature. Probably, however, the complete, non-suspensory condition of the hyoid arch is a primitive character. If this is the case, the suspensory hyomandibulae of elasmobranchs, teleostomes and placoderms must have evolved independently of each other (de Beer and Moy-Thomas, 1935). Some support for this view is found in the different relations of the hyomandibula to neighbouring blood-vessels and nerves in these groups.

REFERENCES

References given in Chapters 8 and 9 are not repeated

Baird, D. (1957) 'A *Physonemus* spine from the Pennsylvanian of West Virginia'. *J. Paleont.*, **31**, 1010–18.

de Beer, G. R. and Moy-Thomas, J. A. (1935) 'On the skull of Holocephali'. *Phil. Trans. R. Soc.*, *(B)* **244**, 287–312.

Bendix-Almgreen, S. E. (1962) 'De Østgrønlandske perm-edestiders anatomi med saerligt henblik på *Fadenia crenulata*'. *Medd. dansk geol. Foren.*, **15**, 152–53.

Bendix-Almgreen, S. E. (1967) 'On the fin-structure of the Upper Permian edestids from East Greenland'. *Medd. dansk geol. Foren.*, **17**, 147–49.

Bendix-Almgreen, S. E. (1968) 'The bradyodont elasmobranchs and their affinities; a discussion'. *Nobel Symposium*, **4**, 153–70.

Bendix-Almgreen, S. E. (1971). 'The anatomy of *Menaspis armata* and the phyletic affinities of the menaspid bradyodonts'. *Lethaia*, **4**, 21–49.

Berman, D. S. (1967) 'Orientation of bradyodont dentition'. *J. Paleont.*, **41**, 143–46.

Eaton, T. H. Jr. (1962) 'Teeth of edestid sharks'. *Univ. of Kansas, Publs Mus. nat. Hist.*, **12**, 347–62.

Hancock, A. and Howse, R. (1870) 'On *Janassa bituminosa*; Schlotheim, from the Marl-slate of Midderidge, Durham'. *Am. Mag. nat. Hist.*, (4) **5**, 47–62.

Jaekel, O. (1899) 'Ueber die organisation der Petalodonten'. *Z. dtsch. geol. Ges.*, **51**, 258–98.

Malzahn, E. (1968) 'Über neue Funde von *Janassa bituminosa* (SCHLOTH.) im niederrheinischen Zechstein'. *Geol. Jb., Hannover*, **85**, 67–96.

Moy-Thomas, J. A. (1935) 'The structure and affinities of *Chondrenchelys problematica* Tr.'. *Proc. zool. Soc. Lond.*, (1935) 391–403.

Moy-Thomas, J. A. (1936) 'On the structure and affinities of the Carboniferous cochliodont *Helodus simplex*'. *Geol. Mag.*, **73**, 488–503.

Moy-Thomas, J. A. (1937) 'On the Carboniferous fish *Eucentrurus paradoxus* Traquair'. *Geol. Mag.*, **74**, 183–84.

Nielsen, E. (1952) 'On new or little known Edestidae from the Permian and Triassic of East Greenland'. *Medd. Grønland*, **144**, 1–55.

Obruchev, D. V. (1967) 'Subclass Holocephali (Chimeras)', in *Fundamentals of*

Palaeontology, 11, Agnatha, Pisces, ed. Obruchev, D. V. (Israel program for scientific translations, Jerusalem) p. 353.

Patterson, C. (1965) 'The phylogeny of the chimaeroids'. *Phil. Trans. R. Soc.*, (B) **249**, 101–219.

Patterson, C. (1968) '*Menaspis* and the bradyodonts'. *Nobel Symposium*, **4**, 171–205.

Radinsky, L. (1961) 'Tooth histology as a taxonomic criterion for cartilaginous fishes'. *J. Morph.*, **109**, 73–81.

Traquair, R. H. (1884) 'On a specimen of *Psephodus magnus* Agassiz, from the Carboniferous Limestone of East Kilbride, Lanarkshire'. *Geol. Mag.*, **2**, 337.

Westoll, T. S. (1960) 'Recent advances in the palaeontology of fishes'. *Liverpool, Manchr. Geol. J.*, **2**, 568–96.

Woodward, A. S. (1919) 'The dentition of *Climaxodus*'. *Q. Jl. geol. Soc. Lond.*, **75**.

Woodward, A. S. (1921) 'Observations on some extinct elasmobranch fishes'. *Proc. Linn. Soc. Lond.*, **133**, 29–39.

CHAPTER ELEVEN

Summary of the
Early Evolution of Fishes

The earliest known fishes were agnathous (jawless) forms with small terminal or subterminal mouths. The majority of known agnathans were armoured with dermal bony plates, but a few possessed only a little armour and it is possible that many unossified and at present unknown forms existed. The known fishes fall into rather sharply defined taxa, the relations of which are not altogether clear. The earliest group, the heterostracans, appears in the Middle Ordovician and like the other two important groups of Palaeozoic agnathans, the osteostracans and anaspids, which do not occur till the Upper Silurian, is not found later than the Upper Devonian. Possibly related to the heterostracans are the little-known denticle-covered fishes, the thelodonts. The heterostracans and osteostracans have the head and front part of the body covered by bony shields, whereas the head of anaspids is only covered by small scales. None of the agnathans have pelvic fins, but some of the osteostracans have pectorals and the anaspids have long lateral fins. The anaspids and heterostracans are peculiar in having hypocercal tails, in which the lower lobe is the larger. The fossil record of lampreys is restricted to one occurrence of a strikingly 'modern' form in the Upper Carboniferous, which shows almost all the specializations of the living species. The famous little fish *Palaeospondylus*, sometimes considered to be an ancestral myxinoid, is of uncertain affinities, and the hagfishes have no fossil record.

Although remains of agnathans are known as early as the Ordovician it is not till the Upper Silurian and Lower Devonian that they become common as fossils, later they become increasingly rare, and are almost extinct by the Carboniferous, surviving at the present time only as the lampreys and hagfishes. It is generally believed, on account of similarities in the brain, cranial nerves, auditory capsules and the nasohypophysial opening, that the lampreys are most closely related to the osteostracans and anaspids, although there is no fossil record linking these groups. Probably the hagfishes are also most closely related to these groups, although it has been suggested that they are the degenerate descendants of the heterostracans.

SUMMARY

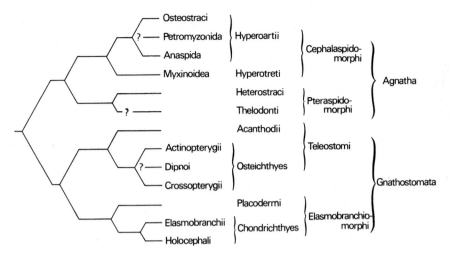

Fig. 11.1. Diagram to summarize the phylogeny and classification of fishes followed in this book.

The gnathostomatous (jawed) fishes, which fed on larger prey, evolved divergently from the agnathans. The mouth was extended backwards and the skeleton of the mandibular arch was utilized as jaws. The origin of gnathostomes is unknown, although there is a slight suspicion that they are related to the heterostracans. The earliest gnathostomes, the acanthodians, are found in the Upper Silurian and became a moderately large and diverse group by Lower Devonian times; they survived into the Permian.

Acanthodians are essentially a group of bony operculate fishes with two pairs of paired fins and a heterocercal tail. Superficially of shark-like appearance, they have characteristically small scales and spines in front of all the fins, both paired and median, except the caudal. The eyes are large and the olfactory organs small, the animals probably relying on sight rather than smell for obtaining their food. Their early success in comparison with other primitive groups, such as placoderms, is probably explained by their mode of life; as nektonic fishes they were not in direct competition with the dominant, benthic agnathans of the Silurian and early Devonian. The decline of acanthodians in the Carboniferous corresponds to the first great radiation of the adaptively similar actinopterygians.

The true bony fishes or osteichthyans appear in the late Upper Silurian and seem to share a common ancestry with the acanthodians. These two groups comprise one of the major branches of gnathostome evolution, the teleostomes, which diverged from the other major branch, the elasmobranchiomorphs, some time before the Upper Silurian. The osteichthyans

247

are typically operculate fishes with some kind of airbladder. There are three well-defined groups of osteichthyans, the crossopterygians, dipnoans and actinopterygians. The first group includes the rhipidistians, related to the ancestors of the tetrapods, and the actinistians. The actinopterygians have become the dominant group of fishes and include almost all the living bony fishes. The dipnoans or lung-fishes survive as three living genera, and the actinistians as one. The crossopterygians, dipnoans and actinopterygians have been distinct groups since their earliest appearance. Crossopterygians and dipnoans differ most strikingly from actinopterygians in the structure of the dermal bones and scales, which are 'cosmoid' in the first two groups and 'ganoid' in the last, and the fins of crossopterygians and dipnoans usually have a concentrated internal skeleton and large fleshy scale-covered lobes. These characters do not necessarily mean that the crossopterygians and dipnoans are more closely related to each other than either group is to the actinopterygians.

The Upper Silurian and Lower Devonian actinopterygians are known only by their detached scales and are of uncertain affinities. The Middle Devonian species belong to the order Palaeoniscida, which have 'palaeoniscoid' ganoid scales and heterocercal tails. This order has its acme in the Carboniferous and Permian but continues almost without change to the Cretaceous. From this type of fish numerous lines of evolution have diverged, the most successful of which has culminated in the teleosts, the dominant group of fishes in the Tertiary and at the present day. Other lines of evolution gave rise to the holosteans, which first appear in the Permian. These fishes lose the open spiracle, the heterocercal tail tends to become homocercal, and the scales, at first still 'ganoid' but of the 'lepidosteoid' type later, lose the outer shiny layer and often become smooth and transparent. Many abortive attempts at achieving the holostean type of structure have appeared but become extinct, forms of this type appearing as early as the Carboniferous, but it is not till the Triassic that they become very common. These have been classed together as the subholosteans. Two other well-known types of fish still alive today appear to have arisen from the palaeoniscids. In the Lower Jurassic the acipenserids (sturgeons) came into existence, retaining the heterocercal tail but losing the ganoine and much of the ossification of the head. The African *Polypterus* is probably related to the palaeoniscids of the Cretaceous, and has retained the palaeoniscoid scales, but has become rather specialized in other ways, especially in the nature of its fins.

As early as the Middle Devonian two groups of crossopterygians, the rhipidistians and actinistians, are distinct. The former have a more generalized dentition and less specialized arrangement of the dermal bones in the head. The rhipidistians, typically represented by *Osteolepis* in the Middle

248

Devonian, are carnivorous fishes which die out in the Lower Permian. They parallel the actinopterygians in the loss of the outer layers of the scales and dermal bones (cosmine) and in the change from a heterocercal to a symmetrical tail. The actinistians or coelacanths have a peculiar trilobed tail and persist until the present day with but little change.

The dipnoans, which are to a great extent a non-predatory, stenophagous group, are represented in the Lower Devonian by *Uranolophus* and *Dipnorhynchus*, which differ from the rhipidistians and actinopterygians in the more numerous dermal bones of the skull, the autostylic jaws and the lack of marginal tooth-bearing bones. However, by Upper Devonian times changes have occurred in the group foreshadowing the modern lung-fishes and by the Carboniferous, fishes are found which differ little from the living *Neoceratodus*, except in the greater degree of ossification. The dipnoans and actinistians show a similar pattern of evolution, with a high initial rate of change as the character complex is 'modernized', followed by a long stable history with little or no adaptive radiation.

The earliest major group of elasmobranchiomorphs, the placoderms, probably appear in the Upper Silurian and persist into the Lower Carboniferous, but they are essentially a Devonian group. The placoderms are operculate fishes characterized by their cranial and thoracic dermal bony shields, which are joined by a pair of hinge joints in the neck region. These shields are especially well developed in early arthrodires and in the antiarchs. The former make up the main placoderm stock, and the latter are particularly remarkable fishes with long, paddle-like pectoral fins, usually jointed, and covered by numerous small bony plates. Placoderms were variously adapted benthic fishes, probably lacking an airbladder like other elasmobranchiomorphs. Primitively they were adaptively similar to the agnathous osteostracans which they ultimately replaced. The rhenanids are less-heavily armoured placoderms which became superficially very like modern rays, most markedly in the shape of the body and form of the paired fins. Another remarkable group, the ptyctodontids, came to resemble the modern rabbit-fishes. The antiarchs, rhenanids, ptyctodontids, and a fourth small group, the petalichthyids, enjoyed most success in the Lower and early Middle Devonian before they were largely replaced by the highly successful arthrodires. The jaws of arthrodires, however, remained in a relatively unevolved condition, and this probably contributed to the rapid replacement of the group by chondrichthyans at the close of the Devonian.

In the late Lower Devonian the cartilaginous chondrichthyans, presumably sharing a common ancestry with the placoderms, appear; and from their earliest appearance two major divisions, the elasmobranchs and holocephalans, can be distinguished. The latter group probably fed mainly on shellfish, and the palatoquadrate was fused to the neurocranium (auto-

249

styly), the dentition was usually modified for crushing and a large operculum closed the gill chamber. The holocephalans are common in the Carboniferous, having replaced the placoderms as the principal durophagous, benthic fishes, where they are represented by such well-known fossils as the helodontoids, but become rare later, surviving to the present day as the chimaeroids or rabbit-fishes. The elasmobranchs, on the other hand, are typically voracious fishes with small eyes and large olfactory organs, relying on smell rather than sight for catching their prey. The jaws are always loosely attached to the neurocranium (primitively amphistylic but later hyostylic) and there is never an operculum. They, too, are common in the Carboniferous and remain a well-established group to the present day. From forms like *Cladoselache* and *Diademodus* in which the pectoral fins have broad bases, a line of evolution can be traced to the modern type of sharks and dogfishes in which the pectoral fins are notched posteriorly. The xenacanthids, with paddle-like fins and prominent head-spines, are a specialized elasmobranch type which appear in the Middle Devonian and continue to the Triassic.

Index

Figures in bold type refer to an illustration

253